Family Circle

GREAT IDEAS

CAREFREE SUMMER MEALS

Editorial Director	**Arthur Hettich**
Editor	**Nancy H. Fitzpatrick**
Art Director	**Marsha J. Camera**
Art Associate	**Walter C. Schwartz**
Food Consultant	**Dora Jonassen**
Production Manager	**Norman Ellers**

All recipes tested in Family Circle's Test Kitchens.

A New York Times Company Publication

CONTENTS

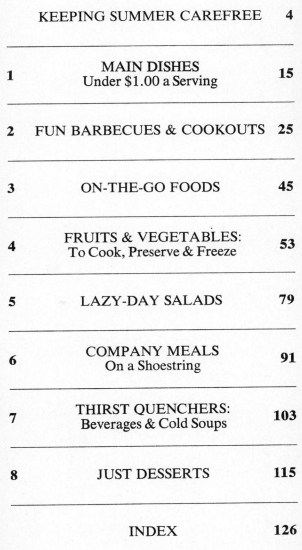

INTRODUCTION

Carefree. Happy. Lighthearted. That's the way your summer cooking's going to be, starting right now with our food tips on this and the following nine pages. Each page offers you a collection of ideas for budgeting your time and money, including specific cooking and measuring charts, a glossary of gourmet terms, barbecue and freezer hints, leftover tips and more. And, as a bonus, we've strategically scattered additional time-and-money-saving suggestions throughout this issue. You'll find them on many of the recipe pages in each chapter. All are geared to making your summer carefree—and keeping it that way!

OVEN-FRESH SNACKS

Freshen stale cookies, potato chips and pretzels by spreading them out on a cooky sheet, and heating in a slow (200°) to moderate (350°) oven for several minutes. The dry heat makes them crisp and ready to serve in a jiffy!

EASY-DO DIP IDEAS

To make a variety of dips the easy way, mix up a blenderful of your favorite dip base, then measure out one-cup portions into several containers. Spice each one differently, then refrigerate. Dips are best made well ahead of time so flavors can blend and dry ingredients can soften. The crunchy add-ins, such as bacon bits, are best stirred in just before serving. Stage your dips dramatically in pretty bowls and dress them up with such eye-feasting garnishes as carrot curls and parsley fringes. Dips served with vegetables are particularly inviting when spooned into vegetable containers such as pepper cups.

BROILING THE RIGHT WAY

When you buy expensive meat to broil, why ruin it with improper techniques? Whether you have a gas or electric range, keep top of meat 4 inches from the heat when meat is 1½- to 2-inches thick. When you have a shallow broiler, and distance between meat and heat is less, the heat may be controlled by lowering the broiler thermostat. With thinner cuts of meat (¾- to 1-inch), the top of the meat should be 2 inches from heat. Broil a 1½-inch steak 8 minutes to a side for rare. Broil a 1-inch steak 5 minutes to a side for rare.

HOW TO HARD-COOK EGGS

Hard-cooked eggs are a must for summertime picnics, but especially for a "pick-up-and-eat" picnic. For an easy way to cook eggs without that unsightly "green ring" around the yolk, follow these directions: Start with the freshest eggs you can buy. Put eggs in a large saucepan. Add cold water to come 1 inch above eggs. Bring to boiling; lower heat to barely simmering. Simmer 15 minutes. Drain; let cold water run over eggs in pan until they are cold. Chill and pack as you would any cold food.

LEFTOVER PASTRY TRIMMINGS

Here's a handy trick for using up leftover pastry trims. Re-roll, sprinkle lightly with grated Parmesan cheese and garlic salt, or with celery salt and sesame seeds, or with seasoned salt and poppy seeds. Then cut into pencil-thin strips about three inches long, slide onto a baking sheet and bake in a hot (425°) oven just until touched with brown, three to five minutes. Delicious as snacks.

SMOOTH AND EASY GRAVIES

To thicken cooking liquids in pot roasts and stews, try the French way: Blend equal parts (2 tablespoons each) butter or margarine and flour (called beurre manie, or kneaded butter). Drop small bits into the bubbling liquid, while stirring briskly. If you need more, just add until gravy is thickened as you like it. The usual flour-water thickening can also be lumpless if you pour the mixture through a sieve into the bubbling liquid.

SUBSTITUTION AND EQUIVALENCY CHART

When the recipe calls for:	You can use:
1 tablespoon cornstarch	2 tablespoons all-purpose flour (for thickening)
1 whole egg	2 egg yolks plus 1 tablespoon water
1 cup homogenized milk	1 cup skim milk plus 2 tablespoons butter or margarine or ½ cup evaporated milk plus ½ cup water
1 ounce unsweetened chocolate	3 tablespoons cocoa powder plus 1 tablespoon butter
1 teaspoon baking powder	½ teaspoon cream of tartar plus ¼ teaspoon baking soda
1 cup sifted cake flour	⅞ cup sifted all-purpose flour (⅞ cup is 1 cup of all-purpose flour less 2 tablespoons)
½ cup (1 stick) butter or margarine	7 tablespoons vegetable shortening
1 cup soured milk or buttermilk	1 tablespoon white vinegar plus sweet milk to equal 1 cup
1 clove fresh garlic	1 teaspoon garlic salt or ⅛ teaspoon garlic powder
2 teaspoons minced onion	1 teaspoon onion powder
1 tablespoon finely chopped fresh chives	1 teaspoon freeze-dried chives
1 teaspoon dry leaf herb	1 tablespoon chopped fresh herbs
1 cup dairy sour cream	1 tablespoon lemon juice plus evaporated milk to make 1 cup

When the recipe calls for:	You start with:
5½ cups cooked fine noodles	8-ounce package fine noodles
4 cups sliced raw potatoes	4 medium-size potatoes
2½ cups sliced carrots	1 pound raw carrots
4 cups shredded cabbage	1 small cabbage (1 pound)
1 teaspoon grated lemon rind	1 medium-size lemon
2 tablespoons lemon juice	1 medium-size lemon
4 teaspoons grated orange rind	1 medium-size orange
4 cups sliced apples	4 medium-size apples
2 cups shredded Swiss or Cheddar cheese	8-ounce piece Swiss or Cheddar cheese
1 cup soft bread crumbs	2 slices fresh bread
1 cup egg whites	6 or 7 large eggs
1 cup egg yolks	11 or 12 large eggs
4 cups chopped walnuts or pecans	1 pound shelled walnuts or pecans

DEEP-FAT FRYING TEMPERATURES WITHOUT A THERMOMETER

A 1-inch cube of white bread will turn golden brown:

345° to 355°	65 seconds
355° to 365°	60 seconds
365° to 375°	50 seconds
375° to 385°	40 seconds
385° to 395°	20 seconds

READY-TO-USE MARINADE

Wine makes an excellent marinade for less tender cuts of meat and adds a touch of glamour to your cooking. Use inexpensive table wines, sold in jugs, for cooking—not so-called cooking wines, which tend to be more expensive. Besides, you can drink the jug wine; you can't drink cooking wine.

FRUITS AND VEGETABLES

• When washing vegetables, do not pour washing water out of bowl as that will merely wash the sand back into the vegetables. Lift vegetables out with your hands or a slotted spoon.
• Do not wash mushrooms; they will become waterlogged. If they need any cleaning at all, lightly rub them with a damp kitchen towel.
• Square off potatoes before cutting them for French fries so there won't be any too-thin slices to burn. Use trimmed scraps in vegetable soups or as thickening for vegetable stews.
• When leaf vegetables such as spinach or chicory have to be thoroughly drained to be used in soufflés or timbales, it is best to squeeze the excess moisture out of them after they're cooked. Do this as you would squeeze water from a sponge.
• When several kinds of vegetables are combined in the same dish, as for a stew, soup or a salad, do not cut all of the vegetables into the same shapes; each should be done in a different way.

ON-THE-GO TIPS

For a no-work picnic start at the supermarket with foods that require little or no preparation for serving. Following is a list of just some you might include. (Note: Be sure to refrigerate any perishables immediately after purchasing.)
- Cold cuts and cheese
- Butter or margarine
- Peanut butter and jelly
- Canned ham, chicken, tuna, salmon, sardines and shrimp
- Barbecued chicken for serving hot or cold
- Coleslaw, potato, macaroni, vegetable and fruit-gelatin salads from the delicatessan section
- Fresh fruits such as melons, grapes and peaches
- Vegetables such as lettuce, tomatoes and celery
- Salad dressing, mustard, catsup, relish, pickles and olives
- Potato chips, pretzels and crackers
- Salted nuts and hard-candy mints
- Bread, rolls, cakes, doughnuts and cookies
- Soft drinks, instant coffee or tea, canned fruit juices and milk
- Canned puddings and fruit.

Packing for the picnic: Department, hardware and variety stores offer a great selection of thermal-type containers, all designed to make it easy and safe to transport your picnic food to lake, camp or boat. Just remember that these containers can keep foods either hot or cold. But you cannot carry both hot and cold foods in the same container.
- Wrap all hot foods in aluminum foil and pack at once in thermal container.
- Hot beverages or soups can be packed in individual thermos bottles or large-size jugs.
- Wrap cold foods in plastic wrap or pack in plastic bags or containers with secure lids, then pack in thermal container. Keep at 40°F or below. Cold foods will stay even colder if you fill a plastic bag or glass jar with tight-fitting lid with ice cubes, then seal securely. Place the cubes in their section of the thermal container, then pack food around it. Or use canned ice.
- Pack salad greens without the dressing. (The dressing can be carried in its store container or, if it's homemade, in a plastic cup with a lid.)
- Mayonnaise or salad dressing—or any salads or sandwiches containing these ingredients—should be kept in an insulated container.
- Wrap sandwiches individually to prevent drying out. Also, you might choose to wrap fillings separately, to prevent soggy bread, or freeze or chill bread ahead of time so it's nice and moist by the time you arrive at your picnic spot.
- Pack small fruits in egg cartons to prevent bruising. Then place the cartons in thermal container with other chilled foods.
- Don't forget the salt and pepper, straws, a can-and-bottle opener, charcoal and fire lighter (if you're barbecuing), barbecue utensils and heat-proof mitt and a first-aid kit.

Simplify cleanups by using foil, paper or plastic plates, cups, utensils and paper napkins. Plus, don't forget:
- A small package of scouring pads if you're barbecuing, plus paper towels and some pre-moistened towelettes; a thermos bottle of water for cooking, and some small-size garbage bags.

MONEY-SAVING MILK IDEA

In all recipes calling for milk, use fortified nonfat dry milk and water. It's better for the figure, tastes the same and costs about 40 percent less than whole milk. Nonfat milk can also be used to boost protein in many dishes. To keep it from getting stale, store nonfat milk in air-tight containers, not in open boxes.

BUYING LARGER CUTS OF MEAT

You can save a lot of money on meat by buying larger cuts. Buy a pork loin, pork butt, whole leg of lamb, chuck roast or bottom round roast. With these cuts it's relatively easy to slice your own steaks and chops. From one bottom round roast, for example, you can cut small portions for stuffed rolled beef, kabobs, plus smaller slices for pepper steak, beef stroganoff, curries and casseroles. The "mini" portions can be frozen.

FLAVORFUL IDEA

Never throw away the liquid from cooked or canned fruits or vegetables (you can even save the water you boil potatoes in). Save them, along with any leftovers, in jars in your refrigerator. Use the vegetable juices for soups, stews, casseroles or liquid to cook meats in. Use the cold fruit juices (instead of cold water) to add to gelatin desserts. These liquids add flavor and vitamins to foods at no extra cost.

EGG TWIRL

If you forget which egg in the refrigerator is raw and which has been hard-cooked, spin the mystery egg on its side; if it twirls in one spot, it is raw; if it works its way all over the surface, it is cooked. Also, to tell if an egg is fresh or stale, slide the egg into a bowl of water. A fresh egg will sink to the bottom; a stale egg will float.

WHOLE CHICKENS SAVE MONEY

Always buy whole chickens and cut them up yourself. You'll save 10¢ to 20¢ on every chicken you buy. And by all means, learn to bone chicken breasts. Chicken cutlets cost three to four times the price of whole chickens. The more you do it, the better you'll get.

WHEN BUYING FROZEN VEGETAGLES

Buy the large, see-through bags of frozen vegetables rather than individual 10-ounce packages. The advantage is twofold: You can use as much or as little as you need—and you can save up to 40 percent on the vegetables you buy. Remember, small pieces or slices are much less costly than whole vegetables (it's very hard to keep them whole during processing).

FONDUE POT FOR PICNICS

A fondue pot or chafing dish is ideal on a picnic if you want to heat up soups and canned foods such as beef stew, chili and chicken à la king. And if the fondue pot is hot enough, you may be able to brown hamburger in it. Here are some ideas for convenient meals you can make using the fondue pot, chafing dish or a small self-contained gas burner or camp stove.
• Make hot open-faced sandwiches by heating canned beef or chicken gravy. Place slices of cooked, sliced and packaged chicken or beef on bread and pour the hot gravy over it. One can of gravy and two packages of meat will serve three or four people.
• Heat a can of chili and pour it over a hot dog on a bun. Top with shredded cheese. Or add two tablespoons of catsup to a can of meatballs, heat, and hollow out unsplit hot dog buns; mash the meatballs and spoon the mixture inside. One can of meatballs makes about three "mini-heros."
• Mix one can cream of mushroom soup and one can drained tuna; heat and serve over bread slices; top with cheese strips. Serves four.
• Canned Spanish rice goes equally well with cooked packaged beef, cut in strips, or drained boned chicken, added and heated. One can of rice plus meat serves two to four.

GOODBYE, TEARY EYES

For a ready supply of onions, it's a good idea to chop them in quantity and store them in a tight plastic container in the freezer. The savings in money might not be tremendous but the savings in time and teary eyes will be!

WHAT TO LOOK FOR WHEN BUYING FISH & SHELLFISH

Fresh fish never has the disagreeable acrid odor usually described as "fishy." It will smell only of the salt-sea air, or fresh water, and then only if you are very close to it. The eyes of a fresh fish are brilliant and translucent, the gills a clear rose color. Shellfish such as lobsters, crabs, oysters, mussels and clams should be alive. When buying boiled lobsters, look for a curled tail, indicating they were alive when boiled.

LEMON JUICE TRICK

Sprinkle lemon juice on any fruits or vegetables that tend to blacken quickly after being cut. This applies to apples, pears, bananas, avocados, artichokes and even mushrooms, if you want them to remain white during cooking.

BEATING EGG WHITES

Egg whites should be allowed to warm to room temperature before they are to be stiffly beaten; that way they can absorb more air and gain greater volume. They give the best volume when beaten with a wire whisk. But even if you do use a rotary beater, begin by hand and give them 10 or 20 hand whisks at the end so they will retain their volume.

"BOUQUET GARNI"

When adding herbs and seasoning such as bay leaves, branch thyme, celery, parsley and carrots, tie them securely with a string into a "bouquet garni" so they can be easily removed.

OVERCOOKED FISH

One of the most frequent errors in preparing fish and shellfish is overcooking. Fish is cooked for flavor, not tenderness, and overcooking will render it dry and flavorless. Fish is done when the meat is solid white and flakes when touched gently with the tines of a kitchen fork.

QUICK DESSERT IDEA

Serve orange slices or Mandarin orange segments with cream cheese and crackers for a quick, very refreshing summertime dessert or snack.

TRIO OF FREEZER USES

Here are three ways to put your time and your freezer to good use:

1. Cooking more than one needs is not twice as much work. To make spaghetti sauce for 12 instead of six, or two meat loaves instead of one, saves time and money. It involves one shopping trip instead of two, the same number of pots and pans, and a savings on the use of the range.

2. Chain cooking is a method in which the week's best meat buy is bought in double or triple quantity. Using ground chuck as an example, the cook then takes a portion of it for spaghetti sauce, another for rolled cabbage, and a third, perhaps, for a casserole. One dish might be for dinner that night; the others for next week or next month.

3. Homemade TV dinners involve the collection of leftovers: A serving of mashed potatoes, one or two chops, a helping of vegetables. Put away in the refrigerator, they usually won't see the light of day until they have to be discarded. Arranged on a sectional aluminum tray, covered with foil and frozen, they make a fine supper when heated the night you're in a real hurry. They're a great way to save, too!

HAMBURGER HINTS

• For a juicier, more tender hamburger, try this idea: Add about ¼ cup cold water to 1 pound of lean ground beef. Then shape into patties.
• To freeze hamburger patties, shape them and place on tray or cooky sheet; place tray in freezer, unwrapped. When patties are frozen, remove them from the tray and wrap individually (or wrap several together with a wax paper divider between each). This keeps the wrapping from sticking to hamburgers when they thaw.
• To store hamburger in the refrigerator, remove store wrapping and re-wrap the meat in wax paper or plastic wrap.

DRESS UP STORE-BOUGHT BREAD

Here's a savory idea for dressing up pumpernickel bread. For each serving desired, spread 1 large slice of black Russian-style pumpernickel with softened butter or margarine that has had caraway seeds crushed and blended into it. Try the same idea with other breads, butter, herbs and cheese. Grated Parmesan, for instance, is delicious when combined with butter and spread on slices of Italian or French bread.

TIMETABLE FOR GRILLING STEAK OUTDOORS

Start by letting steak sit out long enough to reach room temperature. Grill 4 to 5 inches from hot coals for the following lengths of time. Note: On less tender cuts of meat, we suggest you only serve them rare; if cooked longer, they lose flavor and juiciness. These cuts should also be marinated or tenderized (follow label directions when using instant meat tenderizer).

Tender Cuts

| Cut | Weight | Thickness | Approximate Minutes Per Side | | | Servings |
			Rare	Medium	Well Done	
T-Bone	2½ to 3 pounds	1 inch	5	6	8	3
Porterhouse	3 to 3½ pounds	2 inches	10	14	16	4
	3½ to 5 pounds	3 inches	16	20	30	6
Sirloin	3¼ pounds	1½ inches	12	14	16	6
	4½ pounds	2 inches	20	22	24	4 to 5
Rib Steak	12 to 14 ounces	1 inch	5	6	8	1
Filet	4 to 6 ounces	1 inch	4	6	—	1

Less Tender Cuts

| Cut | Weight | Thickness | Approximate Minutes Per Side Rare | Servings |
Round Steak	3 to 3½ pounds	2 inches	17	4 to 6
Flank Steak	1½ pounds	—	5	4
Chuck Steak	1½ pounds	1 inch	12	4
	2 to 4 pounds	1½ inches	17	6 to 8
Sirloin Tip, Sliced	¾ pound	1 inch	17	1 to 2

KITCHEN MATH WITH METRIC TABLES

Measure	Equivalent	Metric (ML)
1 tablespoon	3 teaspoons	14.8 milliliters
2 tablespoons	1 ounce	29.6 milliliters
1 jigger	1½ ounces	44.4 milliliters
¼ cup	4 tablespoons	59.2 milliliters
⅓ cup	5 tablespoons plus 1 teaspoon	78.9 milliliters
½ cup	8 tablespoons	118.4 milliliters
1 cup	16 tablespoons	236.8 milliliters
1 pint	2 cups	473.6 milliliters
1 quart	4 cups	947.2 milliliters
1 liter	4 cups plus 3⅓ tablespoons	1,000.0 milliliters
1 ounce (dry)	2 tablespoons	28.35 grams
1 pound	16 ounces	453.59 grams
2.21 pounds	35.3 ounces	1.00 kilogram

BARBECUE TONGS

When handling meat on a grill, use tongs. If you stick meat with a fork you only allow the juices to escape, and with them a large amount of flavor. Also, before placing meat on grill, score the edges. This will help prevent the meat from curling during cooking. Also trim any excess fat off the meat to prevent grease "flare-ups."

HOW "HOT DOGS" WERE NAMED

The name "wiener," often used for a hot dog, suggests a Viennese origin, but the frankfurter is called a frankfurter in Vienna and a wiener in Frankfurt, as if both cities were trying to disclaim it. Hot dogs were not called hot dogs until 1906, when a cartoonist showed a dachshund inside an elongated bun.

QUICK GARNISHES FOR FISH

Vegetable garnishes add a bright touch of color to almost any fish dish. Some of the more popular vegetables you might use include: Green pepper strips, sliced beets, grated or shredded lettuce, chopped parsley, sliced radishes or radish roses, sliced cucumbers, watercress and carrot curls.

EASY GRILL CLEAN-UP

Before using barbecue grill each time, brush it lightly with salad oil, bacon grease or fat trimmings from meat you're about to cook. The oil or fat will make clean-up easier and will help prevent foods from sticking to grill during cooking.

WHEN YOU FIX PEPPER STEAK

To crush peppercorns for pepper steak, place them in a plastic bag and pound with a rolling pin just enough to crack the tiny balls into large flakes. Sprinkle half on the steak, and pat in lightly so flakes will stick; then turn meat; season other side with pepper flakes.

HOW TO STEAM CLAMS

For 6 servings, buy about 6 pounds, or 3 dozen, shell clams (steamers). Wash the shells thoroughly under cold, running water and place them in a steamer. Add about ½ cup boiling water and cover pot. Steam for 10 minutes, or until clams open. Serve in the shell, with melted butter.

COST PER SERVING

When buying meat, it's the cost per serving that counts—not the cost per pound. The reason is simple. Every pound of meat has a certain amount of lean (protein) and a certain amount of waste (bone, fat, gristle). Obviously, the more lean you get from every pound of meat, the fewer pounds you'll have to buy. To figure the actual cost per serving, you must first know how many servings you can get for every pound of meat. Here's a quick guide:

• Boneless Meats (such as ground beef): 4 to 6 servings per pound.
• Meat with little bone or fat (chuck roast): 3 to 4 servings per pound.
• Medium bone or fat (chuck blade steak): 2 to 3 servings per pound.
• Large amount of bone or fat (turkey): 1 to 2 servings per pound.

To put this guide to work, divide the number of servings you estimate from one piece of meat, into the total price. For example, if you want to buy a package of boneless meat that sells for a total price of $3.00, and you estimate the number of servings you'll get from the package is 4, you can figure the cost per serving by dividing 4 into $3.00—or 75¢ per serving. Compare this to a piece of medium bone meat that sells for $3.69 and yields 2 servings. The cost per serving if you bought this meat would then be about $1.85. Obviously, the $1.85 per serving cost makes this a much more expensive choice.

WAYS TO INCREASE AND DECREASE HEAT ON GRILL

To increase the heat, lower the grill (or raise fire bed), open all drafts, stack coals closer together, or add more coals to fire. Note: When adding coals, place them around edge of fire until they're warm; then move into center of pile. To decrease the heat, raise the grill, spread coals apart, or move coals out from under food to form a circle around it instead of under it.

STORE-BOUGHT CANNED FOODS

Commercially canned foods are considered safe because they are processed under carefully controlled conditions. However, if a canned food shows any signs of spoilage, do not use it. Do not even taste it. Signs to be wary of: Bulging can ends, leakage, spurting liquid, off-odor or mold. For proper processing of home canned foods, see the directions in "The Carefree Summer Preserving Guide," beginning on page 65.

KABOB COOKERY

• In threading kabobs, leave space between meat cubes so they'll brown on all sides. Tongs are handy helpers if meat has been marinated.
• When cooking kabobs over charcoal, place skewers on barbecue rack, about 4 inches from coals. Turn the skewers frequently for even cooking, whether cooking indoors or out.
• When brushing with marinade, remove skewer from barbecue to prevent marinade from dripping onto coals and causing unnecessary flaming.
• Total cooking time will be from 10 to 15 minutes, varying with the number of kabobs as well as the type of food that you grill.
• You can make miniature kabobs using cook-and-serve sausages and cocktail frankfurters. Skewer them alternately with fruit chunks, slices, sections and wedges. For a cold variation of this, substitute cubes of bologna, salami, ham, cervelat and other favorite cold cuts, interspersed with pickles, olives or fruit and vegetable wedges.

TIPS FOR BARBECUEING

1. Line bottom of barbecue with heavy-duty aluminum foil to make cleaning easier and to reflect and conserve heat.
2. Start fire about an hour ahead to ensure a good bed of coals. Lump charcoal may be used, but you may find that compressed charcoal briquets are easier to handle.
3. Use newspapers or thin packing-crate wood to get fire going. Electric starters may be used if an electric outlet is nearby.
4. Coals should have a gray ash over them when ready. At night, the red glow of the coals can be seen. Spread the bed slightly wider than the area to be used for broiling. Unless otherwise noted, food should be 4 to 5 inches above fire. A shallow bed is fine for grilling; rotisserie cooking needs a deeper bed. Keep water handy in a sprinkler or bottle, if necessary, to douse flare-ups.
5. Have on hand: Fork; spatula and tongs, with long, well-insulated handles; two asbestos mitts; a brush and long-handled spoon for basting; a pitcher to hold any sauce; cutting board and sharp knife; and a generously proportioned condiment set.
6. Be sure fire is out before leaving. Just dunk coals in water, gather up foil and let cool.
7. Plan the rest of the menu around the main course, varying the usual potato salad-cole slaw routine. Serve things that are easily portable and handy to heat and serve. Hot food does best in heavy enameled cast-iron pots that can be kept warm in a corner of the grill. Cold things retain freshness best when packed or served in thermal type containers; bring out just before serving time.

FREEZER TIPS YOU SHOULD KNOW

• Freeze food on the shelf in the freezer that has the coils for the fastest freezing.

• Package properly. Use plastic containers with tight-fitting lids for stews and soups. Special glass freezer containers can be used, but allow ½-inch headroom for expansion. For casseroles, cook-and-serve ware are ideal, with over-wrapping of freezer paper or heavy-duty aluminum foil. Waxed paper, lightweight foil and uncoated paper are not enough; frozen dishes can take on "off" flavors.

• Try the disappearing casserole trick: Line a freezer-to-oven baking dish with foil, add the ingredients and freeze. When frozen, remove the food wrapped in the foil, relieving the baking dish for duty. To serve, remove food from foil, return to the same baking dish and bake.

• Label accurately. After food is frozen, it all looks very much the same. Date each package and include the number of portions. A felt-tipped pen or grease pencil does the best marking job.

• Do not keep dishes made with meat for more than four months, with poultry for more than six, and with soups, more than four. They won't endanger one's health, but they might taste peculiar.

• Food may be cooked directly from the freezer. Freezer-to-oven cookware, aluminum or stainless-steel cookware are recommended to prevent breakage due to extreme temperature changes. Remove wrappings to prevent accumulated moisture from falling into the food. Rewrap lightly with fresh wrapping. Before cooking, skim off all excess fat. Cooking may be either in the oven, as with casseroles, or in a heavy saucepan or double boiler.

• Some flavor changes take place in freezing; for example, salt and onions can decrease in potency. Also, cloves, curry and garlic can change, so be sure to taste and adjust seasonings before serving.

• If your freezer should quit due to a power failure or faulty parts, keep the freezer door closed. If it is fully stocked, the contents will remain frozen for at least two days; if half full, for at least one day. For longer periods, buy dry ice (you'll need 25 pounds for each cubic foot of freezer). If thawing takes place, all is not lost. All uncooked foods may be cooked and frozen again. Baked foods can safely be refrozen after thawing, but they may be somewhat dried out and of a lesser quality. If foods have thawed only partially and there still are ice crystals in the package, they can be safely refrozen. A frozen item is "thawed only partially" when the temperature of the package has not risen above 40°.

• The rule of thumb for cooking frozen main dishes is as follows: At 425° to 450°, allow from 40 to 60 minutes per 4 servings in a shallow baking dish; in the top of a double boiler, allow 30 minutes per pint.

FIRST AID FOODS

CHICKEN COATING MIX

Makes enough to coat 4 cut-up chickens.

  1 can (1 pound) unseasoned bread crumbs
  2 tablespoons onion salt
  1 tablespoon paprika
  1 teaspoon pepper
  ¾ cup vegetable oil

Combine bread crumbs, onion salt, paprika and pepper in a large bowl; drizzle oil over; stir in oil until well blended; spoon into a 4-cup jar with a screw top. Store on cabinet shelf up to four weeks.

HOW TO USE:

FOR CHICKEN: Place 1 cup CHICKEN COATING MIX in a plastic bag; add 1 teaspoon crumbled leaf basil, or 1 teaspoon garlic powder, or 2 tablespoons chopped parsley. Shake 1 broiler-fryer, cut-up (about 3 pounds), in coating. Arrange pieces, skin-side up, in single layer on a large baking pan. Bake in moderate oven (375°) 45 minutes, or until tender.

FOR PORK CHOPS: Place 1 cup CHICKEN COATING MIX in a plastic bag; add 1 teaspoon ground ginger, or 1 teaspoon dry mustard, or 1 teaspoon crumbled leaf thyme. Shake 6 one-inch-thick pork chops in coating. Arrange chops in a single layer on a large baking pan. Bake in moderate oven (375°) 50 minutes, or until chops are tender.

CREAMED VEGETABLE BASE

Makes enough for 8 creamed dishes.

  ½ cup (1 stick) butter or margarine
  ½ cup all purpose flour
  ½ cup dry milk powder
  2 tablespoons onion powder
  2 teaspoons salt
  ½ teaspoon pepper

Cut butter or margarine in flour, dry milk powder, onion powder, salt and pepper until very crumbly. (A food processor can do this in seconds; or, use a pastry blender.) Spoon into a 2-cup screw top jar. Store in the refrigerator and use within 2 weeks.

HOW TO USE: Cook 2 packages (10 ounces each) or 1 bag (1 pound) frozen vegetables with 1 cup water and 1 teaspoon salt in a large saucepan, just until tender. Stir in ¼ cup CREAMED VEGETABLE BASE; bring to boiling; lower heat; simmer 3 minutes, stirring often.

SUGGESTED FLAVORINGS:

• For lima beans or whole kernel corn, add 1 teaspoon chili powder.

• For mixed vegetables, add 1 teaspoon crumbled leaf marjoram.

• For carrots and peas, add 1 tablespoon chopped fresh dill or 1 teaspoon dry dillweed.

THE GOURMET'S GLOSSARY OF FOOD

IF YOU ARE dining out at some posh restaurant or preparing a gourmet dish at home, you may run across unfamiliar food words on the menu or in cookbooks. Many are French or Italian or Spanish—*au gratin, al dente, paella,* for example. And what about such everyday recipe words as dredge . . . devil . . . dot . . . draw . . . dice? What do they mean exactly? The quick culinary dictionary that follows defines the food terms and techniques frequently used in today's recipes and restaurant menus.

A

A la: In the manner of; *à la niaison,* in the style of the house, "the house specialty."
A la carte: Dining where the diner selects each course from the menu. The price for each course is listed separately.
Al dente: Italian phrase meaning "to the tooth" used to describe pasta at the perfect stage of doneness—tender but with enough firmness to be felt between the teeth.
Angelica: The "herb of the angels," believed in ancient times to ward off the plague. Today, its pale green celery-like stalks are candied and used to decorate cakes, cookies.
Antipasto: Another Italian word, this one meaning "before the meal." It's the food served before the main course.
Aperitif: A mild alcoholic drink sipped before meals to sharpen appetites.
Aspic: A clear gelatin made from vegetable or meat broth.
Au gratin: Topped with crumbs and/or cheese and browned.
Au jus: A roast dressed with its own pan juices.

B

Baba: A small, round, fruit-studded, cake soaked in syrup.
Baguette: The everyday bread of France.
Bake: To cook, uncovered, in the oven by dry heat.
Bake blind: To bake an unfilled pastry shell.
Barbecue: To roast meat or other food, basting often with a highly seasoned sauce; also the food so cooked.
Baste: To ladle drippings, marinade or other liquid over food as it roasts.
Beurre manié: A French term meaning "kneaded butter." Actually, *beurre manié* is butter kneaded with flour into a soft paste that is used to thicken soups, sauces and gravies.
Beurre noir: French word for "browned" butter.
Bind: To add egg, thick sauce or other ingredient to a mixture to make it hold together.
Bisque: A smooth, creamy soup, often with a shellfish base.
Blanch: To scald quickly in boiling water.
Blend: To mix two or more ingredients until smooth.
Bombe: Frozen dessert of two or more flavors layered in a fancy mold; also the mold itself.
Bouillon: A clear stock made of poultry, beef or veal, vegetables and seasonings.
Bouquet garni: A small herb bouquet, most often sprigs of fresh parsley and thyme plus a dried bay leaf, tied in cheesecloth, then dropped into stocks, stews, sauces and soups.
Braise: To brown in fat, then to cook, covered, in a small amount of liquid.
Bread: To coat with bread crumbs.
Brochette: French for skewer.
Broil: To cook under or on a grill by direct dry heat.

C

Canapé: A small, decorative open-face sandwich.
Capon: A male chicken castrated while young so that it grows plump, fat and tender.
Caramelize: To heat sugar or a sugar-water mixture until it turns a clear amber brown.
Chantilly: Sweetened, flavored cream that has been whipped just until it holds its shape softly.
Clarify: To make stock, aspic or other liquid crystal clear by adding egg shell or egg white; also to clear melted butter by spooning off the milk solids.

Clove of garlic: One segment of a bulb of garlic.
Coat: To cover with flour, crumbs or other dry mixture.
Coat the spoon: Term used to describe egg-thickened sauces when cooked to perfect doneness.
Coddle: To simmer gently in liquid.
Compote: A mixture of sweetened, cooked fruits.
Consommé: Clarified stock or bouillon.
Coquilles: The French word for shells.
Court bouillon: A delicate broth, usually fish-and-vegetable-based, used for poaching fish.
Cream: To beat butter or shortening until fluffy.
Crêpe: Very thin French pancake.
Crimp: To flute the edges of a piecrust.
Crisp: To warm in oven till crisp.
Croquette: A small, savory leg- or cone-shaped patty made of ground meat, poultry or game that is breaded and fried.
Crostini: Fried bread squares served with soup.
Croustade: A toast case used for serving creamed meats, fish, fowl or vegetables.
Croutons: Small fried cubes of bread.
Crumb: To coat with bread or cracker crumbs.
Cube: To cut into cubes.
Cut in: To work shortening or other solid fat into a flour mixture with a pastry blender or two knives.
Cutlet: A small, thin, boneless piece of meat—usually veal.

D

Dash: A very small amount—less than 1/8th teaspoon.
Deep fry: To cook in hot deep fat.
Deglaze: To get up the "browned bits" left in a skillet or sauté pan after meat, poultry, vegetables or other foods have been browned. The technique is to pour off excess fat, to add stock or wine, then to boil and stir.
Demitasse: French for "half cup;" thus, small cups used for after-dinner coffee and the coffee served in them.
Devil: To season with mustard, pepper and other spicy condiments.
Dice: To cut into small uniform pieces.
Dot: To scatter bits of butter or other seasoning over the surface of a food to be cooked.
Draw: To remove the entrails. Also, to melt butter.
Dredge: To coat with flour prior to frying.
Drippings: Fats and juices released by meat as it cooks. They form the basis of many classic sauces and gravies.
Duchesse: Mashed potatoes mixed with butter and cream, piped around meat, poultry or fish dishes as decorative borders, then browned in the oven or broiler.

E-F

En cocotte: "Cooked in a covered baking dish or pot."
Enchiladas: A spicy Mexican classic—tortillas rolled up around meat, vegetables and cheese.
Entremets: Side dishes served at a meal.
Espresso: Robust, dark Italian coffee served in small cups.
Filé: (also known as *filé powder* and *gumbo filé*): A powder made of dried sassafras leaves used to thicken Creole soups and stews. Creole cooks learned the secrets of filé powder from the Choctaw Indians who invented it.
Fillet: A thin boneless piece of meat or fish.
Fines herbes: A mixture of minced fresh or dried parsley, chervil, tarragon and sometimes chives used to season salads, omelets and other dishes.
Flambé or *flambéed:* French words meaning "flaming."
Florentine: In the style of Florence, Italy—which usually means served on a bed of spinach, topped with a delicate cheese sauce and browned in the oven.
Flute: To crimp the edge of a pie crust in a fluted design.
Fold in: To mix a light, fluffy ingredient into a thicker mixture using a gentle over-and-over motion.
Frappé: A mushy frozen fruit dessert.
Fritter: A crisp, golden, deep-fried batter bread, often containing corn or minced fruits or vegetables. Also pieces of fruit or vegetable, batter-dipped and deep-fried.
Frost: To cover with frosting. Also, to chill until frosty.

G-H

Giblets: The heart, liver and gizzard of fowl.
Grate: To rub food across a grater to produce fine particles.
Grease: To rub butter or other fat over the surface of a food or container.
Grind: To put through a food chopper.
Grissini: Long, slim Italian bread sticks.
Gumbo: A Creole stew made with tomatoes and thickened either with filé powder (ground sassafras leaves) or okra.
Hors d'oeuvre: Bite-sized appetizers served with cocktails.
Hull: To remove stems and hulls from berries.
Husk: To remove husks from ears of corn.

I-J-K

Ice: To cover with icing. Also, a frozen dessert.
Jigger: A bartender's measure holding 1½ fluid ounces.
Julienne: Food cut in uniformly long, thin slivers.
Kasha: Buckwheat groats braised or cooked in liquid and served in place of rice or potatoes.
Knead: To manipulate dough with the hands.
Kosher: Food prepared or processed according to Jewish ritual and dietary law.

L

Lard: Creamy-white rendered pork fat; also, the act of inserting small cubes (lardoons) of fat in a piece of meat.
Line: To cover the bottom, and sometimes sides of a pan with paper or thin slices of food.
Lyonnaise: Seasoned in the style of Lyon, France—meaning with parsley and onions.

M-N

Macedoine: A mixture of vegetables or fruits.
Macerate: To let steep in wine or spirits.
Maitre d'hotel: Simply cooked dishes seasoned with minced parsley, butter and lemon.
Marinate: To season or tenderize food by steeping in a piquant sauce prior to cooking.
Marron: The French word for chestnut.
Marzipan: A confection made from almond paste, sugar and egg white, molded into fruit and vegetable shapes.
Mask: To coat with sauce or aspic.
Meringue: A stiffly beaten mixture of sugar and egg white.
Mince: To cut into fine pieces.
Monosodium glutamate: A white crystalline compound used in Chinese and Japanese cookery.
Mousse: A rich, creamy frozen dessert; also a velvety hot or cold savory dish, rich with cream, bound with eggs or, if cold, with gelatin.
Mousseline: A sauce to which whipped cream is added.
Mull: To heat a liquid (often cider or wine) with spices.
Newburg: A rich cream-and-cherry sauce.
Nicoise: Prepared in the manner of Nice, France—with tomatoes, garlic, olive oil and ripe olives.

O-P

Oil: To rub a pan or mold with vegetable oil.
Paella: A popular Spanish one-dish dinner containing rice, chicken, shellfish and vegetables served in their shallow pan. Garlic and saffron are the dominant seasonings.
Panbroil: To cook in a skillet with a very small amount of fat; drippings are usually poured off as they accumulate.
Parboil: To boil food until about half done.
Pare: To remove the skin of a fruit or vegetable.
Paté: A well-seasoned mixture of finely minced or ground meats and/or liver.
Penne: A pasta.
Petits fours: Tiny, fancily frosted cakes.
Pilaf: Rice cooked in a savory broth, often with small bits of meat or vegetables, herbs and spices.
Pinch: The amount of dry ingredient that can be taken up between thumb and index finger—less than ⅛th teaspoon.
Pipe: To press frosting, whipped cream, mashed potatoes or other soft mixture through a pastry bag.
Plank: To broil steak, chops or fish on a well-seasoned (oiled) hardwood plank.
Plump: To soak raisins or other dried fruits in liquid.
Poach: To cook in simmering liquid.
Polenta: A cornmeal porridge popular in Italy. It is often cooled, sliced or cubed, then breaded and fried.
Prick: To punch holes in the surface of pastry or other food with the tines of a fork. It prevents pastry from buckling and potatoes from bursting.
Purée: To reduce food to a smooth, velvety medium by whirling in an electric blender or pressing through a sieve.

Q-R

Quenelles: Delicate fish, chicken or veal dumplings poached in hot liquid and smothered with a silky sauce.
Quiche: An open-faced savory tart.
Ramekin: A small individual-size baking dish.
Reduce: To boil uncovered until quantity of liquid reduces.
Render: To melt solid fat.
Rice: To press food through a ricer to mash or puree.
Risotto: An Italian dish made with short-grained rice and tomatoes or mushrooms, onions or truffles.
Rissole: A small savory meat pie fried in deep fat.
Roe: The eggs of fish.
Roux: A fat-flour mixture used in making sauces.

S

Sauté: French for *pan-fry*.
Savory: An adjective used to describe food that is piquant.
Scald: To heat a liquid almost to boiling—until bubbles form around edge of pan.
Scone: A Scottish bread, shaped into flat round cakes.
Score: To make crisscross cuts over food surface.
Sear: To brown under or over intense heat.
Shirr: To cook whole eggs in ramekins with cream.
Short: An adjective used to describe a bread, cake or pastry that has a high fat content and is thus ultra-tender or crisp.
Shred: To cut in small thin slivers.
Sieve: To put through a sieve.
Sift: To put flour or other dry ingredient through a sifter.
Simmer: To cook in liquid just below the boiling point.
Skim: To remove fat or oil from the surface of a liquid.
Steam: To cook, covered, over a small amount of boiling water so that the steam circulates freely around the food.
Steep: To let food soak in liquid until liquid absorbs its flavor, as in steeping tea in hot water.
Stock: Meat, fowl, fish or vegetable broth.
Strain: To put through a strainer or sieve.
Stud: To stick cloves, slivers of garlic or other seasoning into the surface of a food to be cooked.

T

Table d'hoté: Dining where the diner selects the entree, the price of which determines the cost of the entire meal.
Terrine: A baked paté and/or the name of the earthenware or metal container the paté is baked in.
Thin: To make a liquid thinner by adding liquid.
Timbale: A savory meat, fish, fowl or vegetable custard.
Truss: To tie fowl into a compact shape before roasting.

V-W-Z

Vermicelli: Very fine spaghetti.
Véronique: A dish garnished with white grapes.
Vinaigrette: Dressed with oil, vinegar and herbs.
Vol-ai-vent: Puff pastry shells, filled with creamed chicken, seafood or mushrooms.
Whip: To beat until frothy or stiff with an egg beater.
Wok: A round-bottomed, bowl-shaped Chinese skillet.
Zest: Oily, aromatic, colored part of the skin of citrus fruits.

13

1

MAIN DISHES

UNDER $1.00 A SERVING

*"They dined on mince, and
slices of quince,
Which they ate with a runcible spoon;
And hand in hand, on the edge
of the sand, They danced by
the light of the moon."*
THE OWL AND THE PUSSYCAT, ST. 3
EDWARD LEAR (1871)

"Carefree Summer Meals" begins with some special offerings —main dishes that keep your budget in top-notch condition, and your kitchen clock set for short-order time. These dishes have been planned to feed a family for about $1.00 a serving without ever scrimping on nutrition. It also won't cost you much time to make them, as you'll see when you try Chicken Casserole Spanish Style, shown at left. For further cost-cutting advice, take a look at our introductory section, pages 4-13. The tips you'll find there can help you make summer carefree—all year long.

HERO SALAD

Shown on page 21, this economical sandwich-in-a salad bowl can be made from almost any combination of your favorite coldcuts, cheeses, etc. We used the following.

Makes about 6 servings.

    1 large head Boston lettuce, broken
    ½ pound sliced salami
    ¼ pound sliced ham
    ¼ pound sliced bologna
    ½ pound Swiss cheese
    1 green pepper, sliced
    1 red pepper, sliced
      Hot red cherry peppers (from a 16-ounce jar)
      Italian-style pickled green peppers (from a 12-ounce jar)
      Oil-cured olives (from an 8-ounce jar)
      Oil-and-vinegar dressing

Arrange lettuce around edge of salad bowl. Add all remaining ingredients (except dressing), following arrangement in photograph on page 21. Then drizzle with dressing, or let everyone make up individual salad plates and add dressing to taste. Serve with crusty French or Italian bread.

SPINACH LASAGNA

This recipe makes two big dishes of lasagna so there will be plenty for seconds.

Bake at 350° for 30 minutes.
Makes 12 servings.

    1 pound ground beef
    ½ pound sweet Italian sausages
    2 large onions, chopped (2 cups)
    1 clove garlic, minced
    1 can (2 pounds, 3 ounces) Italian tomatoes with tomato paste
    3 teaspoons salt
    2 teaspoons Italian herbs, crumbled
    ¼ teaspoon pepper
    1 package (1 pound) lasagna noodles
    2 eggs
    2 packages (10 ounces each) frozen chopped spinach, thawed and drained well
    1 carton (1 pound) cottage cheese
    1 cup grated Parmesan cheese
    2 packages (6 ounces each) sliced mozzarella cheese

1. Brown ground beef and Italian sausages in a large kettle; remove with a slotted spoon; reserve. Pour off all but 3 tablespoons of the fat. Sauté onion and garlic until soft in fat in kettle. Return browned meat to kettle with Italian tomatoes, 2 teaspoons of the salt, herbs and pepper. Simmer over low heat, stirring several times, 30 minutes.

2. While sauce simmers, cook lasagna noodles, following label directions; drain and place in a bowl of cold water to keep separated.
3. Beat eggs in a large bowl; add drained spinach, cottage cheese and remaining teaspoon of salt.
4. When ready to assemble: Drain noodles on paper toweling; arrange 3 strips on the bottom of each of two 13x9x2-inch baking dishes. Spoon part of the cheese-spinach mixture over noodles; add part of meat sauce; sprinkle with grated Parmesan cheese. Continue layering until all ingredients have been used. Top each dish with slices of mozzarella cheese.
5. Bake in moderate oven (350°) 30 minutes, or until bubbly-hot. Garnish with sprigs of parsley, if you wish.
Note: These dishes can be made early in the day. Assemble lasagna and keep in the refrigerator until 1 hour before party time. Place in *cold* oven and turn heat to 350°. Bake 1 hour, or until the lasagna is bubbly-hot.

TOMATO-CHEESE TART

This is a high-protein, low-cost main dish you can make in about half an hour.

Bake at 325° for 20 minutes.
Makes 4 servings.

    ½ package piecrust mix
    4 ounces Cheddar cheese, shredded (1 cup)
    2 packages (6 ounces each) process Gruyère cheese, shredded
    3 ripe medium-size tomatoes
    1 teaspoon salt
    1 teaspoon leaf basil, crumbled
    1 teaspoon leaf oregano, crushed
    ⅛ teaspoon pepper
    ½ cup chopped green onions
    2 tablespoons butter or margarine
    2 tablespoons soft bread crumbs

1. Prepare piecrust mix, following label directions, adding ½ cup of the Cheddar cheese. Roll out to a 12-inch round on a lightly floured pastry board; fit into a 9-inch pie plate. Trim overhang to ½ inch; turn under; flute to make a stand-up edge. Prick well with fork.
2. Bake in hot oven (425°) 10 to 15 minutes, or until golden; cool.
3. Spoon remaining Cheddar cheese and Gruyère into piecrust. Slice tomatoes in half lengthwise and then into thin wedges. Arrange, slightly overlapping, in a circular pattern over the cheese. Sprinkle with salt, pepper, basil and oregano.
4. Sauté green onions in butter or margarine until tender in a small skillet. Spoon in the center of pie; sprinkle with bread crumbs.
5. Bake in moderate oven (325°) 20 minutes, or until the tomatoes are tender. Serve immediately.

CHICKEN CASSEROLE SPANISH STYLE

Very little effort is needed on your part when you use the convenience of canned tomatoes and soup to make the sauce. (Shown on page 12.)

Bake at 350° for 1 hour.
Makes 6 servings.

    4 slices bacon
    2 broiler fryers (about 2 pounds each), cut up
    3 medium-size onions, quartered
    2 green peppers, cut into strips
    1 clove garlic, crushed
    ½ cup white wine
    1 can (1 pound) whole tomatoes
    1 can condensed cream of mushroom soup
    1 teaspoon salt
    1 teaspoon leaf marjoram, crumbled
    ½ teaspoon leaf thyme, crumbled

1. Sauté bacon until crisp in large skillet. Drain on paper toweling; reserve.
2. Brown chicken, a few pieces at a time, in bacon drippings in skillet; arrange evenly in 10-cup baking or casserole dish.
3. Add onion, green pepper and garlic to same skillet and cook, stirring often, until lightly browned. Spoon over chicken. Pour wine and tomatoes into skillet. Cook, stirring and crushing tomatoes, until slightly thickened about 5 minutes. Stir in mushroom soup, salt, marjoram and thyme; heat to boiling, stirring constantly; spoon over chicken in baking dish; cover.
4. Bake in moderate oven (350°) 1 hour, or until chicken is tender. Just before serving, sprinkle reserved bacon over the chicken and vegetables. Serve with hot buttered rice or noodles.

BOSTON BAKED BEANS

These beans are the old-fashioned kind that cook the slow lazy way.

Bake at 325° for 4 hours.
Makes 8 servings.

    1 package (1 pound) dried pea beans
    6 cups water
    1 large onion, chopped (1 cup)
    ½ cup firmly packed dark brown sugar
    ½ cup molasses
    2 tablespoons prepared mustard
    1 teaspoon salt
    ½ pound lean salt pork, thinly sliced

1. Pick over beans and rinse. Place in a large saucepan and add water. Heat to boiling; boil 2 minutes; remove saucepan from heat and cover. Allow to stand 1 hour.
2. Add chopped onion to saucepan. Heat to boiling; reduce heat and simmer 1½ hours, or until

the skins of the beans burst when you blow on several of them in a spoon.
3. Stir brown sugar, molasses, mustard and salt into saucepan until well-blended. Layer beans and sliced salt pork into a 10-cup bean pot or casserole. Cover.
4. Bake in slow oven (325°) 3½ hours; remove cover. Bake 30 minutes longer, or until beans are a dark brown. (Should beans begin to get dry during baking, add hot water, just enough to moisten the surface of the casserole.)

RUBY CHICKEN

Cranberry sauce gives this inexpensive main dish its beautiful color—and taste.

Bake at 350° for 2 hours.
Makes 12 servings or 6 servings for two meals.

    3 broiler-fryers (2½ pounds each), quartered
    1 tablespoon salt
    ¼ cup vegetable oil
    3 medium-size onions, chopped (1½ cups)
    1½ teaspoons ground cinnamon
    1½ teaspoons ground ginger
    1 tablespoon grated orange rind
    2 cups orange juice
    3 tablespoons lemon juice
    2 cans (1 pound each) whole-berry cranberry sauce

1. Sprinkle chicken pieces with salt. Brown on one side in hot oil, using two skillets; turn, add onions; brown on second side. Sprinkle on the cinnamon and ginger. Add orange rind and juice and lemon juice. Cover; simmer 20 minutes. Add cranberry sauce. Simmer, covered, 15 minutes longer, or until almost tender. Cool quickly.
2. Line two 10-cup freezer-to-table baking dishes with heavy foil. Remove chicken to dishes.
3. Measure cooking liquid and thicken, if you wish. Allow 1 tablespoon of flour mixed with 2 tablespoons water for each cup of liquid. Bring to boiling; cook 3 minutes; cool, add to chicken.
4. Freeze chicken and sauce. When frozen, remove foil-wrapped food from baking dishes; return to freezer. To serve: Remove foil, place food in same baking dish. Heat, covered, in moderate oven (350°), turning pieces once, 2 hours, or until bubbly-hot.

MONEY-SAVING TIP

Team leftover mashed potatoes or sweet potatoes with bits of leftover roast and/or vegetables, shape into cakes and brown in a skillet for an economical and easy potato pancake. If mixture seems crumbly, add a lightly beaten egg to bind. Tag ends of cheese, incidentally, make savory additions, too. Grate them and mix into potatoes.

ASPARAGUS AND HAM SMITANE

A savory sauce, especially easy to prepare, makes this a gourmet dish.

Makes 4 servings.

  8 thin slices leftover cooked ham
16 stalks cooked asparagus
½ cup dairy sour cream
½ cup mayonnaise or salad dressing
  1 tablespoon lemon juice
    Paprika
    Toast points

1. Preheat the oven to moderate (350°).
2. Arrange ham slices in individual shallow oven-proof baking dishes. Place 4 stalks asparagus over each slice of ham. Cover dishes with foil. Heat in oven for 10 minutes; uncover.
3. Mix sour cream with mayonnaise and lemon juice and spoon over ham and asparagus.
4. Bake 10 minutes longer, then place under broiler about 4 inches from heat until sauce is bubbly-hot. Dust sauce with paprika and garnish ham and asparagus with toast points.

QUICK ROAST BEEF HASH

A hearty, quick and easy supper dish using left-over roast beef and leftover potatoes.

Makes 4 servings.

  3 large leftover baked or boiled potatoes, well-chilled
  1 cup leftover finely chopped lean roast beef or beef pot roast
  2 tablespoons vegetable shortening
½ teaspoon salt
¼ teaspoon pepper
  2 tablespoons butter or margarine
  1 teaspoon Worcestershire sauce
½ cup dairy sour cream
  2 tablespoons minced fresh or freeze-dried chives

1. Adjust broiler rack to about 6 inches under heat. Preheat broiler.
2. Peel and shred the potatoes. Add to chopped beef and toss with a fork to blend.
3. Heat the shortening in a large skillet over medium heat. Sprinkle potato mixture lightly over entire surface of skillet. Don't pack down. Sprinkle with salt and pepper. Cook, without stirring, until underside is lightly browned. (Lift up edge with a spatula.)
4. Melt butter and pour over surface. Place skillet under broiler heat until surface is browned. Turn out onto a warm plate. Mix Worcestershire into sour cream and spoon over surface. Sprinkle with chives and serve this hearty main dish at once.

MONEY-SAVING TIP

Avoid paying for perfection when perfection doesn't count. Why, for example, pay a premium price for fancy whole canned tomatoes when you're going to break them up and cook them down into sauce? And why pay for expensive white-meat tuna when you're going to flake it, then bake it in a casserole? Suit the style of food to the purpose—a few cents saved here and there soon add up to dollars.

COTTAGE POTATO PIE

This is a glamorized version of scalloped potatoes, with sliced frankfurters added for a hearty one-dish meal everyone will enjoy.

Bake at 350° for one hour.
Makes 8 servings.

  6 large potatoes (2¾ pounds)
  1 cup sifted all-purpose flour
½ teaspoon salt
⅓ cup shortening
2-3 tablespoons water
  3 tablespoons all-purpose flour
  1 package (6 ounces) processed Gruyère cheese, shredded
  1 large onion, sliced
  5 frankfurters (½ pound), sliced
  1 tablespoon butter or margarine
  2 cloves garlic, minced
1½ teaspoons salt
¼ teaspoon pepper
⅛ teaspoon ground nutmeg
  1 cup milk
  1 egg yolk
½ cup heavy cream

1. Pare potatoes; slice very thinly. Cover with cold water in a large bowl.
2. Combine the 1 cup flour and salt in a bowl; cut in shortening until mixture is crumbly. Stir in water, 1 tablespoon at a time, until mixture forms a ball.
3. Toss the remaining 3 tablespoons flour with cheese. Drain potatoes thoroughly. Layer in a greased 8-cup shallow baking dish with onion, cheese mixture, frankfurters, butter or margarine, garlic, salt, pepper and nutmeg. Top layer should be potatoes. Pour milk over potatoes.
4. Roll out pastry on a lightly floured pastry board to a 15x11-inch rectangle. Fit over potatoes; turn under and flute edges. Cut 2 slashes in pastry to allow steam to escape. Mix egg yolk with 1 tablespoon cream; brush the egg yolk-cream mixture over pastry.
5. Bake in moderate oven (350°) 1 hour, or until pastry is golden brown and potatoes are done. Remove from oven; pour remaining cream through vents. Let stand for 15 minutes before serving.

BRIDIE'S REALLY GREAT CHICKEN

This oven-baked chicken is quick to prepare and a treat to eat.

Bake at 375° for 1 hour.
Makes 4 servings.

   1 broiler-fryer (about 3 pounds)
   1 can condensed golden mushroom soup
   1 leek, thinly sliced (1 cup) or 1 large onion, chopped (1 cup)
   1 can (3 or 4 ounces) chopped mushrooms
 ¼ cup water
   2 tablespoons lemon juice

1. Cut chicken into serving-size pieces; arrange in a single layer in a 13x9x2-inch baking dish.
2. Combine soup, leek, mushrooms, mushroom liquid, water and lemon juice in a medium-size bowl. Spoon over chicken pieces.
3. Bake in moderate oven (375°) 1 hour, or until chicken is tender and richly browned.

BEEF AND VEGETABLE PIE (PIROGHI)

Of Russian origin, Piroghi is a large meat- or vegetable-filled pastry. Similar individual pastries are called Pirozhki.

Bake at 400° 30 minutes.
Makes 6 servings.

   1 package piecrust mix
   2 tablespoons butter or margarine
   1 large onion, chopped (1 cup)
   2 carrots, sliced (1 cup)
   2 cups chopped green cabbage
   1 pound ground chuck
   1 cup hot water
   1 envelope (¾ ounce) instant brown gravy mix
   2 tablespoons chopped parsley
   1 teaspoon salt
 ½ teaspoon leaf savory, crumbled
 ¼ teaspoon pepper
   1 egg, slightly beaten

1. Prepare piecrust mix, following label directions; chill 30 minutes.
2. Meanwhile, sauté onion, carrots and cabbage in hot butter or margarine in large skillet, stirring often until tender and slightly browned, about 15 minutes. Remove to a large bowl.
3. In same skillet, sauté meat over high heat, stirring constantly until it loses its pink color. Lower heat, stir in water; cook and stir to loosen browned bits in pan. Stir in gravy mix, parsley, salt, savory and pepper; cover, simmer 5 minutes; add to vegetables.
4. Roll pastry to a 16-inch round on a lightly floured surface. Carefully slide a cooky sheet under pastry to within 1 inch from edge of cooky sheet. Spoon meat and vegetable mixture onto pastry half on cooky sheet 2 inches in from edge; fold other half over to make a half circle. Press edges together to seal firmly, turn up and crimp edges. Mix egg with 1 tablespoon water; brush over pie. Make a few slits in top for steam.
5. Bake in hot oven (400°) 30 minutes, or until golden brown. Slide onto a cutting board; cut into slices. Garnish with parsley and tomatoes.

EGGS FOO YOUNG

Now's a great time to try eggs for dinner. They are high in protein, low in cost and about the fastest food to cook—a special point in their favor in the heat of summer.

Makes 4 servings.

   1 can (3 or 4 ounces) chopped mushrooms
   8 eggs
   1 can (1 pound) Chinese vegetables, drained
 ½ teaspoon monosodium glutamate
 ¼ teaspoon pepper
   3 tablespoons vegetable oil
   Hot cooked rice
   Chinese sauce (recipe follows)

1. Drain mushroom liquid into a 2-cup measure and reserve for Chinese Sauce.
2. Beat eggs in a large bowl until foamy; stir in drained mushrooms, Chinese vegetables, monosodium glutamate and pepper.
3. Heat a medium-size skillet until a drop of water will "dance" on it. Brush with part of oil.
4. Pour ¼ cup of the egg mixture onto skillet; cook 1 minute, or until crisp and golden; turn with a wide pancake turner; cook 1 minute longer. Fold in half and arrange on a mound of hot rice on serving platter. Keep warm while using remaining egg mixture to make about 11 more "omelets." Serve with Chinese Sauce.

CHINESE SAUCE: Add water to reserved mushroom liquid to make 1½ cups. Pour into a small saucepan with 2 envelopes or teaspoons instant chicken broth, 1 tablespoon molasses and 1 tablespoon soy sauce. Heat to boiling and simmer 5 minutes to blend flavors. Combine 2 tablespoons cornstarch with ¼ cup cold water to make a smooth paste. Pour into simmering liquid, stirring constantly, until mixture thickens and bubbles 1 minute. Makes about 1½ cups.

MONEY-SAVING TIP

Doing without meat isn't the point so much as doing with *less*. Count on potatoes, rice, pasta, cereals, bread crumbs, dried beans, peas and lentils to accomplish this. They're great meat stretchers, as well as excellent sources of proteins.

JIFFY FONDUE

Few foods are more convivial than cheese fondue, yet few recipes are trickier to make the old-fashioned way. But this zip-quick version, made with frozen Welsh rarebit, is virtually foolproof. And it tastes very much like the real thing.

Makes 4 to 6 servings.

   2 **packages (10 ounces each) frozen Welsh rarebit, thawed to room temperature**
½ **cup dry vermouth**
   Pinch of ground nutmeg
2½ **slices imported Swiss cheese (from a 6-ounce package), cut in small pieces**
   Paprika (optional)
   1 **long thin loaf French bread, cut in 1- to 1½-inch cubes (leave the crust on)**

1. Place Welsh rarebit, vermouth and nutmeg in the top of a double boiler and set over simmering —not boiling—water. Heat and stir until silky-smooth and about the consistency of a medium cream sauce, about 5 minutes.
2. Add pieces of Swiss cheese, a scant handful at a time, heating and stirring after each addition until completely smooth and cheese is melted.
3. Pour into a glazed earthenware fondue pot, set on fondue stand over an alcohol flame turned low. Add a blush of paprika, if you like. Set out a basket of bread chunks, fondue forks and let everyone "dig in," spearing his own bread chunks and twirling them in fondue to coat.

✓ Good

SAUTEED CHICKEN LEGS MOUTARDE

Make sure that you use a very strong light-colored mustard such as Dijon for adequate piquancy.

Makes 6 servings.

   3 **tablespoons vegetable oil**
   6 **chicken legs cut in halves**
   1 **teaspoon salt**
¼ **teaspoon pepper**
¾ **cup chicken broth**
   1 **package (12 ounces) noodles**
   3 **tablespoons butter or margarine**
   1 **tablespoon chopped chives**
   2 **teaspoons cornstarch**
   1 **tablespoon prepared mustard, or more to taste**
   1 **tablespoon chopped parsley**

1. Heat the oil in a large skillet. Brown the chicken pieces on both sides; add ½ teaspoon of the salt and ⅛ teaspoon of the pepper. Discard the browning oil, replace it by ¼ cup of the chicken broth. Cover the pan and cook until tender, or about 30 minutes.
2. Cook and butter the noodles, season them with the remaining salt, pepper and the chopped chives.
3. Remove the chicken pieces to a serving platter. Skim fat from juices. Add ⅓ cup of chicken broth to the pan; scrape well to dissolve all the chicken cooking juices. Bring to boiling. Dissolve the cornstarch in the remaining cold chicken broth, add to the frying pan and stir until thickened. Turn the heat off. Let cool a minute or so and stir in the mustard. Do not reboil. Strain the sauce into a small bowl. Add the tablespoon of parsley.
4. Serve chicken with sauce and noodles.

BRACIOLE

Cook 1 roll for dinner tonight and freeze the other for a non-energetic night.

Makes 2 rolls—12 servings.

   2 **round steaks, 1 inch thick (about 1¼ pounds each)**
   1 **pound Italian sausage**
   1 **medium-size onion, sliced**
   1 **cup herb stuffing mix**
   1 **egg**
¼ **cup water**
   1 **can (4 ounces) pimientos, halved**
   1 **package (8 ounces) sliced mozzarella cheese**

1. Split the steaks butterfly fashion (split, but not all the way; open to 1 large piece). Pound with mallet or edge of heavy plate.
2. Cook the sausage in a large skillet; drain well. In the same skillet, sauté the onion; lift out with a slotted spoon; place on steaks.
3. Add stuffing mix, egg and water to skillet; mix well; spread over steaks.
4. Remove 1 slice of cheese from package; chop and reserve; halve remaining cheese slices lengthwise. Place half of cheese strips and half of the pimientos along one edge of steak. Place sausage on pimientos. Starting at that end, roll up each steak, jelly-roll fashion. Repeat with second steak. Tie rolls every two inches.
5. Place in a shallow baking pan; pour ¾ cup water over rolls. Bake in moderate oven (350°) for 40 minutes, basting occasionally. Sprinkle reserved cheese over rolls. Bake 10 minutes longer, or until cheese melts. Remove strings; slice.
To freeze: Wrap uncooked rolls in foil; label and freeze. To bake frozen rolls: Unwrap; place in baking pan. Pour ¾ cup water over. Bake in moderate oven (350°) for 1 hour and 50 minutes, basting occasionally. Sprinkle cheese on top; bake 10 minutes longer.

At right: Hero Salad—it's a sandwich in a salad bowl! Economical, too, this fun summer idea can include almost any sandwich-salad ingredient you want. See page 16 for ingredients we've included.

SKILLET LAMB A LA GREQUE

Closely related to the famous Greek Moussaka, this quick skillet put-together is delicious even when cold.

Makes 8 servings.

        2 pounds ground lamb
        1 medium-size onion, chopped (½ cup)
        1 clove garlic, minced
        1 large eggplant, pared and cubed (about 8 cups)
        1 can (14 ounces) spaghetti sauce
        2 teaspoons salt
        ⅛ teaspoon pepper
        1 teaspoon leaf basil, crumbled
        1 package (6 ounces) mozzarella cheese slices
          Pitted ripe olives, sliced (about 6)

1. Brown lamb in large skillet, 5 minutes on each side. Break up into chunks with spoon as it cooks; push to one side.
2. Sauté onion and garlic in drippings just until tender. Stir in eggplant, spaghetti sauce, salt, pepper and basil.
3. Cover; bring to boiling; lower heat. Simmer 20 minutes, or until eggplant is tender. Uncover.
4. Cut cheese into strips; arrange in lattice pattern on top of mixture. Place 1 or 2 slices of olive in each space between cheese strips.
5. Cover, simmer 3 minutes longer, or just until cheese begins to melt. Sprinkle with chopped parsley, if you wish.

SPICY LAMB CASSEROLE

Stretching meat is not a new art; people have been practicing it for centuries, producing lovely food. It isn't difficult, either, as this recipe proves.

Makes 6 servings.

        2 pounds lean boneless lamb
        3 tablespoons butter or margarine
        1 large onion, sliced
        2 cloves of garlic, minced
        2 tablespoons flour
     1½ cups water
        2 envelopes instant beef broth
        ½ teaspoon ground cinnamon
        ½ teaspoon ground ginger
        ½ teaspoon ground cardamom
        ⅔ cup golden raisins
        1 teaspoon salt
        ⅛ teaspoon pepper
        3 small yellow squash, cubed
        ¼ cup lemon juice

1. Cut meat into 2-inch strips. Sauté in butter or margarine until brown in a large skillet; transfer to a 10-cup baking dish. Sauté the onion and garlic in the remaining fat until soft.
2. Stir in the flour, water, beef broth, cinnamon, ginger, cardamom, raisins, salt and pepper. Cook, stirring constantly, 2 minutes. Pour the sauce over the meat in baking dish.
3. Simmer, covered, for 35 minutes, or until meat is almost tender. Add the cubed squash and lemon juice; continue cooking until the squash is tender, about 15 minutes.

MONEY-SAVING TIP

Orange and/or lemon peel can add exquisite flavor to meat, fish, poultry and vegetables. So instead of throwing it away after the orange or lemon has been juiced, tuck a strip of peel into the soup or stew pot, casserole dish or vegetable saucepan, and you're on your way to a new flavor treat. To peel an orange or lemon so that you get the colored part of the rind easily (not the bitter white part), run a sharp swivel-blade vegetable peeler over the rind.

FRENCH LIMA BEAN CASSEROLE

Lamb, rosemary and limas bake in a quick version of cassoulet.

Bake at 350° for 2½ hours.
Makes 8 servings.

        1 package (1 pound) dried lima beans
        4 cups water
        1 pound cubed lamb shoulder
        3 tablespoons vegetable oil
        1 large onion, chopped (1 cup)
        2 medium-size carrots, pared and chopped
        2 envelopes or teaspoons instant chicken broth
        2 teaspoons salt
        1 teaspoon leaf rosemary, crumbled
        ¼ teaspoon pepper

1. Pick over beans and rinse. Place in a large saucepan and add water. Heat to boiling; boil 2 minutes; remove from heat and cover saucepan. Allow to stand 1 hour.
2. Brown lamb in vegetable oil in a large skillet; remove with a slotted spoon. Sauté onion and carrot until soft in same skillet.
3. Drain beans and measure liquid. Add enough water to make 3 cups. Stir bean liquid into skillet with instant chicken broth, salt, rosemary and pepper. Heat to boiling.
4. Layer beans and browned lamb in a 12-cup casserole. Pour liquid from skillet over the casserole ingredients. Cover.
5. Bake in moderate oven (350°) 2 hours; remove cover. Bake about 30 to 40 minutes longer, or until the lima beans are tender and soft.

CHICKEN LIVERS PAPRIKASH

This hearty skillet dish goes well with noodles and squash, or any favorite vegetable.

Makes 4 servings.

   1 pound chicken livers
   1 medium-size onion, diced
   3 tablespoons margarine
   ½ teaspoon salt
   ½ teaspoon black pepper
   1 tablespoon sweet paprika
   1 clove garlic, sliced in half
   ½ teaspoon thyme
   1 tablespoon flour
   ¼ cup dairy sour cream

1. Clean livers, removing all fat and connective tissue. Heat margarine in 10-inch skillet and in it sauté onions until soft and bright yellow, but not brown. Add livers and brown on all sides.
2. Sprinkle with salt, pepper and paprika and sauté for a minute or two until paprika loses raw smell.
3. Add 1 cup water, or just enough to half cover livers. Add garlic and thyme and simmer, covered, 15 or 20 minutes, or until livers are done.
4. Blend flour into sour cream, stir into skillet and simmer 3 or 4 minutes. Adjust seasonings and serve the livers immediately.

DUCHESS SAUTÉED BEEF LIVER

Beef liver (instead of expensive calves' liver) is browned and arranged on a platter with a border of fluffy potatoes and topped with onions, pepper strips, tomatoes and beef broth—all for under 50¢ a serving!

Makes 6 servings.

   1 egg yolk
   2 cups mashed potatoes (about 4 medium-size potatoes)
   ¼ cup flour
   1½ teaspoons salt
   ¼ teaspoon pepper
   1½ pounds sliced beef liver
   2 tablespoons vegetable oil
   2 medium-size onions, sliced
   1 green pepper, cut lengthwise into strips
   1 tomato, cut into wedges
   1½ cups water
   1 envelope or teaspoon instant beef broth

1. Beat egg yolk into mashed potatoes; spoon into pastry bag fitted with a star tip. Pipe potatoes in a border around edge of a 10-inch round oven-proof platter or board.
2. Bake in hot oven (400°) 15 minutes, or until

the mashed potatoes are golden-brown in color.
3. Meanwhile mix flour, salt and pepper on wax paper. Cut liver into serving size pieces, if needed; coat with flour mixture.
4. Sauté liver in hot oil in a large skillet 4 minutes on each side, or until brown and done as you like. Arrange slices, overlapping inside border of potatoes. Keep hot at lowest oven temperature.
5. Sauté onions and pepper strips in same skillet, adding more oil if needed, 10 minutes, or until soft and golden. Stir in tomato; sauté 2 minutes longer. Arrange on top of liver.
6. Add water and instant beef broth to skillet. Bring to boiling, stirring and scraping to dissolve browned bits. Simmer, uncovered, 2 minutes. Pour over liver. Sprinkle with chopped parsley, if you wish. Serve at once.

STUFFED CHICKEN BREASTS SUPREME

In less than half an hour you can have this gourmet main dish ready for the oven. The cheese sauce is a snap to make, too.

Bake at 400° for 40 minutes.
Makes 8 servings.

   4 whole chicken breasts (about 12 ounces each)
   1 package (6 ounces) process Gruyère cheese, shredded
   ¼ pound salami, chopped
   ½ cup chopped green onions
   1 egg
   1 package (2⅜ ounces) seasoned coating mix for chicken
   ¼ cup (½ stick) butter or margarine
   ¼ cup flour
   2 cups milk

1. Halve chicken breasts; remove skin, if you wish, then cut meat in one piece from bones. Place each chicken breast between two sheets of wax paper and pound with a wooden mallet to thin.
2. Combine 1 cup of the cheese, salami and green onions in a small bowl. Place about ¼ cup of cheese filling in the center of each chicken breast. Roll up tightly and fasten with a pick.
3. Beat egg in a shallow dish; place seasoned coating mix on wax paper. Dip stuffed breasts in egg; roll in seasoned coating mix. Place in single layer in greased large baking dish.
4. Bake in hot oven (400°) 40 minutes, or until golden-brown.
5. While the chicken is baking, make cheese sauce. Melt butter or margarine in a medium-size saucepan; stir in flour; cook, stirring constantly, just until bubbly. Stir in milk; continue cooking and stirring until sauce thickens and bubbles 1 minute; stir in remaining cheese until melted. Serve the cheese sauce with the chicken.

2
FUN BARBECUES & COOKOUTS

"A man hath no better thing under the sun, than to eat, and to drink, and to be merry."
ECCLESIASTES *8:15*

The barbecue is the oldest kind of cooking known to man. But by no means is it old hat or out-of date. On the contrary, it continues to grow in popularity *and* innovation. The kabobs shown here, for instance, offer classic ingredients seasoned in a new, upbeat way. They include Deviled Chicken Wings plus Herbed Lamb-Vegetable Ka-bobs, with the meat and vegetables on separate skewers—a guarantee against under- or over-done ingredients. The following pages also offer recipes for all kinds of meats including the ever-popular hot dog and hamburger, a clambake you can prepare outdoors or in, plus five-minute sauces and mari-nades. So dust off the old grill and start cooking the way your ancestors did 12,000 years ago.

BARBECUED CHICKEN

*This tangy grilled chicken couldn't be simpler—
the flavorful sauce is both marinade and topping.*

Makes 4 servings.

    2 broiler-fryers (about 1½ pounds each), cut
      in half
    2 tablespoons vegetable oil
    1 medium-size onion
    3 cloves garlic, halved
    ¼ cup lemon juice
    ½ cup vinegar
    1 can (1 pound, 12 ounces) tomatoes
    1 bottle catsup
    1 tablespoon prepared mustard
    ½ teaspoon salt
    ¼ teaspoon pepper
    2 tablespoons chili powder
    2 tablespoons Worcestershire sauce
      Dash of liquid red-pepper seasoning
    2 tablespoons brown sugar or honey (optional)
    2 small red chili peppers

1. Pour oil into a deep, big pot. Add all remaining ingredients (except chicken). Cook over low heat for 1 hour or longer; taste several times during cooking and adjust seasoning to taste.
2. Press sauce through a sieve. Use half of the sauce you have to cover the chickens and let them marinate in it 1 hour or longer before you barbecue them. Refrigerate the other half for later.
3. Cook chickens over a low barbecue fire, turning with tongs, about 30 minutes. Baste with the sauce. Cover with top of barbecue so they'll smoke a little while cooking.
4. Heat the leftover sauce; if it's too thick, add a little vinegar, water or chicken broth. Serve over chicken on a large platter.

SKEWERED SALMON AND SHRIMP

*Pink salmon and juicy shrimp, flavorful with
their wine marinade, make good eating with the
bright green and yellow squash.*

Makes 6 servings.

    1 pound salmon steak, cut 1 inch thick
    1 cup dry white wine
    2 tablespoons vegetable oil
    1 teaspoon salt
    ⅛ teaspoon pepper
    ⅛ teaspoon leaf basil, crumbled
    1 pound raw shrimp, shelled and deveined
    2 small zucchini
    2 small yellow squash
    ¼ cup (½ stick) butter or margarine

1. Remove skin and bones from salmon steak, then cut it into pieces about 1x1½ inches in size.

2. Combine wine, oil, salt, pepper and basil in a large bowl. Add salmon and shrimp. Marinate 4 hours in refrigerator.
3. Trim zucchini and yellow squash; cut into 1-inch pieces. Parboil squash 3 minutes; drain.
4. Drain fish; reserve marinade. Thread salmon, shrimp, zucchini and yellow squash on 6 long skewers. Brush with reserved marinade.
5. Broil or grill, turning and basting vegetables and fish once, 10 minutes.
6. Bring remaining marinade to boiling in a small saucepan; remove from heat. Swirl in butter. Serve with fish skewers.
7. Serve with packaged frozen prepared rice with bell peppers and parsley, if you wish.

LEMON-TARRAGON CHICKEN

*The chicken mellows overnight in a delicately
flavored marinade. Oniony tomato halves and
crispy tiny potatoes make it a whole meal.*

Makes 4 servings.

    1 broiler-fryer, quartered (about 3½ pounds)
    ½ cup frozen chopped onion
    1 small lemon, sliced
    ¾ cup vegetable oil
    ¾ cup red wine vinegar
    2 large cloves garlic, cut in half
    2 teaspoons leaf tarragon, crumbled
    1 teaspoon salt
    2 medium-size tomatoes
    ½ cup vegetable oil or butter
    1 package (9 ounces) frozen fried potato
      rounds

1. Place chicken quarters in large, shallow dish. Add onion and lemon slices.
2. Combine oil, vinegar, garlic, tarragon and salt. Pour over chicken; turn chicken to coat well with marinade; cover with plastic wrap. Refrigerate at least 8 hours, or overnight, turning chicken in marinade several times.
3. Place broiler quarters on lightly oiled grill, bony side down (the bones act as heat conductors and hurry the cooking). Broil over slow coals, 20 minutes. Brush with marinade; turn; broil 20 minutes. Brush again with marinade. Continue broiling, turning occasionally and brushing with marinade 20 minutes, or until tender and golden.
4. For a complete meal: Wash and core tomatoes; cut in half crosswise; place onion pieces from marinade on top of each tomato half. Wrap each tomato half in a 6-inch square of heavy-duty aluminum foil and heat at edge of grill over hot coals 20 minutes—do not turn.
5. In skillet, heat oil or melt butter over grayed coals; add potato rounds. Heat over coals, turning with large pancake turner until potatoes are browned and piping hot, about 15 minutes.

HIBACHI PORK KABOBS

It takes only 10 minutes to prepare these savory kabobs for your picnic grill.

Makes 6 servings.

1½ **pounds very thin pork chops**
  2 **cooking apples**
1½ **cups white grape juice**
  1 **tablespoon freeze-dried chopped shallots**
⅓ **cup ham glaze (from a 12-ounce jar)**
  1 **package (12 ounces) frozen rice with peas and mushrooms in cooking pouch**

1. Cut chops into ½-inch-wide strips; quarter, core and cut apples into wedges.
2. Thread pork strips and apple wedges, alternately, onto 12 bamboo skewers. Arrange in a single layer in a shallow pan; pour grape juice over and sprinkle with shallots. Marinate at least 20 minutes, longer if possible.
3. Heat coals in hibachi or heat a table-model broiler, following manufacturer's directions.
4. Cook rice following package directions; keep warm while preparing kabobs.
5. Grill kabobs, brushing with marinade, 15 minutes, turning and brushing several times; brush kabobs with ham glaze and grill 5 minutes longer, or until richly glazed. Serve on cooked rice.

FROZEN FRENCH FRIES AT YOUR COOKOUT

Here are three outdoor ways to conveniently prepare either regular, thin or shoestring frozen French fries.

Grill in a popcorn popper: Use a long-handled popcorn popper with a metal pan (or a wire basket) and sliding wirecloth lid. Layer frozen French fries in the pan and brush or drizzle each layer with salad oil or melted butter. (Don't fill the pan too full.) Place popper on the grill over medium-hot coals. Cook, shaking occasionally with lid in place, for 20 to 25 minutes, or until fries are tender and lightly browned. Sprinkle with salt.

Grill in foil packets: Place individual servings of frozen French fries in the center of sheets of heavy-duty aluminum foil. Spoon 1 tablespoon salad oil or melted butter over each serving and sprinkle with salt. Make packets of the potatoes by bringing the 2 opposite edges of the foil up over the potatoes and sealing together with a tight double fold. Seal each end in the same manner. Place the packets, sealed edges down, on grill over hot coals. Cook 10 minutes. Using asbestos mitts or barbecue tongs, turn packets over and open, pushing back foil. Cook, stirring occasionally, 20 to 25 minutes longer, or until French fries are tender and lightly browned. Serve immediately.

Grill in a foil pan: Use a disposable foil pan (or make one of double thicknesses of heavy-duty foil) to hold the desired number of servings of frozen French fries. (For best results, put no more than four servings in a pan.) Layer potatoes in the pan and drizzle or brush salad oil or melted butter over each layer. Place the pan(s) on grill over hot coals. Cook, stirring occasionally, for 30 to 40 minutes, or until fries are tender and lightly browned. Sprinkle with salt and pepper—and pass the catsup bottle, if you wish!

THE PARISIAN

Not to be outdone, the Parisian haute cuisine influence creates a most elegant and luscious burger. (Shown in photograph on page 29.)

Makes 4 servings.

¼ **cup white wine vinegar**
¼ **cup water**
  1 **tablespoon finely chopped shallots or green onions**
½ **teaspoon dried tarragon, crumbled**
  2 **egg yolks**
½ **cup (1 stick) butter or margarine**
  1 **teaspoon chopped parsley**
  1 **pound ground round or chuck**
⅓ **cup dry red wine**
  1 **tablespoon finely cut chives**
  1 **teaspoon salt**
¼ **teaspoon pepper**
  1 **tablespoon butter or margarine**
    Watercress
  4 **hamburger rolls, split, buttered and toasted**

1. For Béarnaise Sauce: Combine vinegar, water, shallots and tarragon in a small saucepan. Heat to boiling, then simmer 8 to 10 minutes, or until mixture is reduced to ¼ cup. Strain into top of double boiler. Cut butter or margarine into 8 pieces. Add egg yolks to double boiler; beat with wire whisk until foamy. Set over simmering, not boiling, water. Add butter or margarine, 1 piece at a time, stirring constantly; each piece should melt before you add the next; sauce should be fluffy-thick. Season with salt and pepper, if needed. Stir in parsley. Remove top saucepan from hot water immediately.
2. Lightly mix beef with wine, chives, salt and pepper in a large bowl. Shape into 4 equal-size patties, about the size of the rolls.
3. Melt 1 tablespoon butter or margarine in a heavy skillet. Add hamburgers; sauté over medium heat for about 4 minutes on each side, or until done as you like them.
4. Place a few sprigs of watercress on each bottom half of 4 rolls; top with hamburger; spoon Bearnaise Sauce over; garnish with sliced cherry tomatoes and sliced mushrooms, if you wish. Top each hamburger with the remaining half of roll.

THE ALL-AMERICAN SUPERBURGER

Make the homestyle version of America's No. 1 favorite—the big stacked hamburger.

Makes 6 double burgers.

    Jumbo Burger Rolls (recipe follows)
½ cup mayonnaise or salad dressing
¼ cup chili sauce
¼ cup sweet pickle relish
1½ pounds ground round or chuck
1½ teaspoons salt
¼ teaspoon pepper
  2 tablespoons butter or margarine
  6 crisp, washed lettuce leaves
  6 tomato slices
  6 slices process American cheese
  6 thin slices sweet Bermuda onion

1. Combine mayonnaise or salad dressing, chili sauce and sweet pickle relish in a small bowl; mix well; cover. Refrigerate until ready to use.
2. Mix beef lightly with salt and pepper; shape into 12 patties, pressing them very thin.
3. Melt butter or margarine in a large skillet. Pan-fry hamburgers over medium heat 2 minutes on each side, or until done as you like them.
4. To assemble hamburgers: Cut rolls evenly into three layers; place a lettuce leaf on bottom layer, then a hamburger, tomato slice, sauce, middle roll layer, another burger, cheese slice, onion slice, more sauce and top of roll. Serve with French Fried Onion Rings, if you wish.

JUMBO BURGER ROLLS

You need a really big roll to make the All-American Superburger. These are simple and so delicious.

Bake at 325° for 25 minutes.
Makes 6 large rolls.

  1 package hot-roll mix
¾ cup very warm water
  2 eggs
  2 tablespoons sesame seeds

1. Prepare hot-roll mix with water and 1 egg and let rise, following label directions.
2. Turn dough out onto a lightly floured pastry board; knead 8 to 10 times. Divide into 6 even pieces; shape into smooth balls, then flatten to make about a 4-inch round. Place on a greased cooky sheet.
3. Cover with a towel; let rise 30 minutes, or until double in bulk. Beat remaining egg; brush over rolls; sprinkle with sesame seeds.
4. Bake in moderate oven (325°) 25 minutes, or until rolls are golden and give a hollow sound when lightly tapped. Let rolls cool on wire rack.

FRENCH FRIED ONION RINGS

A kicky go-with that you'll be glad you tried.

Makes 4 to 6 servings.

  1 large Bermuda onion
  2 eggs
½ cup milk
  1 cup sifted all-purpose flour
  1 teaspoon baking powder
½ teaspoon salt
    Vegetable oil

1. Peel onion; cut into ¼-inch-thick slices; separate into rings.
2. Beat eggs and milk until frothy in a large bowl; sift in flour, baking powder and salt; stir with a wire whisk, just until blended.
3. Pour enough vegetable oil into a large skillet to make a depth of 1 inch; heat to 375°.
4. Dip onion rings, a few at a time, into batter; drop into heated oil. Fry, turning once, 3 to 4 minutes, or until crisp and golden. Drain on paper toweling. (If batter is too thick, add 1 or 2 tablespoons milk.) Sprinkle with salt, if you wish.

DEVILED CHICKEN WINGS

Mustard, Worcestershire sauce, catsup and fiery pepper sauce make a memorable spread-on for charcoal-ready chicken or beef.

Makes 4 servings.

10-12 chicken wings (about 1½ pounds)
  1 small orange, sliced (optional)
  2 teaspoons prepared mustard
  2 teaspoons Worcestershire sauce
  3 tablespoons catsup
¼ teaspoon liquid red-pepper seasoning
⅛ teaspoon garlic salt
⅛ teaspoon pepper
½ teaspoon parsley flakes

1. Rinse and dry chicken wings; cut off and discard wing tips. Thread wings onto skewers alternately with orange slices.
2. Combine mustard, Worcestershire sauce, catsup, red-pepper seasoning, garlic salt, pepper and parsley flakes in a small bowl. Brush on chicken.
3. Grill chicken 6 inches from white-hot charcoal, turning frequently, about 30 to 35 minutes.

Shown at right in large photograph: The All-American Superburger, loaded with cheese, onion, pickle and tomato. Then for an around-the-world sampling of burgers, we've added (from top, clockwise): The Iberian Burger, The Neapolitan, The Toreador, The Islander, The Parisian and The Athenian. Recipes for all are in this chapter.

THE ATHENIAN

Flavors borrowed from the Greek moussaka make this topping uniquely different.

Makes 4 servings.

   1 can (4¾ ounces) eggplant appetizer
   ½ cup coarsely chopped peeled tomatoes
   ¼ cup chopped green onions
   ¼ teaspoon leaf basil, crumbled
   1 pound ground round or chuck
   1 teaspoon salt
   ⅛ teaspoon pepper
   1 tablespoon butter or margarine
   4 hamburger rolls, split, buttered and toasted

1. Combine eggplant appetizer, tomatoes, green onion and basil in a small bowl; cover. Refrigerate until ready to use.
2. Mix beef lightly with salt and pepper; shape into 4 equal-size patties about the size of the rolls.
3. Pan-fry hamburgers in butter or margarine in a large skillet over medium heat, 4 minutes on each side, or until done as you like them.
4. Place each hamburger on bottom half of roll; spoon some eggplant mixture on top of each; sprinkle with more chopped green onion, if you wish. Top each with remaining half of roll. Garnish with green onion, olives and pimiento.

THE TOREADOR

The wide-awake taste of a pungent Mexican chili topping deserves a hearty olé!

Makes 4 servings.

   1 tablespoon vegetable oil
   1 medium-size onion, chopped (½ cup)
   1 clove garlic, chopped
   1 tablespoon chili powder
   1 can (1 pound) tomatoes
   1 can (1 pound) red kidney beans, drained
   ½ teaspoon salt
   ⅛ teaspoon pepper
   ⅛ teaspoon liquid red-pepper seasoning
   1 pound ground round or chuck
   1 teaspoon salt
   ⅛ teaspoon pepper
   2 tablespoons butter or margarine
   4 hamburger rolls, split, toasted and buttered
   Shredded lettuce
   4 ounces (1 cup) shredded Cheddar cheese

1. Heat oil in a saucepan; sauté onion and garlic until tender. Add chili powder; stir 1 minute. Add tomatoes, beans, the ½ teaspoon salt, pepper and red-pepper seasoning. Simmer 30 minutes, or until the mixture is thick.
2. Season beef with remaining salt and pepper; shape into 4 equal-size patties, about roll size.

3. Melt butter or margarine in a skillet. Pan-fry hamburgers about 4 minutes on each side, or until done as you like them.
4. Arrange shredded lettuce on bottom halves of rolls; top with burger. Spoon chili mixture over burgers. Place more shredded lettuce and cheese atop chili. Garnish with red-onion rings, if you wish. Top each with remaining half of roll.

TRICKS WITH GRILLED BURGERS

Grill burgers good and brown before turning. And flip only once. Prevent sticking by brushing patties with a little vegetable oil mixed with a seasoner of your choice. Or brush grill with oil; will not only prevent sticking, but will cut down considerably on cleanup time.

DUXBURY BURGERS

A cranberry glaze adds zest to ground beef.

Makes 8 servings.

   1 package (8 ounces) ready-mix herb-seasoned stuffing
 1¼ cups hot water
   ½ cup (1 stick) butter or margarine, melted
   2 eggs, lightly beaten
   3 pounds ground beef
     Salt
   1 can (8 ounces) whole cranberry sauce
   2 tablespoons vegetable oil
   1 tablespoon prepared mustard
   1 can (about 11 ounces) beef gravy
   8 hero rolls, split

1. Combine stuffing mix, hot water and melted butter or margarine in a large bowl; toss until evenly moist. Stir in eggs; cool completely.
2. Divide ground beef into 8 parts. Shape each into a 4-inch square, then roll between sheets of wax paper to an 8-inch square. (Tip: To prevent slipping, lay wax paper on top of damp paper toweling.) Sprinkle meat lightly with salt.
3. Spread about ⅓ cup of the cooled stuffing mixture over each square; roll up, jelly-roll fashion. Place in a single layer on a cooky sheet; cover. Chill until cooking time.
4. Combine cranberry sauce, vegetable oil and mustard in an electric-blender container; cover; beat until smooth. (If you do not have a blender, beat at high speed with an electric beater.)
5. When ready to cook meat, place on grill about 6 inches above hot coals. Grill 10 minutes; turn. Cook 10 minutes longer; brush with part of the cranberry mixture. Continue cooking, turning and brushing often, 5 minutes, or until meat is richly glazed and done as you like it.
6. While meat cooks, heat gravy in a small saucepan and warm the hero rolls on edge of grill.

7. Place each burger in a roll; garnish with small onion rings, if you wish. Serve gravy separately. *Note:* Stuff and shape meat and fix cranberry mixture at home; carry to your eating spot in a keep-cold container.

THE NEAPOLITAN

Top your burger with all those great pizza flavors and back a winner.

Makes 4 servings.

  1 pound ground round or chuck
  1 egg
  ¼ cup packaged bread crumbs
  1 clove garlic, crushed
  ½ teaspoon salt
  ½ teaspoon leaf basil, crumbled
  ½ teaspoon leaf oregano, crumbled
  ¼ cup grated Parmesan cheese
  ⅛ teaspoon pepper
  1 tablespoon butter or margarine
  4 tomato slices
  4 ounces mozzarella cheese, sliced and cut into strips
  4 hamburger rolls, split, buttered and toasted

1. Mix beef lightly with egg, bread crumbs, garlic, salt, basil, oregano, Parmesan cheese and pepper until well-blended in a large bowl. Shape into 4 equal-size patties, about the size of the rolls.
2. Pan-fry in butter or margarine in a large skillet over medium heat 4 minutes on each side, or until done as you like them.
3. Place a tomato slice on each burger and criss-cross 2 strips of cheese. Place under the broiler just until cheese is melted. Place on bottom half of hamburger roll; sprinkle with additional oregano and parsley, if you wish. Top with remaining half of roll. Garnish with olives, if you wish.

THE ISLANDER

No doubt about it, with the zip of curry and the sun-ripe touch of pineapple, you can almost see the palm trees.

Makes 4 servings.

  3 tablespoons butter or margarine
  1 small onion, finely chopped (¼ cup)
  2 teaspoons curry powder
  1 can (8¼ ounces) sliced pineapple
  2 teaspoons chopped chutney
  1 pound ground round or chuck
  1 envelope or teaspoon instant beef broth
  2 tablespoons water
  4 hamburger rolls, split, toasted and buttered
  Flaked coconut
  Watercress

1. Melt 2 tablespoons of the butter or margarine in a small saucepan; add onion; sauté 6 to 8 minutes, or until tender. Stir in curry powder; continue cooking, stirring constantly, 2 minutes.
2. Drain juice from pineapple (⅓ cup); add to curry along with chutney. Cook, uncovered, over low heat, stirring occasionally, until thickened slightly, about 10 minutes. Add pineapple slices; keep warm.
3. Lightly mix beef with instant beef broth and water. Shape into 4 equal-size patties, about the size of the rolls.
4. Heat remaining 1 tablespoon butter or margarine in a large skillet; pan-fry hamburgers over medium heat, 4 minutes on each side, or until done as you like them.
5. Place a hamburger on bottom half of each roll; top each with pineapple slice and curry sauce. Garnish with flaked coconut and watercress. Top each with remaining half of roll. Serve with slices of lime, if you wish.

THE IBERIAN

The bright peppers and mellow sherry lend a touch of sunny Spain.

Makes 4 servings.

  1 pound ground round or chuck
  1 teaspoon salt
  ¼ teaspoon pepper
  2 tablespoons butter or margarine
  2 tablespoons vegetable oil
  1 tablespoon finely chopped shallots or green onions
  ½ green pepper, cut into strips
  ½ red pepper, cut into strips
  1 tablespoon bottled steak sauce
  1 tablespoon prepared mustard
  4 tablespoons dry sherry
  2 tablespoons chopped parsley
  4 hamburger rolls, split, buttered and toasted

1. Lightly mix beef with salt and pepper. Shape into 4 equal-size patties, about the size of the rolls.
2. Melt butter or margarine in a large skillet. Pan-fry hamburgers 4 minutes over medium heat; turn and push to one side of skillet. Add oil, shallots and peppers; after 4 minutes, remove hamburgers and keep warm. Continue to cook peppers, stirring often, 5 more minutes, or until crisply tender. Remove and keep warm.
3. Stir steak sauce, mustard and sherry into skillet; stir over low heat until well-blended with drippings. Cook, uncovered, until reduced to about half, 2 to 3 minutes; stir in parsley.
4. Arrange hamburgers on bottom halves of rolls; pile peppers on top and spoon sauce over. Top each with remaining half of roll. Garnish with a few fresh, quartered mushrooms, if you wish.

EL RANCHO HOT DOGS

From the Southwestern United States, where the natives enjoy food "heated."

Makes 6 servings.

   1 tablespoon vegetable oil
   1 clove garlic, chopped
   ½ cup frozen chopped onion
   1 can (1 pound) red kidney beans
   1 can (8 ounces) tomato sauce
   2 tablespoons diced green chili peppers (from a 4-ounce can)
   ½ teaspoon salt
   ⅛ teaspoon pepper
   6 hot dogs
   6 toasted hot dog rolls
   1 cup shredded iceberg lettuce
   4 ounces Monterey Jack cheese, shredded (1 cup)

1. Heat oil in a skillet; sauté garlic and onion until tender, about 5 minutes. Add kidney beans with liquid, tomato sauce, chili peppers, salt and pepper. Bring to boiling; lower heat. Simmer, uncovered, 5 minutes.
2. Add hot dogs to bean mixture; simmer 10 minutes longer, or until hot dogs are hot and bean mixture has thickened.
3. Fill toasted rolls with hot dogs and beans. Top with lettuce and cheese.

SAMURAI KABOBS

Broil the skewered hot dogs and vegetables right in their marinade.

Makes 6 servings.

   ⅓ cup soy sauce
   ⅓ cup cider vinegar
   ⅓ cup peanut or vegetable oil
   1 teaspoon ground ginger
   ¼ teaspoon crushed red pepper
   1 pound hot dogs
   8 small white onions, peeled
   1 medium-size green pepper
   1 medium-size red pepper
   6 toasted hot dog rolls

1. Combine soy sauce, vinegar, oil, ginger and red pepper in a 13x9x2-inch metal pan. (The bottom half of a small broiling pan is just right.)
2. Cut hot dogs into thirds, crosswise. Parboil onions 5 minutes in salted boiling water; drain. Halve and seed peppers; cut into squares.
3. Thread hot dog pieces, pepper squares and onion onto bamboo skewers. Place in a single layer in pan of marinade. Allow to marinate at least 30 minutes, turning kabobs several times.
4. Broil, 4 inches from heat, in metal pan in marinade, 4 minutes; turn kabobs; broil about 4 minutes longer.
5. Brush remaining marinade onto toasted rolls and place a kabob in each.

CALIFORNIA HOT DOGS

Avocado dip, a new item in the frozen food case, makes a quick and delicious topping.

Makes 8 servings.

   1 pound hot dogs
   ½ cup bottled barbecue sauce
   1 can (7¾ ounces) frozen avocado dip, thawed
   8 toasted hot dog rolls
     Pitted ripe olives, chopped
     Thin onion slices

1. Brush hot dogs with barbecue sauce.
2. Broil, 4 inches from heat, 4 minutes; turn; brush with barbecue sauce; broil 4 minutes longer.
3. Spread avocado dip onto toasted rolls; place a broiled hot dog on each roll; top with chopped ripe olives and thin slices of onion.

ALL-AMERICAN HOT DOGS

Hot dogs teamed with bacon, cheese and ready-to-cook hash brown potatoes are certain to make a big hit with the whole family.

Bake at 400° for 10 minutes.
Makes 8 servings.

   1 package (12 ounces) frozen shredded hash-brown potatoes
   1 pound hot dogs
   2 slices process American cheese
   8 slices bacon, partially cooked
   8 toasted hot dog rolls

1. Thaw hashbrown potatoes for 15 minutes. Cut each potato brick into 4 strips, crosswise, with a long sharp knife.
2. Split hot dogs almost in half, lengthwise, with a sharp knife; cut each cheese slice into 4 strips.
3. Tuck a potato strip inside each hot dog; top with a cheese strip; wrap a slice of partially cooked bacon around hot dog and secure with wood pick. Place on a cooky sheet.
4. Bake in hot oven (400°) 10 minutes, or until bacon is crisp. Remove wood picks. Place the hot dogs on toasted rolls and serve with mustard.

At left: Imaginative new ways to serve hot dogs. Starting at the top: All-American Hot Dogs; California Hot Dogs; El Rancho Hot Dogs; Samurai Kabobs. The recipes for all four are included on this page.

FIVE-MINUTE GARNISHES FOR MEATS

Vegetable and Fruit Kabobs are easy to make by spearing green pepper cubes, radishes, cauliflowerettes, olives and cucumbers on small wooden skewers; or combine banana wedges, crab apples, pineapple chunks, cherries, orange slices, etc. Serve these with grilled steaks, hamburgers or any backyard meat platter.

Orange Cups go well with all kinds of poultry dishes. Mound whole-berry or jellied cranberry sauce into orange cups and broil or bake until hot or make ahead and refrigerate until serving time; serve iced cold.

Bacon wraps are a nice flavor addition to calves' liver. To make them, halve bacon slices and wrap each around a cherry tomato or tomato wedge. Fasten with wood pick; broil until bacon is crisp.

Green-Grape Garnish, made with small bunches of seedless grapes, looks pretty around a ham. Brush grape bunches with egg whites that have been beaten until frothy, then dip bunches in sugar. Shake off excess, then allow sugar to set.

Relishes go well with meats as you'll see when you read Chapter 4 which contains excellent homemade relish recipes. But here's a really quick relish idea you'll want to try also. Fill canned peach, pear or apricot halves with store-bought pickle relish. Serve cold or broil until hot.

ART'S FOOLPROOF BARBECUED SPARERIBS

The secret for crisp juicy spareribs is the pre-barbecue cooking they get in peppy seasoned broth. (Shown on opposite page.)

Makes 6 to 8 servings.

- 3 pounds spareribs
  Water
- 1 tablespoon salt
- 1 tablespoon mixed pickling spices
- 1 medium-size onion, sliced
- ½ cup barbecue sauce (from an 18-ounce bottle)
- ¼ cup dark corn syrup

1. Place ribs in a large kettle (cut, if necessary, to fit kettle). Cover ribs with water and add salt, pickling spices and onion slices.
2. Heat slowly to boiling; lower heat; cover; simmer ribs 1 hour. Remove kettle from heat and allow ribs to cool in liquid.
3. When ready to broil ribs: Remove ribs from liquid and arrange in single layer on rack of broiler pan or on grill.
4. Combine barbecue sauce and corn syrup in a cup or small-size bowl. Brush over the spareribs.
5. Broil, 4 inches from heat, turning and basting often, 20 minutes, or until ribs are evenly glazed. To serve, cut into serving-size pieces.

SPARERIB VARIATIONS

Deviled Beef Bones—Follow recipe for Art's Foolproof Barbecued Spareribs through Step 2, substituting 3 pounds beef short ribs for the pork spareribs. Arrange ribs on wax paper. Combine ¾ cup bottled barbecue sauce with ¼ cup prepared mustard in a small bowl; brush over ribs. Sprinkle 1 cup seasoned bread crumbs on another piece of wax paper. Roll ribs in crumbs to coat, then arrange in single layer on rack of broiler pan. Broil, 4 inches from heat, turning and basting often with sauce, 20 minutes.

Honeyed Veal Riblets—Follow recipe for Art's Foolproof Barbecued Spareribs through Step 2, substituting 3 pounds breast of veal for the pork spareribs. Arrange ribs in single layer on rack of broiler pan. Combine ½ cup bottled barbecue sauce and ¼ cup honey in a cup; brush over ribs. Broil, 4 inches from heat, turning and basting with sauce, 20 minutes, or until ribs are glazed.

Glazed Lamb Riblets—Follow recipe for Art's Foolproof Barbecued Spareribs through Step 2, substituting 3 pounds lamb riblets for the pork spareribs. Arrange ribs in a single layer on rack of broiler pan. Combine ½ cup bottled barbecue sauce with ¼ cup bottled chutney, chopped, in a cup; brush over ribs. Broil, 4 inches from heat, turning and basting often with sauce, 20 minutes, or until ribs are evenly glazed.

GARLIC HOT DOGS

For a zesty taste treat, try marinating hot dogs in garlic and oil before cooking.

Makes 8 servings.

- ½ cup olive or vegetable oil
- 2 cloves garlic, minced
- 1 pound hot dogs
- 1 package (12 ounces) frozen chopped onions
- 8 toasted hot dog rolls
  Hot mustard

1. Heat oil and garlic in a medium-size saucepan for 5 minutes; remove from heat; add hot dogs; cover saucepan. Marinate hot dogs, turning several times, at least 2 hours.
2. Measure 2 tablespoons of the garlic oil into a large skillet. Sauté onions in oil until golden; remove from skillet; reserve.
3. Add remaining oil and hot dogs to skillet; brown hot dogs, turning several times, 5 minutes.
4. Divide onions among toasted rolls; add hot dogs; top with mustard.

At right: Art's Foolproof Barbecued Spareribs, an easy-to-make specialty you can prepare indoors or out. The recipe is in the column at left.

BAVARIAN HOT DOGS

Try this hearty Old World-inspired treat with its beer and sauerkraut topping.

Makes 8 servings.

- 1 large onion, chopped
- 2 tablespoons butter or margarine
- 1 can (1 pound, 11 ounces) sauerkraut, drained and rinsed
- ½ teaspoon caraway seeds
- 1 can (12 ounces) beer
- 1 pound hot dogs
- 8 toasted hot dog rolls
  Mustard

1. Sauté onion in butter until soft in a large skillet; stir in rinsed sauerkraut and caraway seeds and cook for about 2 minutes; add the can of beer; lower heat; cover skillet.
2. Simmer 20 minutes; arrange hot dogs over sauerkraut; simmer 10 minutes longer, or until hot dogs are heated through.
3. Spoon sauerkraut into toasted rolls; add hot dogs; spread with mustard.

ORIENTAL SKEWERED SHRIMP

A fine appetizer from the hibachi.

Makes 4 to 6 servings.

- ¾ cup medium dry California sherry
- ¼ cup soy sauce
- 1 teaspoon sugar
- ½ teaspoon ground ginger
- 36 raw medium-size shrimp, shelled and deveined (about 1¼ pounds)
  Wooden or bamboo skewers, about 9 inches long
  Cherry tomatoes
  Yellow pickled peppers

1. Combine sherry, soy sauce, sugar and ginger in a small saucepan. Heat just to boiling; remove from heat; cool to room temperature.
2. Wash shrimp. Thread 3 shrimp lengthwise, through the center, heads doubled up against the tails, on each skewer. Thread a cherry tomato or yellow pickled pepper at end of each skewer. Place on a platter and brush with sauce on all sides. Refrigerate for 1 hour.
3. Grill over medium coals for 6 to 10 minutes, turning once and brushing frequently with the sauce, until nicely glazed. Serve piping hot.

At left: Oriental Skewered Shrimp is a fine appetizer for outdoor dinners. The shrimp, threaded with cherry tomatoes and peppers, is brushed with a ginger-soy sauce. Recipe is above.

FIVE-MINUTE BARBECUE SAUCES & MARINADES

YOGURT MARINADE

Use this creamy marinade on chicken or lamb.

Makes about 1½ cups.

- ½ teaspoon fennel seeds
- ½ teaspoon ground cardamom
- ¼ teaspoon ground ginger
- 1 envelope instant chicken broth
- 1 cup unflavored yogurt
- ½ cup milk
- 1 tablespoon bottled chili sauce
- 2 tablespoons chopped fresh mint or 2 teaspoons dried mint

1. Place fennel seeds, cardamom, ginger and instant chicken broth in small bowl. Crush seeds against side of bowl with back of wooden spoon.
2. Add yogurt, milk, chili sauce and mint; stir to mix. Use to marinate meat for several hours.

FLORENTINE MARINADE

Try this sassy marinade on fish or poultry.

Makes 1 cup.

- ¼ cup lemon juice
- ¼ cup dry vermouth
- 1 envelope Italian flavored salad-dressing mix
- ½ cup olive oil

Combine lemon juice, vermouth, salad-dressing mix and oil in a jar with tight-fitting cover; shake well. Note: For variation, add ½ teaspoon dried mint.

BASIC BARBECUE SAUCE

Here's a simple basic sauce and four zippy variations to brush on steaks or burgers as they grill.

Makes 3 cups.

- 1 cup light molasses
- 1 cup prepared mustard
- 1 cup cider vinegar

Combine all ingredients in a 4-cup jar with tight-fitting lid; shake well to mix. Store in refrigerator.

Left: Barbecue sauces and marinades you can make in five minutes or less! Clockwise, starting at top: Basic Barbecue Sauce, Yogurt Marinade, Florentine Marinade, Pineapple Baste and Super Simple Sauce. Recipes for all are in this chapter.

Variations on Basic Barbecue Sauce:
Ginger-Rich Sauce—Mix 1 cup Basic Barbecue Sauce with ½ cup ginger marmalade and 1 teaspoon ground ginger. Makes 1½ cups.
Zing Sauce—Mix 1 cup Basic Barbecue Sauce with ¼ cup catsup, ¼ cup vegetable oil and 2 tablespoons Worcestershire. Makes 1½ cups.
Italian Herb Sauce—Mix 1 cup Basic Barbecue Sauce with ½ cup chili sauce and ½ teaspoon oregano. Makes 1½ cups.
Peppy Tomato Sauce—Mix 1 cup Basic Barbecue Sauce with ½ cup tomato juice and ½ teaspoon freshly ground pepper. Makes 1½ cups.

SUPER SIMPLE SAUCE

Brush on steaks, hamburgers and shish kabobs.

Makes about 2¼ cups.

- 1 bottle (8 ounces) oil and vinegar salad dressing
- 1 cup bottled chili sauce
- ¼ cup bottled steak sauce

Combine dressing, chili sauce and steak sauce in a small bowl. Use to baste meats as they grill. Note: For variation, add ½ teaspoon dried oregano.

FRUITED GLAZE

Try it on pork and poultry.

Makes about 1¼ cups.

- ½ cup orange or ginger marmalade or apricot preserves
- ½ cup bottled barbecue sauce
- ¼ cup light molasses
- 2 teaspoons prepared mustard

Combine marmalade or preserves, barbecue sauce, molasses and mustard in small bowl. Stir to mix. Brush on meat for last 30 minutes of cooking time.

RUMAKI MARINADE

Use this soy-based marinade for steak, hamburger and liver.

Makes about 1½ cups.

- 1 cup soy sauce
- ½ cup dry sherry
- 2 tablespoons honey
- 2 tablespoons vegetable oil
- 1 clove garlic, crushed

Combine soy sauce, sherry, honey, oil and garlic. Use to marinate meat or liver, refrigerated, for several hours; then broil, basting with marinade.

PINEAPPLE BASTE

This tangy tropical sauce is perfect for livening up fish and chicken dishes.

Makes about ¾ cup.

- ¼ cup frozen concentrate for pineapple juice, thawed
- ¼ cup lime juice or dry white wine
- ¼ cup soy sauce
- 1 clove garlic, crushed
- 1 teaspoon ground ginger
- 2 tablespoons olive or vegetable oil

Combine pineapple juice, lime juice or wine, soy sauce, garlic, ginger and oil in small cup; stir to mix well. Use as basting sauce on fish or chicken.

SKEWERED CHICKEN LIVERS WITH MUSHROOMS

Tender, crumb-coated chicken livers, paired with fresh mushrooms and a delicate wine sauce, are an epicure's delight.

Makes 4 servings.

- 1 pound chicken livers
- 3 tablespoons butter or margarine, melted
- ¼ cup dry white wine
- ½ cup fine dry bread crumbs
- ¼ teaspoon onion salt
- ¼ teaspoon leaf basil, crumbled
- 4 large mushrooms, quartered
- 8 cherry tomatoes
  White Wine Sauce (recipe follows)

1. Halve chicken livers; combine 2 tablespoons melted butter or margarine and wine in a medium-size bowl; add chicken livers and marinate for ½ hour in the refrigerator.
2. Combine bread crumbs, onion, salt and basil on wax paper. Drain excess liquid from chicken livers and roll in bread-crumb mixture until the livers are completely coated.
3. Thread chicken livers, mushrooms and cherry tomatoes alternately on 4 skewers; brush with remaining butter or margarine.
4. Broil or grill 15 minutes, turning once, or until liver is slightly brown. Serve with White Wine Sauce and parslied hot noodles, if you wish.

WHITE WINE SAUCE—Sauté ¼ cup chopped green onions in 2 tablespoons butter or margarine in a medium-size saucepan 5 minutes, or until tender; stir in 2 teaspoons flour, ¼ teaspoon salt and ⅛ teaspoon pepper. Cook, stirring constantly, just until bubbly. Stir in 1 cup dry white wine; continue cooking and stirring until sauce thickens and bubbles for 1 minute.

SWEET-SOUR SAUSAGE KABOBS

Convenient, ready-cooked sausage combines with a packaged sweet-sour mix for Far East twist to a kabob.

Makes 6 servings.

- 1 can (5¾ ounces) pineapple tidbits
- ¼ cup water
- ¼ cup vinegar
- 1 envelope (2 ounces) sweet-sour sauce mix
- 2 tablespoons brown sugar
- 2 packages (8 ounces each) brown-and-serve link sausages, halved
- 1 can (1 pound) whole onions
- 1 large green pepper, seeded and cut into 12 squares

1. Drain pineapple tidbits, reserving syrup and pineapple separately.
2. In a small saucepan, combine pineapple syrup, water, vinegar, sweet-sour sauce mix and brown sugar. Bring to boiling, stirring constantly; lower heat; simmer 1 minute, or until sauce thickens.
3. Thread sausages, onions, green pepper pieces and pineapple alternately on 6 long skewers; brush with sauce.
4. Broil or grill 8 minutes, turning once and brushing with sauce. Keep remaining sauce warm to serve with the kabobs. Serve with packaged chicken-flavor rice and vermicelli, if you wish.

SKEWERED CHICKEN CANTONESE

Flavors borrowed from mild Cantonese cooking give this chicken a special difference.

Makes 6 servings.

- 4 whole chicken breasts, skinned and boned
- 1 cup dry sherry
- 2 tablespoons vegetable oil
- 1 tablespoon soy sauce
- ½ teaspoon salt
- ⅛ teaspoon pepper
- ¼ teaspoon sugar
- 4 slices fresh ginger root (optional)

1. Cut chicken breasts into 1-inch pieces.
2. Combine sherry, oil, soy sauce, salt, pepper, sugar and ginger root in a large bowl; add chicken pieces. Marinate 4 hours in refrigerator.
3. Drain chicken; reserve marinade. Thread pieces on 6 short skewers with pieces just touching.
4. Broil or grill, turning and basting once, 8 minutes, or until chicken is golden.
5. Bring remaining marinade to boiling in a small saucepan; pour into shallow dish. Turn cooked chicken skewers in sauce immediately as they are removed from the broiler. Serve the chicken on packaged noodles with almonds, if you wish.

RANCH-STYLE BARBECUED CHICKEN

Pungent flavors of the Southwest liven this dish.

Makes 4 servings.

    1 whole broiler-fryer (about 3 pounds)
    1 teaspoon salt
    ¼ teaspoon pepper
    2 tablespoons vegetable oil
    ⅔ cup catsup
    ⅓ cup cider vinegar
    ⅓ cup water
    ¼ cup finely chopped onion
    1 tablespoon brown sugar
    1 tablespoon Worcestershire sauce
    1 teaspoon chili powder

1. Rinse chicken inside and out; pat dry with paper toweling. Rub salt and pepper onto skin and inside body cavity of chicken. Fasten neck skin to back with skewer; tie legs to tail.
2. Place chicken on spit, following manufacturer's directions; brush with part of the oil. Set spit in position over hot coals; start rotisserie. Roast, brushing several times with the oil, 1 hour.
3. Combine catsup, vinegar, water, onion, brown sugar, Worcestershire sauce and chili powder in a small saucepan. Bring to boiling; cover. Simmer for about 30 minutes.
4. Brush barbecue sauce over chicken. Roast ½ hour longer, brushing warm sauce over chicken several times until the chicken has become tender and skin is richly glazed.
5. Remove chicken from spit to a cutting board. Remove skewers and string. Cut chicken into quarters with kitchen scissors. Pass remaining barbecue sauce to spoon over.

TAHITIAN CHICKEN

The exotic flavors of curry and tropical fruits go so well with chicken.

Makes 8 servings.

    4 whole chicken breasts, split (about 12 ounces each)
    ¾ cup bottled oil-and-vinegar salad dressing
    2 teaspoons curry powder
    1 can (15¼ ounces) sliced pineapple
    2 medium-size bananas or 1 large papaya
    8 preserved kumquats
    2 large limes
    ½ cup honey

1. Bone chicken breasts (or buy chicken fillets already boned), and cut each split chicken breast into 4 pieces.
2. Combine oil-and-vinegar salad dressing and curry powder in a medium-size bowl; add chicken. Marinate chicken for 2 hours in the refrigerator.

3. Cut pineapple slices in half. Just before cooking, peel bananas and cut into 2-inch pieces. Halve, seed and pare papaya; cut into 1-inch cubes; cut limes into wedges.
4. Drain chicken; reserve the marinade. Thread chicken, pineapple, banana or papaya, kumquats and lime wedges, alternately on 8 long skewers. Stir honey into remaining marinade and brush generously over kabobs.
5. Broil or grill, turning and basting often, 10 minutes, or until chicken is golden.
6. Serve kabobs with kasha or packaged frozen prepared fried rice with almonds, if you wish.

HERBED LAMB-VEGETABLE KABOBS

When lamb is on special, try this Middle East favorite. Lean cubes are seasoned with herbs, then broiled with vegetables.

Makes 6 servings.

    ½ leg of lamb, butt or shank end, weighing about 4 pounds
    ½ cup lemon juice
    ¼ cup olive or salad oil
    2 tablespoons catsup
    1 clove garlic, minced
    ½ teaspoon rosemary, crushed
    ½ teaspoon thyme
      Few drops liquid red-pepper seasoning
    3 tablespoons honey
    2 ears of corn, cut crosswise into 1½-inch pieces
    2 zucchini, cut crosswise into 1-inch pieces
    2 medium-size yellow onions, cut into wedges
    ½ pound mushroom caps
    1 pint cherry tomatoes
    1 green pepper, cut into 1-inch pieces

1. Trim all fat from lamb, then cut lamb into 18 two-inch cubes; place in a single layer in a shallow glass or plastic dish. (Use any remaining lamb and bone to make a hearty soup.)
2. Mix lemon juice, olive or salad oil, catsup, garlic, rosemary, thyme and red-pepper seasoning in a 1-cup measure; pour over lamb. Chill, turning cubes often to season evenly, 2 to 3 hours.
3. Thread lamb cubes and vegetables on separate skewers as pictured on page 26.
4. Strain marinade from lamb into a cup; stir in honey; brush on both lamb and vegetables.
5. Place lamb and corn kabobs on grill 4 inches from heat or broil, following range manufacturer's directions, turning kabobs often and brushing them with more marinade, 15 minutes, or until lamb is done as you like it.
6. After 5 minutes, add tomato kabobs. Cook 10 minutes longer, turning the kabobs often and brushing frequently with marinade.
7. Serve kabobs plain or with hot buttered rice.

CHICKEN IN THE ITALIAN STYLE

Chicken grills with zucchini, and both are basted with herb seasoned butter.

Makes 4 servings.

½ **lemon**
1 **broiler-fryer, quartered (about 3½ pounds)**
1 **teaspoon salt**
¼ **teaspoon pepper**
½ **cup (1 stick) butter or margarine**
2 **cloves garlic, cut in half**
½ **teaspoon leaf oregano, crumbled**
½ **teaspoon leaf basil, crumbled**
2 **medium-size zucchini, cut in half lengthwise**

1. Squeeze lemon juice over chicken. Sprinkle with salt and pepper. Let stand 30 minutes.
2. Melt butter in saucepan; add garlic, crumbled oregano and crumbled basil.
3. Place broiler quarters on lightly oiled grill, bony side down. Broil over hot coals 25 minutes; brush with the herbed butter; turn; broil 20 minutes, or until chicken is tender and golden brown.
4. Brush zucchini with the herbed butter and place cut side down on grill for last 20 minutes.
5. Heat remaining herbed butter to pass in bowl.

PARTY STEAK DIANE

Many gourmet dishes are easy to prepare outdoors, as this recipe proves.

Makes 8 to 10 servings.

1 **sirloin steak, cut 2 inches thick and weighing 5 pounds**
1 **teaspoon freshly ground pepper**
½ **cup (1 stick) butter or margarine**
2 **teaspoons dry mustard**
¾ **pound fresh mushrooms, washed, trimmed and sliced**
1½ **cups sliced green onions**
1 **tablespoon lemon juice**
1 **tablespoon Worcestershire sauce**
1 **teaspoon salt**
¼ **cup chopped parsley**

1. Remove steak from refrigerator 1 hour before cooking. Trim off any excess fat, then score remaining fat edge every inch so that the meat will lie flat on grill. Sprinkle pepper over both sides of the steak; rub in well.
2. Melt butter or margarine in a medium-size frying pan on grill over hot coals; stir in mustard, mushrooms and onions. Sauté 10 minutes, or until onions are soft. Stir in lemon juice, Worcestershire sauce, salt and parsley; remove from heat.
3. When ready to cook meat, rub hot grill with a few fat trimmings to help prevent sticking. Place steak on grill about 6 inches above hot

coals. Grill 15 minutes; brush lightly with part of butter mixture from sauce; grill 5 minutes longer. Turn steak; grill 20 minutes; brush lightly with sauce. Grill 5 minutes longer for rare, or until steak is done as you like it. To test for doneness, cut a small slit near bone. Place steak on a cutting board; garnish with a tomato rose and parsley, if you wish.
4. Reheat remaining sauce. Slice steak ¼-inch thick; serve remaining sauce separately.

BACKYARD CLAMBAKE

This is a one-pot meal seafood fans will find irresistible, as well as a cinch to make.

Makes 8 servings.

4 **dozen steamer clams in the shell (or 2 dozen steamer clams and 2 dozen fresh mussels)**
8 **ears of corn in the husks**
8 **medium-size baking potatoes or 8 sweet potatoes**
8 **carrots**
8 **small onions or 4 medium-size onions, peeled and halved**
2 **live lobsters (about 3 pounds each) or 8 live lobsters (about 1 to 1¼ pounds each)**
2 **cups water or 2 cans light beer**
  Lemon wedges
  Melted butter or margarine

1. Scrub clam shells thoroughly under cold, running water, using a stiff brush to remove sand. Cut a piece of cheesecloth, about 18"x36" and center washed clams on cloth; tie ends around clams to form a neat little bundle. Repeat same procedure for mussels.
2. Remove outer husks from corn, fold back inner ones; remove silks. Pull inner husks back over ears. (Or, if you prefer, remove both husks along with silk.) Wash potatoes; peel completely or just cut off ends. Wash and peel carrots and onions. Wrap in foil or cheesecloth packets.
3. Using a large metal container, lobster pot or galvanized can, layer all ingredients as follows: Clams and mussels in cheesecloth bags, potatoes, carrots, onions, lobsters and fresh corn.
4. Pour in water or beer; cover with tight-fitting lid. Place over medium heat on stove or over a hot grill, 4 inches from heat. Steam for about 1 hour, or until potatoes and onions are tender.
5. Remove ingredients from pot; place on serving plates (or leave lobsters on platter, crack apart and serve in individual-size portions). Serve with lemon wedges and melted butter or margarine.

At right, all the ingredients that make our Backyard Clambake scrumptious—without much work. The recipe for this meal-in-a-pot is above.

3

ON-THE-GO FOODS

"O beautiful for spacious skies,
For amber waves of grain,
For purple mountain majesties
Above the fruited plain! . . ."
AMERICA THE BEAUTIFUL
[*1893*] KATHARINE LEE BATES

We're on the go. From indoors to out, from winter garb to carefree clothes and casual pursuits. Hand-in-hand with this beautiful change of pace goes the picnic basket, and it's brimming with foods that taste sumptuous no matter how simple they are. Perhaps it's the ambiance of the day—the play of sunlight on a stream, the cool splash of a waterfall, the bleating sound of a goat in some faraway meadow. Whatever the reason, there's no denying appetites are ready for a hearty luncheon sandwich such as the one here. To make it: Mound your favorite cold cuts on a half loaf of Italian or French bread with lettuce, tomato, sardines, olives, pickles, etc. Drizzle all with oil and vinegar, and slice into small portions. For other picnic ideas, turn the page.

PÂTÉ STUFFED HERO ROLLS

Looks like a lot of work; who will guess that it took less than 10 minutes to put these totable sandwiches together?

Makes 8 servings.

    4 hero rolls, about 8 inches long
    2 cans (4½ ounces each) deviled ham
    4 tablespoons prepared mustard with onion
      Butter or margarine, softened
    6 hard-cooked eggs, shelled
    2 cans (4¾ ounces each) liver pâté

1. Cut a ½-inch-thick slice, crosswise, from each roll. Hollow out soft centers of rolls with a serrated knife. (Save crumbs to make bread pudding or crumb topping for casseroles.)
2. Combine deviled ham and 2 tablespoons of the mustard in a small bowl. Spread the insides of 2 rolls with softened butter or margarine. Spread deviled-ham mixture inside rolls and on cut sides of 2 tops. Halve 3 eggs lengthwise and place 3 halves, cut side up, in each roll; spread remaining deviled-ham mixture between and over egg halves; place tops on heroes.
3. Wrap each hero tightly in plastic wrap and chill at least 2 hours.
4. Repeat Steps 2 and 3 with remaining heroes, liver pâté, remaining mustard and butter.
5. To serve: Unwrap hero rolls and cut each into ½-inch-thick slices with a sharp knife.

SPICY RELISH STUFFED EGGS

A picnic without eggs isn't a picnic!

Makes 6 servings.

    6 hard-cooked eggs, shelled
    ¼ cup mayonnaise or salad dressing
    1 tablespoon pickle relish
    ½ teaspoon prepared mustard
    ¼ teaspoon salt
    ⅛ teaspoon pepper

1. Cut eggs in half lengthwise; carefully remove yolks to a bowl. Mash thoroughly with a fork.
2. Add mayonnaise or salad dressing, relish, mustard, salt and pepper. Mix well.
3. Spoon yolk mixture into whites. Cover; refrigerate. Just before serving, garnish with parsley.

Left: A light summer dinner that includes Carolina Coleslaw and Homestyle Fried Chicken with Quick Tomato Sauce and Orange-Curry Sauce. Round out your picnic with fruit, cookies and milk. Recipes for chicken and sauces are in this chapter; coleslaw recipe is in Chapter 5.

APPIAN SAMPLER

Inspired by popular Italian antipasto, this sandwich combines a variety of foods.

Makes 4 servings.

    1 small loaf Italian bread
    ⅓ cup bottled Italian salad dressing
      Romaine
    4 tomatoes, each cut in 6 thin slices
    2 packages (6 ounces each) assorted sliced cold cuts (bologna, salami, ham, cappicola sausage)
    4 slices provolone cheese, halved
    8 large fresh mushrooms, washed, trimmed and sliced thin
    1 small can sardines, drained
   12 small onions, washed and trimmed
      Watercress
      Red and green pepper strips
      Ripe and green olives
      Sweet pickles

1. Cut bread in half lengthwise; drizzle with salad dressing; top with romaine.
2. Layer bread this way: Tomatoes, meat, tomatoes, cheese, meat, mushrooms and sardines; lay 3 green onions across top of each sandwich. Tuck sprigs of watercress between layers or around edge of plates. Garnish with pepper strips, olives, pickles and additional salad dressing.

GALWAY STACKS

It's cold-cut corned beef with a chili cabbage slaw.

Makes 4 sandwiches.

    ½ medium-size head of cabbage, trimmed and finely shredded (6 cups)
    1 can (4 ounces) red chili peppers, drained and chopped
    1 medium-size onion, chopped fine (½ cup)
    ¼ cup cider vinegar
    3 tablespoons vegetable oil
    ¼ cup sugar
    1 teaspoon salt
    ⅛ teaspoon pepper
    4 poppy seed rolls
    4 tablespoons (½ stick) butter or margarine
    2 packages (4 ounces each) sliced corned-beef

1. Place cabbage, peppers and onion in a bowl.
2. Combine vinegar, vegetable oil, sugar, salt and pepper in a cup; stir until sugar dissolves. Pour over cabbage mixture; toss lightly to mix. Let stand, stirring often, 1 hour to season; drain.
3. Split rolls; spread with butter or margarine. Place about ¼ cup of the cabbage mixture on each slice of corned beef; roll up tightly, jelly-roll fashion. Place 3 meat rolls on bottom half of each buttered roll; cover with remaining half of roll.

HAM STUFFED ZUCCHINI

This is a good way to use those bits and pieces of leftover ham from Sunday's dinner.

Bake at 325° for 45 minutes.
Makes 8 servings.

- 8 small zucchini
- 2 teaspoons salt
- 4 cups ground cooked ham (about 2 pounds)
- 2 eggs
- ¼ teaspoon pepper
- 1 teaspoon leaf basil, crumbled
- ½ cup chopped pimiento
- ½ cup chopped green pepper
- ¼ cup grated Swiss cheese (1 ounce)
- 1 tablespoon vegetable oil

1. Cut off the ends of the zucchini; hollow out with an apple corer, removing all pulp and leaving only the shell. Sprinkle the insides of zucchini with 1 teaspoon of salt.
2. Combine ground ham, remaining teaspoon of salt, eggs, pepper, basil, pimiento, green pepper and cheese in a medium-size bowl. Pack ½ cup of filling into each zucchini shell, using your fingers or a teaspoon.
3. Place zucchini into a greased, large baking dish. Brush with oil. Bake in moderate oven (325°) 45 minutes, or until tender. Serve hot or cold.

TUNA FILLED CHEESE PUFFS

Make your own puffy cheese shells to pack with tuna salad.

Bake at 425° for 30 minutes.
Makes 12 servings.

- ½ cup water
- 3 tablespoons butter or margarine
- ½ teaspoon salt
  Pinch of pepper
- ½ cup sifted all-purpose flour
- 2 eggs
- 3 one-ounce wedges (from a 6-ounce package) process Gruyère cheese, finely diced

FILLING:
- 2 cans (7 ounces each) tuna, drained
- ½ cup mayonnaise or salad dressing
- 1 small onion, chopped (¼ cup)
- 1 cup chopped celery
- 2 tablespoons drained capers
- 2 tablespoons chopped pimiento
- 1 teaspoon salt
- ⅛ teaspoon pepper

1. Measure water, butter or margarine, salt and pepper into saucepan; bring to boiling. Remove from heat; add flour all at once. Stir briskly over low heat just until mixture leaves the side of the pan and forms a ball. Remove from heat.
2. Beat in eggs, one at a time. Stir in all but 2 tablespoons of the process Gruyère cheese.
3. Spoon 12 mounds onto greased cooky sheets. Sprinkle with remaining cheese.
4. Bake in hot oven (425°) 30 minutes, or until crisp and brown. Cool on wire rack.
5. Make filling: Flake tuna; add mayonnaise or salad dressing, onion, celery, capers, pimiento, salt and pepper. Mix well. Split puffs, fill.

TIME-SAVING TIP

Shape your own throwaway pans from heavy aluminum foil for heating potatoes or vegetables on the grill. Turn up edges 1½ to 3 inches for sides; pinch corners so pans won't leak. These pans also make good juice catchers when you're barbecuing on a spit. Still another cook-saver: Bundle single servings of meat or fish in aluminum foil and, after cooking, fold back and use for serving.

HOMESTYLE FRIED CHICKEN

It's finger-food—crackly-crisp outside, juicy all the way through. Pictured on the cover and on page 46, it's a perfect choice for all kinds of picnics.

Makes 6 servings.

- 2 broiler-fryers (about 2 pounds each), cut up
- 1 cup flour
- 2 teaspoons salt
- ½ teaspoon pepper
  Bacon drippings
  Orange-Curry Sauce (recipe follows)
  Quick Tomato Sauce (recipe follows)

1. Wash and dry chicken pieces well. Shake in mixture of flour, salt and pepper in paper bag to coat well.
2. Heat bacon drippings in large heavy frying pan or electric skillet. It'll take about 1 cup, for fat should be about ½-inch deep. (If you like, use part shortening or salad oil.)
3. Place chicken in single layer in hot fat; cover lightly. Cook over *low heat* 20 minutes, or until golden; turn; cover again and cook 20 minutes to brown other side. (If using an electric skillet, follow manufacturer's directions.) Remove browned chicken and set aside while cooking any remaining pieces, adding more drippings, if needed, to keep fat ½-inch deep.
4. Drain fat from frying pan, leaving just enough to keep chicken from sticking; return all chicken to pan. Cover; cook, turning once or twice, over very low heat, 30 minutes longer, or until chicken is tender and golden brown.
5. Serve hot or cold, plain or with dunking sauces.

ORANGE-CURRY SAUCE

Just sweet, just tart enough to go with mild-flavor chicken.

Makes 2 cups.

    1 cup orange marmalade
    ⅓ cup vinegar
    ¼ cup granulated sugar
    2 tablespoons brown sugar
    1 tablespoon curry powder
    1 tablespoon Worcestershire sauce
    1 teaspoon salt
    ½ teaspoon ground ginger

Combine all ingredients in small saucepan; heat to boiling, then simmer, stirring constantly, until marmalade is melted and sauce is blended. Serve the sauce warm or cold with poultry.

QUICK TOMATO SAUCE

It's tomato-rich and spicy—a good all-round sauce to keep on hand.

Makes 1½ cups.

    1 can (8 ounces) tomato sauce
    ½ cup finely chopped green pepper
    ½ cup finely chopped celery
    2 tablespoons vinegar
    2 tablespoons light molasses
    1 tablespoon Worcestershire sauce
    ¼ teaspoon liquid red-pepper seasoning

Combine all ingredients in small saucepan; heat to boiling; then simmer, stirring constantly, 5 minutes, or until vegetables are softened and sauce is blended. Serve warm or cold.

PICNIC POTATO CONES

Here's a zippy mashed-potato mixture to serve with ham-bologna slices.

Makes 8 servings.

    6 medium-size potatoes, pared and diced
    1½ cups dairy sour cream
    1 envelope blue-cheese salad dressing mix
    1 cup finely chopped celery
    2 packages (6 ounces each) sliced ham-bologna (16 slices)
    Parsley

1. Cook potatoes, covered, in boiling salted water in a large saucepan 15 minutes, or until tender; drain. Return potatoes to pan and shake over low heat until dry and fluffy. Press through a ricer or mash in a large bowl; cool slightly.
2. Blend sour cream and blue-cheese dressing mix in a small bowl; beat into potatoes; stir in celery.
3. Curl each slice of ham-bologna into a cornucopia; fasten with a wooden pick. Spoon potato mixture into each to fill. (Or press through a pastry bag into cornucopia.) Arrange in a single layer on a large serving platter; cover. Chill at least 2 hours to season.
4. Just before serving, garnish each cornucopia with a tiny sprig of parsley; garnish platter with lettuce and radish roses, if you wish. *Note:* Wrap platter tightly and carry as is to your eating spot.

WEIGHT-WATCHING TIP
Make the most of your sandwich spreads by adding lots of chopped celery and onions. Every sandwich looks more festive with a crunchy fresh lettuce leaf. Don't forget sliced tomatoes, green pepper strips, dill pickle slices, cucumber chips, carrot sticks and other calorie-shy side snacks.

KETTLE VEAL DINNER

Add slices of crusty French bread and this savory stew makes an easy one-pot dinner.

Makes 6 servings.

    2 pounds boneless veal shoulder
    2 tablespoons butter or margarine
    2½ cups water
    2 teaspoons salt
    1 teaspoon leaf thyme, crumbled
    1 bay leaf
    ¼ teaspoon pepper
    1 envelope instant chicken broth or 1 teaspoon granulated chicken bouillon
    1 can (1 pound) whole boiled onions, drained
    1 package (10 ounces) frozen peas
    1 can (3 or 4 ounces) sliced mushrooms
    ¼ cup flour
    1 small loaf French bread, sliced

1. Trim any fat from veal; cut meat into 1-inch cubes. Brown in butter or margarine in a heavy kettle or Dutch oven.
2. Stir in 2 cups of the water, salt, thyme, bay leaf, pepper and broth. Heat to boiling; cover.
3. Simmer 1 hour and 15 minutes, or until veal is almost tender; remove bay leaf. Stir in onions, frozen peas, mushrooms and liquid; cover again. Cook mixture for about 15 minutes, or until peas and veal are tender.
4. Mix flour with remaining ½ cup water until smooth in a cup; stir in veal mixture. Cook, stirring constantly, until the mixture thickens and boils for about 1 minute.
5. Ladle over French bread in soup plates.
Note: Chill stew if made ahead; reheat in kettle on a grill at picnic spot. Be sure kettle has heat-proof handles and that you have barbecue mitts.

49

POTATO SALAD STUFFED TOMATOES

How to carry your salad and eat it, too: The small meaty summertime tomatoes may even be from your own garden.

Makes 16 servings.

    8 small tomatoes, halved and seeded
    3 medium-size potatoes (about 1 pound)
  ½ cup dairy sour cream
    2 teaspoons vinegar
    1 teaspoon salt
  ½ teaspoon sugar
  ½ teaspoon dry mustard
  ⅛ teaspoon pepper
    1 clove garlic, crushed
  ¼ cup chopped green pepper
    2 tablespoons chopped pimiento
    1 tablespoon freeze-dried or fresh chopped
      chives

1. Scoop out tomatoes; turn upside down on paper toweling to drain.
2. Cook potatoes in boiling salted water in a medium-size saucepan 30 minutes, or until tender; drain; cool until easy to handle, then peel and cut into small cubes. Place in a medium-size bowl.
3. Blend sour cream, vinegar, ½ teaspoon of the salt, sugar, dry mustard, pepper and garlic in a small bowl. Add green pepper and pimiento to potatoes; toss with dressing. Cover; chill at least 1 hour to season and blend flavors.
4. Sprinkle remaining ½ teaspoon salt into tomato shells; spoon 2 tablespoons potato-salad mixture into each tomato. Sprinkle with chives.

JUMBO SAUSAGE LOAF

For a complete picnic menu, add pound cake or brownies, milk, punch, baked beans, fresh salad and bread—and you're ready to take off.

Bake at 425° for 40 minutes.
Makes 8 servings.

    1 package (12 ounces) smoked sausages
    1 package (8 ounces) process American cheese
    2 hard-cooked eggs, shelled and diced
    2 eggs, slightly beaten
    2 teaspoons Worcestershire sauce
    1 package piecrust mix
      Melted butter or margarine

1. Slice sausages thin; dice cheese. Combine both with hard-cooked eggs in a large bowl. Add beaten eggs and Worcestershire sauce; toss lightly to mix.
2. Prepare piecrust mix, following label directions. Roll out directly on a small cooky sheet to a rectangle, 14x12.
3. Spread sausage mixture evenly in center of pastry, leaving 4-inch borders at sides, and 2

inches at ends. Moisten pastry edges; fold ends over filling, then fold sides up over top and overlap; press edges together to seal. Cut several slits in top to let steam escape. Brush lightly with melted butter or margarine.
4. Bake in hot oven (425°) 40 minutes, or until pastry is golden and filling bubbles up.
5. Cool completely on cooky sheet on a wire rack. To carry to picnic, wrap with foil.

PICNICS FOR DIETERS

Saving on bread calories: Ordinary ("soft") white bread is about 70 calories a slice, but you can slim a sandwich from the outside-in by switching to a leaner bread. Here are some pointers:
• "Sandwich-thin" bread is only around 55 calories a slice.
• "Diet," "protein," or "special formula" breads may be anywhere from 30 to 55 calories a slice, so look for the calorie count printed on the label. Breads made from soy flour have a protein boost. "Gluten" bread, made from low-starch flour, is the slimmest bread of all—only 35 calories a slice.
• Dark breads (rye, pumpernickel, cracked or whole wheat) are leaner in calories than white bread, ounce-for-ounce, but the slices are usually larger. Look for skinny-slice types, or buy it whole and cut it yourself.
• Hard rolls, "Jewish rolls," English muffins, hamburger and hot dog rolls are about 150 calories each, but you can trim them down to about 78 by serving your sandwiches open-face.
• Serving a sandwich open-face on one slice of bread automatically cuts the bread calories in half.

CHEDDAR-PEAR OPEN FACE SANDWICH

Here's a new approach to a popular combination —cheese and fruit.

Makes 6 servings.

    1 package (10 ounces) Cheddar cheese
  ½ cup dairy sour cream
  ¼ cup mayonnaise or salad dressing
  ¼ teaspoon ground ginger
    6 slices whole-wheat bread
      Butter or margarine, softened
    6 lettuce leaves
    6 canned pear halves (from a 1 pound, 13-
      ounce can)

1. Shred cheese; combine with sour cream, mayonnaise or salad dressing and ginger until well-blended in a medium-size bowl.
2. Spread each slice of bread with butter or margarine and arrange a lettuce leaf on top. Spread cheese mixture over lettuce and top with a pear half. Garnish with fresh mint sprigs, if you wish.

MEXICAN SOMBREROS (TOSTADAS)

This dish is a must for bean fans. (Shown above.)

Makes 18 tostada stacks.

- 1 package (10 ounces) Monterey Jack cheese, shredded
- 2 cups shredded romaine lettuce
- 1 cup diced tomatoes
- 1 cup sliced ripe olives
- 1 cup sliced radishes
- 1 cup diced onion
- ⅔ cup vegetable oil
- 1 can (10 ounces) tortillas
- 2 cans (15¼ ounces each) kidney beans
- ¼ teaspoon garlic powder
- ⅛ teaspoon chili powder
- 1 cup dairy sour cream

1. Arrange cheese, romaine, tomatoes, olives, radishes and onions in separate small bowls. Chill.
2. Heat oil in small skillet. Fry tortillas one at a time until brown and crispy, about 1 minute. Remove each "tostada" from oil with tongs. Drain on paper toweling. Keep warm.
3. Put kidney beans into container of electric blender. Whirl until smooth.
4. Combine beans, garlic powder and chili powder in a medium-size saucepan. Heat until bubbly-hot at home or on backyard grill.
5. To serve: Spread some beans on tostada, then cheese and vegetables. Garnish with sour cream.

DUNKIN' RIBS

A soy dip gives these ribs an Oriental touch.

Makes 4 servings.

- 3½ pounds country-style spareribs
  Salt
  Pepper
  Soy Dip (recipe follows)

1. Trim any excess fat from ribs; cut ribs apart, if needed. Season with salt and pepper.
2. Rub hot grill with a few fat trimmings to help prevent sticking. Place ribs 8 inches above coals.
3. Grill slowly, turning often, 1½ hours, or until meat is tender. Place ribs on a large serving platter; serve hot with Soy Dip.

SOY DIP—Mix 1 tablespoon cornstarch with ¼ cup water until smooth in a small saucepan; stir in ½ cup peach preserves, ¼ cup soy sauce and 1 teaspoon salt. Cook, stirring constantly, until mixture thickens and boils 3 minutes. Remove from heat; stir in 2 tablespoons dry sherry. Serve warm. Makes about 1 cup.
Note: Make dip at home and carry to your eating spot in a jar with a tight lid, then reheat on grill.

Mexican Sombreros (above) offer everyone a chance to add their favorite fresh vegetables to bean-filled tortilla shells. Recipe is on this page.

4

FRUITS & VEGETABLES

TO COOK, PRESERVE & FREEZE

"The earth bringeth forth fruit of herself; first the blade, then the ear, after that the full corn in the ear."
THE GOSPEL ACCORDING TO
ST. MARK 4:28

In celebration of summer we've gathered together a bumper crop of garden recipes — one that can transform fields of golden corn, ripe tomatoes and juicy red watermelons into memorable feasts you'll enjoy throughout the year. In addition to ready-to-serve recipes, you'll find ones for making preserves —jams, jellies, marmalades, relishes, etc.—all geared to small quantities so you don't need a gargantuan garden or grocery purchase. And, our complete step-by-step directions take the guesswork out of freezing and canning foods. Turn the page and join the celebration.

BASIC SAUCE MIX FOR VEGETABLES

Be a super-sauce maker and save both vitamins and money at the same time when you keep this sauce base in the refrigerator. Just stir a few spoonfuls into the cooking liquid when the vegetables are crisply tender; add the distinctive herb or seasoning, and you're done.

Makes 2 cups.

- ½ cup (1 stick) butter or margarine
- ½ cup all-purpose flour
- ½ cup nonfat dry milk powder
- 2 tablespoons onion powder
- 2 teaspoons salt
- ¼ teaspoon pepper

Cut butter or margarine into flour, dry milk, onion powder, salt and pepper with a pastry blender or 2 knives until mixture is very crumbly. Spoon into a 2-cup container with a tight cover. Store in the refrigerator. Will keep up to 2 weeks.

HOW TO USE BASIC SAUCE MIX WITH FROZEN VEGETABLES

- 4 cups frozen vegetables (from a 2-pound bag) or 2 packages (10 ounces each) frozen vegetables
- 1 cup water
- 1 teaspoon salt
- 4 tablespoons Basic Sauce Mix (recipe above) Additions (recipes follow)

1. Combine frozen vegetables, water and salt in medium-size saucepan. Heat to boiling; cover saucepan; lower heat and cook 5 minutes, or just until vegetables are crisply tender.
2. Drain vegetables and measure cooking liquid. (You should have 1 cup. If you have more, boil liquid in saucepan to reduce it to 1 cup; if you have less than 1 cup, add water to make 1 cup.)
3. Return drained vegetables to saucepan with Basic Sauce Mix and suggested additions. Cook, stirring constantly, until mixture thickens and bubbles 3 minutes. Spoon into heated bowl.

The secret behind the vegetables at left lies, not in any fancy cooking, but in very special, easy-to-make sauces. The string beans and cauliflower start off with a basic cream sauce mix, with mustard added to the green bean sauce and curry to the cauliflower. The cherry tomatoes are served with a brown butter sauce; the onions are stuffed with vegetables and topped with cheese sauce. The carrots and beets are covered with a cornstarch glaze, the carrots flavored with orange juice, the beets with a sweet-and-sour mixture. Recipes for all are in this chapter.

Suggested Additions:

Carioca Combo: Cook 2 cups frozen whole-kernel corn, and 2 cups frozen Fordhook lima beans, following directions, bottom left. Additions: ¼ cup chopped sweet red pepper *or* 2 tablespoons chopped pimiento and ½ teaspoon chili powder. Makes 6 servings.

Green and Gold Vegetable Medley: Cook 2 cups frozen cut green beans and 1 package (10 ounces) frozen cut wax beans, following directions, bottom left. Additions: ¼ cup finely chopped parsley, ½ teaspoon leaf thyme, crumbled; and ¼ teaspoon garlic powder. Makes 6 servings.

Green Peas Superb: Cook 4 cups frozen peas, following directions, bottom left. Additions: 1 small cucumber, pared, seeded and chopped, 1 teaspoon dried dillweed. Makes 6 servings.

HOW TO USE BASIC SAUCE MIX WITH FRESH VEGETABLES

- 1 head, bunch, or pound of fresh vegetables
- 1 cup water
- 1 teaspoon salt
- 4 tablespoons Basic Sauce Mix (recipe above) Additions (recipes follow)

1. Prepare vegetables; combine with water and salt in medium-size saucepan. Heat to boiling; cover saucepan; lower heat; cook 10 minutes, or just until crisply tender. Remove vegetables to serving bowl with slotted spoon; keep warm.
2. Measure cooking liquid; add more water, if necessary to make 1 cup. Add Basic Sauce Mix and suggested additions. Beat with wire whisk until smooth. Return to heat; cook, stirring constantly, until mixture thickens and boils 3 minutes. Spoon over vegetables and serve at once.

Suggested Additions:

Cauliflower with Curry Sauce: Wash 1 small cauliflower; remove green leaves; trim root end. Cook and drain, following directions above. Additions: 1 teaspoon curry powder and 1 bay leaf. Remove bay leaf before spooning over cauliflower; sprinkle paprika on top. Makes 6 servings.

Tangy Green Beans: Wash 1 pound green beans; tip and trim to an even length. (The trims can go into the soup pot.) Cook with 1 teaspoon rosemary, crumbled, following directions above. Strain and measure cooking liquid. Addition: 1 tablespoon prepared mustard. Makes 6 servings.

Broccoli Au Gratin: Wash and separate 1 bunch broccoli; trim into 3-inch pieces. Cook with 1 teaspoon leaf basil, crumbled, following directions above. Place broccoli in a heat-proof serving dish. Strain and measure cooking liquid. Additions: ¼ cup grated Swiss cheese. Spoon over broccoli and top with ½ cup buttered bread crumbs. Bake in moderate oven (350°) 10 minutes, or until golden. Makes 6 servings.

BROILED TOMATOES NESTED WITH SPINACH

One of Finland's most colorful and delicious vegetable dishes is creamed spinach baked in juicy-ripe tomatoes. To short-cut preparation time, we've substituted thick tomato slices and mounded the spinach on top.

Makes 6 servings.

   1 package (10 ounces) frozen chopped spinach, completely thawed
   ¼ cup frozen chopped onion
   3 tablespoons butter or margarine
   ⅛ teaspoon ground nutmeg
   1 teaspoon salt
   ¼ teaspoon pepper
   3 tablespoons mayonnaise or salad dressing
   2 tablespoons grated Parmesan cheese
   3 medium-size ripe tomatoes
   1 hard-cooked egg

1. Press thawed spinach as dry as possible in a strainer; reserve.
2. Brown onion in 2 tablespoons of the butter in a medium-size skillet. Add nutmeg, ½ teaspoon of the salt, ⅛ teaspoon of the pepper and spinach. Mix well, cover; lower heat to moderate and cook 4 to 5 minutes, just until spinach is cooked through. Mix in mayonnaise and 1 tablespoon of the Parmesan.
3. Cut tops and bottoms off tomatoes, then divide center portion of each into two thick slices (about 1¼ inches thick). Lay slices flat in a shallow 9-inch flameproof dish. Dot with remaining butter and sprinkle with the remaining salt, pepper and Parmesan. Broil, with tops 4 to 5 inches from the heat, about 3 minutes, just until bubbling. Remove from broiler, mound spinach in center letting tomato show around the edges. Broil 2 to 3 minutes longer, until sizzling, and serve. Just before serving, scatter sieved hard-cooked egg yolk and chopped egg white on top of spinach.

ORANGE GLAZED CARROTS

Orange juice in the sauce brings out the fresh taste in carrots.

Makes 6 servings.

   2 pounds carrots
   1 tablespoon sugar
   2 teaspoons cornstarch
   ½ teaspoon salt
   ¾ cup orange juice

1. Wash carrots thoroughly; scrape; cut into 2-inch pieces.
2. Bring about 1 inch water to boiling in a large saucepan. Add salt and carrots. Cook, covered, 10 minutes, or until carrots are just tender. Drain.
3. Combine sugar, cornstarch and salt in saucepan; add orange juice. Cook over medium heat, stirring constantly, until sauce thickens.
4. Add cooked carrots to sauce; heat 3 minutes.

SWEET-SOUR GLAZED BEETS

Just the right amount of vinegar makes this sauce so good with beets.

Makes 4 servings.

   2 bunches beets
   ¼ cup sugar
   1 tablespoon cornstarch
   ¼ teaspoon salt
   ½ cup cider vinegar

1. Wash beets. Cut off all but 2 inches of tops; leave root ends intact.
2. Place beets in saucepan; add water to cover. Bring water to boiling. Cook beets, covered, 35 to 45 minutes, or until tender. Drain.
3. Allow beets to cool slightly; trim root and stem ends; slip skins off. Slice beets. You will have about 2 cups.
4. Combine sugar, cornstarch and salt in saucepan; add vinegar. Cook over medium heat, stirring constantly, until sauce thickens and bubbles.
5. Add beets to sauce; heat about 3 minutes.

SAUCY ASPARAGUS SPEARS

You can use fresh or frozen asparagus for this vegetable treat.

Makes 6 servings.

   1 bunch fresh asparagus, weighing about 2 pounds or 2 packages (10 ounces each) frozen asparagus spears
   1 cup mayonnaise or salad dressing
   1 tablespoon lemon juice
   1 teaspoon leaf basil, crumbled
   ¼ teaspoon freshly ground pepper
   1 medium-size tomato, peeled and finely chopped

1. Wash and trim asparagus. Stand upright in a deep saucepan; pour in boiling water to a depth of about an inch; cover. Cook 15 minutes, or just until crisply tender; or, cook frozen asparagus, following label directions. Drain and keep warm.
2. While asparagus cooks, combine mayonnaise or salad dressing, lemon juice, basil and pepper in a small heavy saucepan. Heat slowly, stirring constantly, until mixture is very warm. Remove saucepan from heat and stir in chopped tomatoes.
3. Place asparagus spears on heated serving plate and carefully spoon the hot sauce over.

SWEDISH GREEN BEANS IN DILL-MUSTARD SAUCE

Dill is Scandinavia's favorite herb, and in spring and summer you see feathery bouquets of it at open air markets everywhere. If you cannot obtain fresh dill, try this recipe with dillweed.

Makes 4 to 6 servings.

     2 packages (9 ounces each) frozen whole green
       beans

SAUCE:
     3 tablespoons butter or margarine
     3 tablespoons flour
     2 teaspoons sugar
     1 teaspoon dry mustard
     1 tablespoon chopped fresh dill or 1 teaspoon
       dillweed
     ½ teaspoon salt
       Pinch of pepper
     ¾ cup milk
     3 tablespoons prepared mustard
     1 egg yolk, lightly beaten with 1 tablespoon
       cider vinegar

1. Cook beans, following label directions; drain; return to saucepan.
2. While beans cook, prepare Sauce: Melt butter in a small saucepan over moderate heat; blend in flour, sugar, dry mustard, dillweed, salt and pepper; cook 1 minute. Add milk, stirring until thickened and smooth, 2 to 3 minutes. Blend in prepared mustard. Mix a little hot sauce into egg-yolk mixture, stir back into saucepan, turn heat down to lowest point and keep warm, stirring now and then, until beans are done.
3. Pour sauce over beans, toss to coat well.

STUFFED ONIONS

Cheese soup makes a ready sauce for sweet onions.

Bake at 375° for 20 minutes.
Makes 6 servings.

     6 large sweet Spanish onions
     1 package (10 ounces) frozen mixed
       vegetables, cooked and drained
     1 can condensed Cheddar cheese soup
     ½ teaspoon salt
     ⅛ teaspoon pepper
     1 tablespoon butter, melted
     ¼ cup seasoned bread crumbs

1. Peel onions; cut slice from top of each. Cook in boiling salted water, in a large saucepan, just until tender, about 45 minutes. Drain.
2. Carefully remove onion centers, leaving 3 outer rings intact. Chop enough of the centers to measure 2 cups. Wrap remaining onion centers in plastic, foil or freezer wrap; freeze for later use in casseroles, stews or meat loaves.
3. Combine the chopped onion with cooked vegetables, soup, salt and pepper. Place onion shells in shallow 6-cup baking dish, fill with vegetables.
4. Combine butter with bread crumbs; sprinkle over filled onions.
5. Bake in a moderate oven (375°) 20 minutes, or until crumbs are browned.

POTATO, BACON AND EGG CASSEROLE

Sliced potatoes are layered with eggs, bacon and chives.

Bake at 350° for 25 minutes.
Makes 6 servings.

     ½ pound bacon
     ¼ cup packaged bread crumbs
     2 pounds potatoes, cooked and peeled
     6 hard-cooked eggs, sliced
     2 tablespoons minced chives
     ½ teaspoon salt
     ⅛ teaspoon pepper
     1 cup dairy sour cream
     ½ cup milk
     1 tablespoon flour

1. Cook bacon in a large skillet until crisp; drain and reserve. Pour off all but 1 tablespoon of drippings. Sauté crumbs in drippings until brown.
2. Slice potatoes. Crumble bacon.
3. Arrange half of sliced potatoes in a buttered shallow 8-cup baking dish. Spread sliced eggs, bacon and chives over potatoes; sprinkle with salt and pepper. Top with remaining sliced potatoes.
4. Combine sour cream, milk and flour; mix well. Pour over potatoes. Sprinkle with crumbs.
5. Bake in a moderate oven (350°) 25 minutes.

CHERRY TOMATOES IN BROWN BUTTER SAUCE

The French have a way with sauces for vegetables and this is one of the most delightful of them all.

Makes 4 servings.

     4 tablespoons (½ stick) butter or margarine
     1 tablespoon lemon juice
     ¼ cup finely chopped parsley
     1 teaspoon leaf tarragon, crumbled
     1 pint cherry tomatoes, washed and stemmed

1. Melt butter or margarine over low heat in a medium-size heavy skillet until a deep golden brown; stir in lemon juice, parsley and tarragon.
2. Add tomatoes and cook, swirling the skillet constantly, just until skins begin to burst, about 3 minutes. Spoon into a heated vegetable bowl.

STUFFED ARTICHOKES ROMANO

If you've never tried artichokes before this is a great recipe to start with—it will make you a fan!

Makes 6 servings.

       3 cups fresh bread crumbs (6 slices)
    ¾ cup chopped parsley
    ½ cup grated Romano cheese
    ¼ cup sliced green onions
       1 clove garlic, crushed
       1 teaspoon salt
          Dash of pepper
       6 large artichokes
       6 tablespoons olive or vegetable oil
          Melted butter or margarine

1. Combine bread crumbs, parsley, cheese, green onions, garlic, salt and pepper in a medium-size bowl; toss lightly to mix.
2. Cut stems from artichokes close to base; slice about an inch from top with a sharp knife and snip off any spiny leaf tips. Carefully spread leaves open. Pull out small yellow center leaves, then scrape out fuzzy chokes with a teaspoon. Rinse artichokes in cold water.
3. Spoon stuffing mixture into hollow in each artichoke; stand in a deep kettle. Drizzle 1 tablespoon of the olive oil over each; pour boiling water into kettle to a depth of 2 inches. Heat to boiling; cover.
4. Cook 40 minutes, or until a leaf pulls away easily from base; drain well. Serve with small bowls of melted butter or margarine as a dip.

PETITS POIS FRANCAIS

A continental favorite, these peas are simmered with shredded lettuce and green onions in a buttery dressing.

Makes 8 servings.

       4 pounds fresh peas in pods, shelled (4 cups)
       2 cups shredded lettuce
    ¼ cup sliced green onions
    ½ teaspoon salt
    ⅛ teaspoon pepper
    ½ cup water
       4 tablespoons (½ stick) butter or margarine
       2 tablespoons flour

1. Combine peas, lettuce, green onions, salt, pepper, water and 3 tablespoons of the butter or margarine in a large saucepan; heat to boiling; cover. Simmer 10 minutes, or until peas are tender.
2. While peas cook, blend remaining 1 tablespoon butter or margarine with flour to a paste in a cup.
3. Stir into pea mixture, a small amount at a time; continue cooking and stirring until mixture thickens and boils 1 minute. Spoon into a heated bowl.

DANISH CAULIFLOWER WITH SHRIMP SAUCE

One of Denmark's loveliest vegetables is a light meal in itself. And you get it all on the table in less than 30 minutes.

Makes 6 servings.

       1 medium-size cauliflower, trimmed of outer green leaves
       6 cups water with 2 teaspoons salt mixed in

SAUCE:
    ¼ pound frozen, shelled, deveined shrimp
    ¼ cup frozen chopped onion
       3 tablespoons butter or margarine
       3 tablespoons flour
    ½ teaspoon dillweed
          Pinch of ground mace
          Pinch of white pepper
    ¾ teaspoon salt
       1 cup milk
       1 tablespoon lemon juice
    ¼ cup mayonnaise or salad dressing
       2 egg yolks, lightly whisked with 1 tablespoon dry vermouth

1. Make a deep X-shaped cut in base of cauliflower, then place on a vegetable steamer rack (so you can ease the whole cooked cauliflower out of the pan without breaking it). Bring salted water to boiling in a large heavy kettle. Lower rack and cauliflower into water, cover tightly and cook 20 minutes, or until the cauliflower is tender but *slightly* crisp.
2. Cook shrimp, following label directions. Drain on paper toweling and slice fairly thin; reserve.
3. Prepare sauce: In a small saucepan sauté onion in butter 2 to 3 minutes until soft. Blend in flour, dillweed, mace, pepper and salt; add milk; heat and stir until smooth and quite thick, about 2 to 3 minutes.
4. Smooth in lemon juice and mayonnaise; whisk a little hot sauce into egg yolks, then stir back into pan. Add shrimp, turn heat down to lowest point and keep warm, stirring now and then, just until cauliflower is done.
5. Lift cauliflower from kettle, slide onto a large serving plate and spoon some of the shrimp sauce on top; pour the rest into a sauceboat so that everyone can help himself to more. Garnish with tomato and egg wedges, cooked shrimp and dill, if you wish.

Scandinavian vegetable classics include (at right from top, clockwise): Danish Cauliflower with Shrimp Sauce, Broiled Tomatoes Nested with Spinach and Swedish Green Beans in Dill Mustard Sauce. The recipe for the cauliflower is on this page. The recipes for the tomatoes and the green beans can be found on pages 56 and 57.

FIVE-MINUTE VEGETABLE SAUCES YOU CAN MAKE AHEAD OF TIME

In five minutes or less, you can make some delicious sauces guaranteed to turn vegetable dishes into gourmet treats. The secret lies in using either prepared mayonnaise, salad dressing or sour cream as the basis for each of these sauces.

MAYONNAISE OR SALAD DRESSING SAUCES

Start with ½ cup of mayonnaise or salad dressing for each of the following sauces:

Caper Sauce—Stir ½ cup light or table cream and 2 tablespoons drained chopped capers into mayonnaise in a small bowl. Spoon over freshly cooked potatoes. Makes about 1 cup.

Deviled Egg Sauce—Combine mayonnaise, 3 tablespoons milk and 1 teaspoon prepared mustard in a small saucepan. Heat, stirring constantly, just until bubbly, then stir in 1 chopped, hardcooked egg. Serve over any green vegetable. Makes about ½ cup.

Caesar Sauce—Toast ¾ cup tiny bread cubes in a small frying pan. Stir in 1 tablespoon bottled Caesar salad dressing, then fold in mayonnaise. This is a spreadable sauce—delicious on asparagus or cauliflower. Makes about ¾ cup.

Blue-Cheese Sauce—Blend 2 tablespoons blue cheese and ½ teaspoon dry mustard into mayonnaise. Serve over asparagus, broccoli, green beans or cauliflower. Makes about ½ cup.

Puffed Derby Sauce—Beat 1 egg white until stiff in a small bowl; fold in mayonnaise, 1 tablespoon lemon juice and a dash of nutmeg. Layer over a hot vegetable (asparagus, broccoli, lima beans, green beans or squash) in a heatproof serving dish. Slide into heated broiler for 2 to 3 minutes, or until top is puffed and golden-brown. Makes about 1 cup.

SOUR CREAM SAUCES

Start with 1 cup sour cream for each of the following sauces:

Caraway Cream—Stir in 1 teaspoon caraway seeds, 1 teaspoon Worcestershire sauce and ¼ teaspoon salt. Try it on crisply cooked, shredded green cabbage. Makes 1 cup.

Cucumber Cream—Blend in 2 tablespoons each mayonnaise and lemon juice, 1 tablespoon sugar, ½ teaspoon onion salt and a few drops of liquid red-pepper seasoning. Finely chop the white part of 1 pared medium-size cucumber (no seeds) and stir in. Try it on mild-flavor zucchini or yellow squash. Makes about 1½ cups. (See page 63.)

Left: A bumper crop of delicious fruits and vegetables, ready for preserving. See pages 65-77.

Horseradish Cream—Stir in 1 tablespoon each prepared horseradish and chili sauce and 1 teaspoon prepared mustard. Add a sprinkling of salt and pepper and serve over tiny cooked white onions. Makes about 1 cup.

Curry Cream—Stir in ½ cup finely chopped celery, 1 teaspoon minced onion and ¼ teaspoon curry powder. Season to taste with salt and pepper. Spoon over hot drained green beans. Makes about 1¼ cups.

PICKLED BEETS

Here's a quick recipe that can be served as a vegetable course or as part of an appetizer tray.

Makes 6 servings.

    1 can (1 pound) sliced beets
    1 tablespoon mixed pickling spices
    1 tablespoon cider vinegar

Drain liquid from beets into a small saucepan; add pickling spices and vinegar. Heat to boiling; lower heat; simmer 5 minutes. Place beets in a small bowl. Strain beet liquid over and chill.

ORANGE-STUFFED SWEET POTATOES

The potatoes are mashed with spices and orange segments, for a really new flavor change.

Bake at 400° for 1¼ hours.
Makes 6 servings.

    3 large sweet potatoes (about 1½ pounds)
    1 jar (11 ounces) mandarin oranges
    2 tablespoons butter or margarine
    1 teaspoon salt
    ¼ teaspoon pepper
    ¼ teaspoon ground ginger
      Toasted slivered almonds (optional)

1. Scrub potatoes. Place on a cooky sheet.
2. Bake in hot oven (400°) 1 hour, or until potatoes are tender when pierced with a fork.
3. Drain oranges; reserve syrup.
4. Halve potatoes lengthwise; scoop out insides into a bowl and mash until smooth. Blend in ¼ cup syrup, butter, salt, pepper and ginger.
5. Stir orange segments into potatoes. Pile mixture into potato shells. Top with toasted slivered almonds. Place on cooky sheet.
6. Return to hot oven (400°) and bake for 15 minutes, or until piping hot.

Left: Fruits to serve as salads or desserts. The recipes for Pineapple Crown (with sour cream dressing), and Melon Basket Medley are in Chapter 8.

SAUTÉED ZUCCHINI

This favorite summer vegetable takes only about 8 minutes to cook.

Makes 4 servings.

    ¾ pound zucchini
    2 tablespoons margarine
    1 tablespoon minced parsley
      Salt and pepper to taste

Wash zucchini well and dry. Cut in thin rounds. Heat margarine in a 10-inch skillet and when hot, add zucchini and toss lightly, stirring constantly with a wooden spatula, turning pieces two or three times. After about 5 minutes, zucchini should become a bit translucent. Cover pan and simmer 3 minutes. Add parsley, salt and pepper.

COUNTRY CREAMED CORN

Raw kernels simmer in a buttery sauce for the freshest flavor.

Makes 6 servings.

    4 tablespoons (½ stick) butter or margarine
    ⅓ cup cream
    ½ teaspoon salt
    ¼ teaspoon sugar
    ¼ teaspoon seasoned pepper
    3 cups uncooked corn kernels (4 to 5 ears)
      Thinly sliced green onions

1. Melt butter or margarine in a medium-size saucepan; stir in cream, salt, sugar, seasoned pepper and corn; heat to boiling; cover.
2. Simmer, stirring several times, 15 minutes, or until corn is tender.
3. Spoon into serving bowl; sprinkle with onions.

MUSHROOMS IN SOUR CREAM

Here's a classically good recipe that's extra easy.

Makes 4 servings.

    ¼ cup chopped green onions
    3 tablespoons butter or margarine
    1 pound mushrooms, washed, trimmed and sliced (¼-inch thick)
    1 teaspoon salt
    ⅛ teaspoon pepper
    ½ cup dairy sour cream

1. Sauté green onions in butter or margarine until soft, in a large skillet, about 5 minutes. Add mushrooms and cook quickly until tender, 5 minutes.
2. Sprinkle with salt and pepper; stir in sour cream and heat slowly just until piping hot.

SESAME BROCCOLI

An Oriental touch will add a lively lift to your next dinnertime.

Makes 8 servings.

- **1 bunch broccoli, weighing about 1½ pounds**
- **4 tablespoons (½ stick) butter or margarine**
- **¼ cup water**
- **1 tablespoon soy sauce**
- **1 cup thinly sliced celery**
- **1 can (5 ounces) water chestnuts, drained and sliced**
- **1 tablespoon sesame seeds**

1. Trim outer leaves and tough ends from broccoli. Cut stalks and flowerets into 2-inch lengths, then slice thin lengthwise.
2. Combine butter or margarine, water and soy sauce in a large frying pan; heat to boiling. Stir in broccoli, celery and water chestnuts; heat to boiling again; cover. Steam 10 minutes, or just until broccoli is crisply tender.
3. While broccoli cooks, heat sesame seeds in a small heavy frying pan over low heat, shaking pan constantly, just until lightly toasted; stir into broccoli mixture. Spoon into a heated serving bowl. Serve with more soy sauce.

HOW TO ROAST CORN

In Aluminum Foil: Husk and remove silks from freshly picked corn; spread with softened butter or margarine; season with salt and pepper; wrap well in heavy-duty or double-thick regular aluminum foil. Place in shallow pan and roast in oven, the same as for corn in husks (see below), or grill out of doors over hot coals, 15 to 25 minutes, turning corn several times to grill evenly.
In Husks: Remove only outer husks; fold back inner ones, being careful not to split them; remove silks. Spread corn with softened butter or margarine, sprinkle with salt and pepper or with seasoned salt. Pull husks back up over ears; tie tips with string to keep corn covered and moist; place in baking pan; roast in hot oven (400°) 20 to 25 minutes.
On the Grill: Remove outer husks from freshly picked corn; pull back inner husks; remove all silk; turn inner husks back into place; soak ears in cold water for at least 30 minutes. Place around edge of grill over hot coals; roast, turning 2 or 3 times, 10 to 15 minutes, or until husks and kernels are toasty-browned. Serve with butter or margarine and salt and pepper.
OR: Instead of soaking corn you can remove outer husks, pull back inner husks, remove silk and spread corn with softened butter or margarine. Then salt and pepper, replace inner husks and tie with string to keep in moisture. Roast on the grill same way as water-soaked ears.

HOW TO COOK CORN ON THE COB

Allow 1 or 2 ears of corn for each serving. Peel husks back and break off with stub; pick off all silks. Fill a large kettle with enough water to cover corn; season each quart with ½ teaspoon sugar and 1 teaspoon salt. (Sugar brings out all of the natural sweetness of the corn.) Heat water to boiling; add corn; cover. Simmer 5 to 10 minutes, or until tender. Lift out ears with tongs; drain well. Serve piping-hot with your choice of plain or seasoned butter.

Lemon Butter—Stir 1 teaspoon lemon juice into ½ cup whipped butter or margarine in a small bowl. Let everyone add salt to taste.

Chive Butter—Stir 1 tablespoon finely cut chives into ½ cup whipped butter or margarine in a small bowl. Let everyone add salt to taste.

Chili Butter—Stir ½ teaspoon chili powder into ½ cup whipped butter or margarine in a small bowl. Let everyone add salt to taste.

CORN SCALLOP

This sunny vegetable teams with zucchini, tomatoes and a sprinkle of herbs for an inviting triple-good dish.

Bake at 400° for 1 hour and 10 minutes.
Makes 6 servings.

- **4 small zucchini, trimmed and sliced thin (about 3 cups)**
- **6 tablespoons (¾ stick) butter or margarine**
- **4 medium-size tomatoes, peeled and sliced**
- **1 teaspoon sugar**
- **½ teaspoon salt**
- **2 cups coarse saltine crumbs**
- **1 teaspoon Italian seasoning**
- **2 cups uncooked corn kernels (3 to 4 ears)**

1. Sauté zucchini lightly in 2 tablespoons of the butter or margarine in a large frying pan; remove. Sauté tomatoes in 2 more tablespoons of the butter or margarine in same pan; sprinkle with sugar and salt. (Set remaining butter or margarine aside for Step 4.)
2. Mix saltine crumbs and Italian seasoning in a medium-size bowl.
3. Sprinkle ¾ cup of the seasoned crumbs over bottom of an 8-cup shallow baking dish; top with layers of ⅔ of the tomatoes, another ¾ cup crumbs, zucchini and corn. Place remaining tomato slices, overlapping, in a row on top; cover.
4. Bake in hot oven (400°) 1 hour, or until bubbly; uncover. Sprinkle tomatoes with remaining ½ cup seasoned crumbs; dot corn with remaining 2 tablespoons butter or margarine. Bake 10 minutes longer, or until crumbs are toasty.

The Carefree Summer Preserving Guide

CANNING FRUITS & VEGETABLES

Learning to preserve summer's bounty is by no means difficult, as the following guide illustrates. It's simply a matter of having a little extra time and a bit of patience until you get the knack of things. And the rewards are generous—low-cost, fresh-tasting food you can enjoy throughout the coming months. Start by reading the step-by-step directions below. They cover all you need to know for canning and freezing food from the garden (or the supermarket). Then, go on to our recipes.

THREE METHODS OF CANNING

Water-Bath Method & Canner: Modern scientists are discovering that great-grandmother knew what she was doing when she used the hot-water-bath method for preserving foods. This method—suggested for fruits, tomatoes, pickles, relishes and other acid foods—is a way of processing foods with boiling water (212°F). The boiling water destroys spoilage micro-organisms.

In following the water-bath method of preserving foods, use a water-bath canner (available in department stores) or a large metal container or kettle deep enough for water to cover tops of jars 2 to 4 inches without boiling over. The canner must also have a tight-fitting cover and a rack or basket to keep jars from touching the bottom of the kettle. If you don't already own a canner, you can puchase one for about $10.

The canner can also be used for butters, conserves, jams, marmalades and preserves. (See Step 9 under General Directions.)

Steam-Pressure Method & Canner: For foods such as beans, beets, corn and other low-acid foods, we recommend preserving them by freezing (see DIRECTIONS FOR FREEZING, page 67). However, you can use the steam-pressure method if you choose. The method requires a higher water temperature (240°) in order to destroy bacteria spores which cause flat-sour, botulism and other types of spoilage in low-acid foods. You will need a steam-pressure canner, or cooker—specially designed for higher temperatures—and it is necessary to follow manufacturer's directions carefully.

The Open Kettle Method is recommended *only* for jellies. The food is cooked in an uncovered kettle and poured boiling hot into sterilized hot jars, which are then sealed immediately.

PLANNING YOUR CANNING

Before using any of the three methods outlined above, you should do a little planning:
1. Check the condition of hot-water-bath canner, if you have one; otherwise, consider buying one. (Again, you can use any deep kettle, but it must be large enough to take the height of the mason jars, at least a 2-inch depth of water above the jars, with space for the boiling water, plus a rack of ½-inch under the jars.)
2. Check the condition of the jars and metal bands on hand. Be sure that the jars have no cracks and that the metal rings are not bent.
3. Buy new domed lids (you should never use them more than once). Buy jars in the half-pint, pint or quart size, depending on your needs. (Half-pints are ideal for jams and relishes; pints are the right size for 2 or 3 servings and quarts are for larger servings or for pickles.)

GENERAL DIRECTIONS

Follow all the directions carefully and *do not* take any shortcuts. Your time is too valuable and food too costly to have your preserves spoiled.
1. Spend only a few hours at a time and put up just one kind of food at a time.
2. Place hot-water-bath canner onto surface burner; add water to half fill canner (a teakettle does this job easily); cover canner; bring water to boiling while preparing jars and food.
3. Wash jars in hot sudsy water; rinse well; leave in hot water until ready to use.
4. Place new domed lids in a bowl and cover with boiling water; keep in water until ready to use.
5. Follow individual recipe directions.
6. Remove jars from water, one at a time; place on paper toweling or a clean cloth.
7. Pack and/or ladle food into jars, leaving ½-inch headroom.
8. Wipe top and outside rim of jar with a clean cloth; place domed lid on top; screw metal rings on tightly, but do not use force.
9. Place jars in canner rack and lower into rapidly boiling water, adding additional boiling water to kettle if the level of the water is not 2 inches above the jars; cover kettle. Return to a full boil.*
10. Process, following the times given in the individual recipes and calculated from the time that the water comes to the second boil.
Note: For those who live at altitudes above sea level, when recipe directions call for processing 20 minutes or less, add 1 minute for each 1,000 feet; when processing more than 20 minutes, add 2 minutes for each 1,000 feet.
11. Remove jars from canner and place on wire racks or cloth-lined surface at least 3 inches apart, out of drafts, until cool, about 12 hours.
12. Test all jars to be sure that they are sealed by tapping with a spoon. (A clear ringing sound means a good seal. If jars are not sealed properly, either store in refrigerator and plan to use within a month or re-process beginning with Step 6.)
13. Remove metal rings; wipe jars with a clean dampened cloth; label, date and store jars in a cool, dark, dry place.

*In the case of butters, conserves, jams, marmalades and preserves, lower jars into simmering water (180°-185°), and process at simmering.

WHEN MAKING JELLIES

There are two other safe methods of sealing foods with a high acid and sugar content.

A. *Using jelly jars with domed lids:* Fill one hot sterilized jar* at a time to within ⅛-inch of top; wipe off top and outer rim; top with domed lid and screw metal ring on tight. Cool 12 hours. Label, date and store in a cool, dark, dry place.

B. *Using jelly glasses:* Fill hot sterilized glasses* to within ¼-inch of top; wipe off top and outer rim; pour a ⅛-inch layer of hot paraffin over. Prick any air bubbles in paraffin. Cool 12 hours. Cover glasses; label, date and store in a cool, dark, dry place.

To sterilize jelly jars and glasses, wash jars or glasses in hot sudsy water; rinse well; place in a kettle fitted with a rack to keep the jars at least ½-inch from bottom of kettle. Fill kettle to 1-inch depth above jars with water; cover kettle. Bring to boiling; boil 10 minutes. Keep jars in water until just before filling, then invert onto a clean towel, away from draft, to drain. Cover lids and bands with water in a small saucepan. Bring water to simmering (180°-185°). Remove from heat and leave in water until ready to seal jars.

FREEZING FRUITS & VEGETABLES
GENERAL DIRECTIONS

• *Check Freezer Temperature.* Before you start, be sure your freezer or freezer section of your refrigerator will go as low as 0° and hold that temperature. It is best to check this with a freezer thermometer. Set freezer control to lowest setting before you begin processing the food.

• *Choose the Right Packaging Material.* Packaging for the freezer should be moisture- and vapor-proof. For vegetables and fruits, the following are available:

1. *Rigid Containers of Plastic* with snap-on lids, or glass freezer jars tempered for freezing, with screw tops. Both are reusable. Leave head space as marked (usually ½ inch).

2. *Plastic Bags.* Have advantage of taking less space in freezer, but should be protected against possible puncture. Press filled bags to exclude as much air as possible; close with wire-twists.

3. *Heat-in-Pouch Containers* (boilable bags) are the newest thing in food containers. Can go from freezer to saucepan of boiling water. However, they are only for use when vegetables are frozen in a sauce, so there will be some liquid in the pouch when reheating. See recipe for Special Herb-Butter Sauce for Vegetables in next column.

4. *Heavy-Duty Aluminum Foil* or plastic wrap. Good for odd shapes such as corn on the cob. Seal with freezer tape.

• *Select Quality.* Your final product can be no better than the quality you start with. Freeze only the best, and freeze it soon after picking.

• *Freeze in Small Quantities.* Freeze in containers that will hold just enough for one meal. Smaller containers are easier to store in the freezer, too!

• *Don't Overload Freezer.* The U.S. Department of Agriculture recommends that you do not freeze more than 2 to 3 pounds of food per cubic foot of freezer space at any one time. Place containers of food on or next to freezing surfaces, leaving a little space all around. When frozen, stack containers to make more room.

SIX QUICK-AND-EASY STEPS FOR FREEZING VEGETABLES

1. *Sort and Wash.* Pick over vegetables and discard the imperfect ones. Sort according to size, if there are differences. Wash gently in running cold water.

2. *Prepare for Freezing.* Follow instructions for individual vegetables (*see guide on page 68*).

3. *Blanching.* Plunging the prepared vegetables in boiling water is a necessary step. It stops the action of the natural enzymes that aided the growth of the vegetables but would now affect taste and color.

To Blanch: Bring 1 gallon of water to boiling in a kettle large enough to hold a colander or wire basket. Put 4 cups prepared vegetables in the colander; lower into boiling water; cover kettle. Start timing the blanching period at once, following the time for each suggested vegetable. (Note: Blanching is not necessary for chopped onion, chopped green and red peppers, fresh herbs or whole tomatoes.)

4. *Chilling.* Lift colander from boiling water at end of blanching time. Plunge into a container of cold water immediately. Add a tray of ice cubes to keep water cold. Chill for about the same length of time that you have kept the vegetables in the boiling water. If preparing more than three batches, change the water after the third batch.

5. *Drain Thoroughly.* Paper toweling will absorb most of the moisture. Pack loosely in containers you have selected.

6. *Seal and Label.* Be thorough. After you have stashed your prize vegetables away in the freezer, don't lose them. Label containers with name of contents and the date. Freeze, following GENERAL DIRECTIONS. Properly processed vegetables are in A-1 condition for 8 to 12 months.

SPECIAL HERB-BUTTER SAUCE FOR VEGETABLES IN BOILABLE BAGS

To each 2 cups of vegetables processed and ready to freeze, add 3 tablespoons water, 1 tablespoon butter or margarine, pinch of oregano, thyme or basil, dash of salt and pepper. Seal, label and freeze. When ready to cook, bring water to boiling in saucepan. Add pouch of frozen, seasoned vegetables. Be sure top of pouch above tie closure is above the water level. Cook 15 minutes after the water has come to boiling again.

FREEZER GUIDE FOR VEGETABLES

Green or Wax Beans: Wash and tip; divide into different thicknesses, leave whole, cut into 2-inch pieces or French. Blanch: Cut-up and Frenched beans, 3 minutes. Whole beans, 4 minutes. Chill.

Lima Beans: Shell and sort beans, using only the perfect beans. Blanch: Baby lima beans, 1½ minutes. Fordhook lima beans, 3½ minutes. Chill.

Beets: Choose only young and tender beets, no larger than 3 inches in diameter. Wash and trim tops to within ½-inch of beet. Divide into sizes. Cook in boiling water until tender: Small beets, 25 to 30 minutes. Medium-size beets, 45 to 50 minutes. Cool immediately by plunging into a bowl of ice and water. Peel and slice or dice. Pack in rigid containers, allowing ½-inch head room.

Carrots: Use young tender carrots. Remove tops; scrub and pare. Leave whole, slice or dice. Blanch: Sliced or diced, 3 minutes. Whole, 5 minutes. Chill.

Corn *(On the Cob):* Husk ears; remove silks; separate into different sizes. Blanch: Small, 6 minutes. Medium-size, 8; large-size, 10. Chill.

Corn *(Whole Kernel):* Prepare and blanch corn, following directions, page 67. Cut kernels from cobs about two-thirds the depth of the kernel.

Spinach, Beet Greens, Chard, Turnip Greens, Collard: Pick over leaves using only the tender ones. Wash and trim. Blanch: 2 minutes. Chill.

Herbs *(mint, dill, parsley, rosemary, thyme, sweet basil, fennel, leek, marjoram, tarragon):* Wash and trim herbs; dry on paper towels; chop into fine pieces. Blanch: Not necessary.

Onions: Peel, slice and chop. Blanch: No need.

Peas: Shell and pick over, using only young and perfect peas. Blanch: 1½ minutes. Pack: Dry-pack into rigid containers or plastic bags.

Peppers (Red and Green, Sweet and Hot): Use only firm, crisp, thick-walled ones. Wash; halve; seed. To use uncooked: Cut into thin slices or dice. Blanch: Not necessary. To use cooked: Cut into wedges, strips or halves. Blanch: Wedges or strips, 2 minutes. Halves, 3 minutes. Chill.

Summer Squash or Zucchini: Use only young and tender squash. Wash, tip and cut into ½-inch slices. Blanch: 3 minutes. Chill.

Tomatoes *(Whole):* Freezing tomatoes this way is not the most recommended way to keep them, but if you have a few beauties that you would like to keep for no more than three months: Wash and dry tomatoes. Blanch: Not necessary. Pack: Wrap individually in plastic bags or plastic wrap.

Tomatoes *(Stewed Tomatoes):* This is the best way to freeze tomatoes for use throughout the year. By just stewing them, you have the basis for making spaghetti sauce, vegetable soup or stewed tomatoes as a vegetable anytime you are ready to serve them. Wash, peel and quarter tomatoes. Place in a large kettle; heat to boiling; cover kettle; simmer for 20 minutes, or until tomatoes are tender. Spoon into a large bowl. Place bowl in a sink filled with ice and water until tomatoes are cool. You can add 1 teaspoon salt for each 4 cups of tomato, if you wish. Blanch: Not necessary. Pack: Spoon them into rigid containers, allowing ¾-inch head room.

Tomatoes *(Tomato Puree):* Wash, peel and quarter tomatoes. Place in a large kettle; heat to boiling; cover kettle; simmer 20 minutes, or until very tender. Press through a strainer into a large bowl; place bowl in a sink filled with ice and water until puree is cool. You can add 1 teaspoon salt for every 4 cups of tomatoes, if you wish. Blanch: Not necessary. Pack: Pour into rigid containers, allowing ¾-inch head room.

Tomatoes *(Tomato Juice):* Wash, peel and quarter tomatoes. Place in a large kettle; heat to boiling; cover kettle; simmer 5 to 10 minutes, or until almost tender. Press through a sieve into a large bowl. Place bowl in a sink filled with ice and water until juice is cool. You can add 1 teaspoon salt for each 4 cups of juice, if you wish. Blanch: Not necessary. Pack: Pour into glass freezer jars, allowing ¾-inch head room.

Turnips, Parsnips, Rutabaga: Cut into ½-inch slices; pare slices; cut into cubes. Blanch: 2 minutes. Chill. Pack: Dry-pack into rigid containers.

FIVE QUICK-AND-EASY STEPS FOR FREEZING FRUITS

1. *Sort and Wash.* Pick over fruit and discard bruised or immature ones. Wash gently, a few at a time, in running cold water.

2. Prepare fruit as you would for serving *(see individual fruits, page 69).*

3. Choose the method you wish to use. The two most popular methods for freezing fruits are:

• *The Syrup Pack:* A 40 percent sugar-water syrup helps keep the shape of the fruit quite well. It is preferred when the fruit is to be thawed and served as is. Or you may use:

• *The Sugar Pack,* which mixes the fruit with sugar in the correct proportion, drawing out some of the juices. This pack is good for fruits that will be cooked. If you wish to freeze some especially perfect berries for garnishing, arrange the washed berries on a tray; freeze. When *just* frozen, fill them into rigid containers. Seal, label and return to freezer. The berries will not stick together, as they have been individually frozen, and may be used one by one as you wish.

4. *Choose the Right Container.* Fruits are best packed for freezing in rigid containers. The same types of container mentioned under vegetables may be used. Rigid containers are preferred to keep fruit from damage in the freezer, and to contain the fruit syrups without spilling. Leave head space, as marked on container.

5. *Seal and Label.* Always label with contents and date. It is often frustrating to try to guess the contents of a container when it is frozen solid. Freeze, following GENERAL DIRECTIONS for freezing fruits and vegetables, on page 67.

USING THE FRUITS FROM THE FREEZER

Fruit should be thawed before using. When they are to be served as is, the texture and flavor are best if there are still a few ice crystals. For cooking, you need only thaw slightly if you have to measure or separate the pieces of fruit. Otherwise, the heat of cooking will be enough.

Sugar-pack fruit thaws fastest. Syrup-pack fruit may be thawed in an hour in a bowl of cold water or 5 to 7 hours in the refrigerator.

How to Sugar-pack Fruit: Put part of the prepared fruit *(see individual fruits)* in a large bowl. Sprinkle with the amount of sugar recommended. Add ascorbic acid, as suggested, to prevent darkening. Mix gently until juices start to flow. Fill containers, allowing head space. Seal; label; freeze.

How to Syrup-pack Fruit: Prepare sugar syrup following directions for individual fruits. Cool; chill. Fill containers with prepared fruit. Pour chilled syrup over fruit, leaving head space. Seal; label; freeze.

Note: For each pint of fruit you will be needing from ½ to ⅔ cup of the chilled syrup.

HANDY FREEZING GUIDE FOR FRUITS

Apples *Prepare Syrup:* Dissolve 3 cups sugar in 4 cups hot water. (Makes 5½ cups.) Cool; chill. Just before pouring over fruit, stir in ¾ teaspoon pure ascorbic acid powder to keep the fruit colors bright. Pure ascorbic acid is available from drugstores, or you may use the commercial ascorbic acid mixtures. Follow package directions for amount to use. Wash, pare, core and cut apples into thin slices. Slice directly into a bowl containing a solution of 2 tablespoons salt to 4 cups of cold water to prevent darkening. Don't leave in this solution more than 15 minutes. Drain well. Fill containers; pour in chilled syrup. Seal; label; freeze.

Applesauce: Wash, pare, core and cut apples. Cook until tender in a small amount of water. Either puree or leave in chunks. Add sugar, if you wish. Fill containers. Seal; label and freeze.

Strawberries, Raspberries, Blackberries, Blueberries, Boysenberries *Prepare Fruit:* Select plump, ripe, firm berries. Discard immature or bruised ones. Wash gently and drain. Remove hulls from strawberries. Slice strawberries or leave whole. Use either of following packs.

Sugar Pack:
Add ¾ cup sugar to each quart of strawberries. Mix gently. Fill containers, leaving head space. Seal; label and freeze.

Syrup Pack:
Prepare syrup as for Apples. Chill. Fill containers. Pour syrup over berries, leaving head space. Seal; label and then freeze.

Peaches (Apricots, Nectarines) *Prepare Fruit:* Select firm, ripe fruit. Wash, halve and pit. Peaches make a better frozen product if they are very thinly peeled rather than peeled with boiling water.

Sugar Pack:
Add ⅔ cup sugar to each quart of peaches. To preserve best color, sprinkle peaches with a mixture of ¼ teaspoon ascorbic acid dissolved in ¼ cup cold water for each quart of peaches.

Syrup Pack:
Prepare syrup as for Apples. Chill. Fill containers. Pour syrup over peaches, leaving head space. Seal; label and then freeze.

Pears: Select firm, well-ripened pears. Wash, peel, halve and core. Prepare a double amount of syrup as for Apples. Chill one half; heat remainder to boiling. Cook pears in this syrup for 1 to 2 minutes. Drain and cool. Fill containers. Add 1 teaspoon ascorbic acid to the chilled syrup. Pour over pears, leaving head space. Seal; label and then freeze.

EMERGENCY TACTICS—In the event of power failure, which can happen to the best of us, leave freezer *closed.* A fully loaded freezer will keep the food frozen from 1 to 2 days, even in the heat of summer.

GRAPE-LEMON JELLY

It's inexpensive and delicious—who could ask for more!

Makes 8 eight-ounce glasses.

    2 cups grape juice
    7 cups sugar
    1 bottle liquid fruit pectin
    1 cup water
    1 can (5¾ ounces) frozen lemon juice, thawed
      Few drops yellow food coloring

1. Prepare jelly glasses or jars following directions for *sterilizing jelly jars* (see "When Making Jellies," on page 67).
2. Grape Jelly Layer: Measure grape juice and 3½ cups of the sugar into a large saucepan. Bring to boiling over high heat, stirring constantly.
3. Stir in ½ bottle of the fruit pectin. Bring to a full rolling boil; boil hard 1 minute.
4. Remove from heat; skim off foam with a metal spoon. Ladle into 8 hot, sterilized glasses, filling each half full. Hold ladle close to jar to prevent air bubbles in jelly. Allow to cool slightly while preparing Lemon Jelly Layer.
5. Lemon Jelly Layer: Measure water and remaining 3½ cups of the sugar into a large saucepan. Bring to a full rolling boil over high heat; stirring constantly; boil 1 minute.
6. Remove from heat; stir in lemon juice and food coloring to tint a pale yellow. Add remaining ½ bottle of the fruit pectin.
7. Carefully ladle hot Lemon Jelly over slightly cooled Grape Jelly in glasses. Immediately cover with thin layer of hot paraffin, following directions on page 67, "When Making Jellies."

SWEET PEPPER AND ORANGE JAM

Delicious served in orange cups with a ham.

Makes 7 half pints.

25 sweet red peppers (about 6 pounds)
 1 large seedless orange, peeled and cut into pieces
 2 cups cider vinegar
4½ cups sugar
 1 teaspoon salt

1. Prepare jars and lids following General Directions, Steps 3 and 4, page 66.
2. Wash peppers; cut in half; remove seeds and white membrane; cut into large pieces; put through food chopper using coarsest blade.
3. Drain peppers well and discard liquid. Grind orange.
4. Combine chopped peppers, orange, vinegar, sugar and salt in a large kettle. Bring quickly to boiling, stirring constantly. Cook over high heat, stirring often, 30 minutes; or just until mixture is thick and clear like jam. (Do not overcook.)
5. Ladle into hot jars following General Directions, Steps 6-8. Process at simmering for 10-15 minutes following General Directions, Steps 9-13.

PARSLIED APPLE JELLY

Try this with a leg of lamb!

Makes 6 half pints.

 8 pounds tart cooking apples, washed
 8 cups water
4½ cups sugar
 ⅔ cup white vinegar
 1 cup chopped parsley
  Several drops green food coloring

1. Remove stem and blossom ends of apples; do not pare or core; slice or chop. Combine with water in a very large kettle.* Bring to boiling; reduce heat; cover. Simmer 20 minutes, or until apples are soft.
2. Pour cooked apple mixture into a damp jelly bag. (Make your own from unbleached muslin or several thicknesses of cheesecloth.) Let stand without squeezing for at least 4 hours, or until clear liquid has stopped dripping out. (Or pour apple mixture through several layers of wet cheesecloth in a colander placed over a large bowl.) You will get about 4 cups.
3. Combine apple juice with sugar and vinegar in a large kettle; bring to a full rolling boil; continue to boil for about 20 minutes, stirring and skimming occasionally, or until mixture registers 220° on a candy thermometer at sea level. (For higher elevations use temperature 8° higher than temperature at which water boils.) If you do not

have a thermometer, test with clean metal spoon; jelly is done when the drops run together and fall off the spoon in a sheet or flake.
4. When jelly is done, remove from heat; stir in parsley and a few drops of food coloring to tint a pleasing green. Continue to skim and stir for 7 minutes.
5. Ladle into hot sterilized jars or glasses. (See: "When making Jellies" on page 67.)

*If you do not have a very large kettle, divide recipe in half; prepare one half at a time.

PINEAPPLE-ORANGE WINE JELLY

Rich topaz in color and irresistible on breakfast muffins.

Makes 4 six-ounce glasses.

3¼ cups sugar
1¼ cups white wine
 ½ bottle liquid fruit pectin (from a 6-ounce bottle)
 1 can (6 ounces) frozen concentrated pineapple-orange juice, thawed

1. Combine sugar and wine in a large saucepan.
2. Bring quickly to a full rolling boil, stirring constantly; boil hard 1 minute.
3. Remove from heat; stir in liquid fruit pectin and thawed juice. Mix well.
4. Ladle jelly quickly into hot sterilized jelly glasses following directions on page 67, WHEN MAKING JELLIES. Top each with a thin layer of melted paraffin; cool jars; cap, label and date following directions on page 67.

TOMATO AND PEAR MARMALADE

A lovely wintertime reward to pass with the holiday roast!

Makes 6 eight-ounce jars.

1½ pounds tomatoes
 1 pound pears
 ¼ cup lemon juice
 2 teaspoons grated lemon rind
1½ inches stick cinnamon
 1 package (1¾ ounces) powdered fruit pectin
 5 cups sugar

1. Prepare jars and lids following General Directions, Steps 3 and 4, page 66.
2. Place tomatoes in scalding water for 30 seconds; peel and cut into eighths; place in a medium-size saucepan. Bring to a boil; reduce heat; simmer 10 minutes; measure 2¼ cups.
3. Pare, core and dice pears to measure 2 cups.

Toss pears with the lemon juice and rind in a bowl.
4. Combine tomatoes, pears, cinnamon stick and pectin in a kettle. Bring quickly to a boil, stirring occasionally. Add sugar; bring again to a full rolling boil; boil rapidly 1 minute.
5. Remove from heat; skim off foam. Discard cinnamon stick. Stir and skim for 7 minutes to cool and prevent floating fruit; ladle into hot jars following General Directions, Steps 6-8. Process at simmering for 10-15 minutes, following General Directions, Steps 9-13.

SPICED BLUEBERRY PRESERVES

Blackberries, boysenberries, dewberries, logan- berries or youngberries can be substituted for the blueberries in this recipe.

Makes 8 half pints.

    12 cups blueberries (3 quarts)
    ¼   cup lemon juice
    6   cups sugar
    ½   teaspoon ground mace

1. Prepare jars and lids following General Direc- tions, Steps 3 and 4, page 66.
2. Wash berries and place in a large kettle with juice; cook slowly, stirring constantly, until juice flows from berries; stir in sugar and mace.
3. Bring to boiling; lower heat; simmer 20 min- utes, stirring often, until mixture thickens.
4. Ladle into hot half-pint jars following General Directions, Steps 6-8. Process at simmering for 15 minutes following General Directions, Steps 9-13.

LEMONY PEAR PRESERVES

Serve as a dramatic topping for vanilla ice cream or lemon sponge cake.

Makes 7 half pints.

     4 cups sugar
     2 cups water
    10 medium-size pears, pared, halved, cored
        and sliced (about 3 pounds)
     1 lemon, sliced
     2 tablespoons chopped preserved ginger
        (optional)

1. Combine 2 cups of the sugar with water in a large kettle. Bring to boiling; simmer 2 minutes. Lower pear slices into kettle with a slotted spoon; bring to boiling. Lower heat; simmer 10 minutes; add remaining 2 cups sugar, lemon slices and pre- served ginger, if used.
2. Cook, stirring often, 20 minutes, or until pear slices are translucent.
3. Remove kettle from heat; cover; let stand 12 to 18 hours at room temperature. Next day, bring

mixture to boiling and prepare jars and lids follow- ing General Directions, Steps 3 and 4, page 66. Ladle mixture into hot half-pint jars, leaving ¼- inch headroom, and following General Directions, Steps 6-8 on page 66. Seal and process 20 minutes in water-bath following General Directions, Steps 9-13, page 66.

PEAR HONEY

This preserve will be a bright new flavor treat for honey fans.

Makes 6 half pints.

    6 large ripe pears, pared and cored
    1 lemon, thinly sliced
    5 cups sugar

1. Prepare jars and lids following General Direc- tions, Steps 3 and 4, page 66.
2. Put pears through a food chopper, using the fine blade. (There should be about 4 cups.)
3. Combine with lemon and sugar in a large kettle. Bring to boiling, stirring constantly. Reduce heat; simmer, stirring occasionally, until mixture is thickened and clear, about 30 minutes.
4. Ladle into hot jars or glasses; seal and process 10 minutes following General Directions, Steps 6-13, page 66.

STRAWBERRY-APRICOT PRESERVES

The luscious taste of summer berries is yours year- round in this shimmering crimson preserve.

Makes 6 eight-ounce jars.

    4 cups (2 pints) strawberries, washed and
       hulled
    4 cups sugar
    1 package (1¾ ounces) powdered fruit pectin
    1 can (6 ounces) apricot nectar

1. Prepare jars and lids following directions for sterilizing jars found on page 67 under the heading "When Making Jellies."
2. Crush strawberries, a layer at a time, in a large bowl; measure. (There should be 2 cups.)
3. Stir in sugar, let stand, stirring occasionally, until sugar is dissolved, about 15 minutes.
4. Heat pectin and apricot nectar to boiling in a small saucepan; boil hard, stirring constantly, 1 minute; stir into fruit and continue stirring 3 minutes. (Some sugar crystals will remain.)
5. Ladle quickly into hot sterilized jars or freezer containers; cover tightly. Let stand 24 hours at room temperature; label and date. Store in freezer. (If preserves are to be eaten within 2 or 3 weeks, store in refrigerator.)

CRANBERRY-APPLE JELLY

Two flavors in one glass for very little extra effort.

Makes 8 eight-ounce glasses.

  2 cups apple juice
  7 cups sugar
  1 bottle liquid fruit pectin
  2 cups cranberry juice
    Red food coloring

1. Apple Jelly Layer: Measure apple juice and 3½ cups of the sugar into a large saucepan. Bring to boiling over high heat, stirring constantly.
2. Stir in ½ bottle of the fruit pectin. Bring to a full rolling boil; boil hard 1 minute.
3. Remove from heat; skim off foam with a metal spoon. Ladle into 8 hot sterilized glasses, filling each half full. (Follow directions on page 67, "When Making Jellies," for sterilizing glasses or jars.) Allow to cool slightly while preparing cranberry layer.
4. Cranberry Jelly Layer: Follow recipe for Apple Jelly, substituting cranberry juice for apple juice, using remaining sugar and pectin. After skimming foam from jelly, stir in a little red food coloring to tint to a nice deep pink.
5. Carefully ladle hot Cranberry Jelly over slightly cooled Apple Jelly in glasses. Immediately cover with thin layer of paraffin or with domed lid (see directions on page 67, "When Making Jellies").

RASPBERRY-PEACH CONSERVE

Now you can capture all the flavor of two summer favorites, to serve in the fall.

Makes 8 half pints.

1½ pounds ripe peaches
  2 cups fresh raspberries
  1 cup raisins
  2 tablespoons lemon juice
  1 package (1¾ ounces) powdered fruit pectin
  7 cups sugar
  ½ cup coarsely chopped walnuts

1. Prepare jars and lids following General Directions, Steps 3 and 4, page 66.
2. Dip peaches into boiling water for 30 seconds; peel, halve, pit and chop.
3. Combine peaches, raspberries, raisins, lemon juice and pectin in a large kettle. Bring quickly to boiling, stirring occasionally. Add sugar; bring again to a full rolling boil; boil rapidly 1 minute. Remove from heat; skim off foam. Add walnuts.
4. Stir and skim for 7 minutes to cool and prevent floating fruit.
5. Ladle into hot jars following General Directions, Steps 6-8. Process at simmering for 10-15 minutes, following General Directions, Steps 9 through 13.

PLUM CHUTNEY

We used plums, but this recipe will work as well with your bounty of peaches, pears or nectarines.

Makes 5 pints.

2½ pounds purple plums, halved, pitted and diced (8 cups)
  2 large onions, chopped (2 cups)
  1 clove garlic, minced
  2 cups firmly packed brown sugar
  1 cup raisins
  1 tablespoon chili powder
1½ teaspoons salt
  4 cups cider vinegar

1. Combine plums, onions, raisins, garlic, brown sugar, chili powder and salt in a large kettle; stir in cider vinegar.
2. Bring to boiling, stirring often; lower heat; simmer 1 hour, stirring often, or until mixture thickens. While mixture cooks, prepare jars and lids (see General Directions, Steps 3-4, page 66).
3. Following General Directions, Steps 6-8, ladle into hot pint jars, leaving ¼-inch headroom. Seal and process 5 minutes following General Directions, Steps 9-13.

BRANDIED FRUITS

Here is a glamorous melange of fruits for special gift-giving. The bonus syrup is great over ice cream.

Makes 16 eight-ounce jars of fruit plus 6 eight-ounce jars of syrup.

  5 cups granulated sugar
  5 cups (2½ pounds) firmly packed brown sugar
  1 bottle (4/5 quart) brandy
  2 three-inch pieces stick cinnamon
  1 tablespoon whole cloves
  2 pints (4 cups) strawberries, washed and hulled
  1 medium-size pineapple, sliced, peeled, cored and cut into quarters
  4 large pears, pared, quartered, cored and sliced
  4 large peaches, pared, halved, pitted and sliced
  1 pound sweet cherries, washed and stemmed
  1 pound seedless green grapes, washed and stemmed

1. Combine granulated and brown sugars with brandy in a 24-cup crock or glass container. (A punch bowl or very large bean pot will work perfectly.) Stir until sugars dissolve. Add spices.
2. Gradually add fruits, stirring gently until all fruits have been added.
3. Allow container to stand at room temperature 1 hour, stirring twice. Cover fruit with plastic

wrap and then cover the container with lid.
4. Refrigerate container, removing plastic wrap and stirring fruits once each day for one week.
5. Wash and rinse 16 eight-ounce canning jars and their lids or fancy jars and bottles you may wish to use. Sterilize in boiling water for 10 minutes, following directions for sterilizing given on page 67 under section titled "When Making Jellies." Spoon fruits and syrup from container into prepared jars to within ½ inch of tops. Pour remaining syrup into sterilized jars or bottles. (You will have about 6 cups.) Seal jars and bottles.
6. Process fruits and syrup that have been packed in standard canning jars, 10 minutes in the water-bath canner, following General Directions, Steps 6-13 on page 66. Fruits and syrup packed in other sterilized jars and bottles should be stored in the refrigerator and used within a month.

SPICED WATERMELON RIND

Sweet, with a hint of sour, this watermelon pickle uses the part of the melon usually discarded.

Makes 8 eight-ounce jars.

     Rind from large (20 pound) watermelon
 16 cups water
  1 cup salt
SYRUP:
  8 cups sugar
  2 lemons, thinly sliced
  2 tablespoons whole cloves
  2 tablespoons whole allspice
  8 one-inch pieces stick cinnamon
  4 cups cider vinegar
  4 cups water

1. Pare outer green skin from rind. Cut pared rind into 1-inch cubes. (There should be about 16 cups.) Combine 8 cups of the water with ½ cup salt in a large bowl; add 8 cups rind; repeat with remaining water, salt and rind in second large bowl. Refrigerate both bowls overnight.
2. Drain rind; place in kettle or Dutch oven. Cover rind with fresh water. Heat to boiling; lower heat, simmer 10 minutes, or until rind is tender; drain.
3. While the rind drains, combine sugar, lemons, cloves, allspice, cinnamon, vinegar and the 4 cups of water in same kettle. Heat to boiling, stir in drained rind. Return syrup to boiling; lower heat. Simmer, stirring often from bottom of kettle, for 1 hour, or until rind is clear and syrup is thickened. While mixture cooks, prepare jars and lids, following General Directions, Steps 3 and 4, page 66.
4. Ladle into hot jars following General Directions, Steps 6-8, leaving ¼-inch head space (instead of ½). Process for 10 minutes following General Directions, Steps 9 through 13, page 66.

PICKLED EGGPLANT

A vegetable combo that's great served as a side dish or on the relish tray.

Makes 3 to 4 pints.

  2 pounds eggplant, trimmed and cut into
     1-inch cubes (8 cups)
  1 cup thinly sliced celery
  1 large onion, thinly sliced
  1 green pepper, seeded and cut into strips
  1 red pepper, seeded and cut into strips
 ⅓ cup salt
     Ice cubes
1½ cups sugar
  1 tablespoon dill seeds
1½ cups cider vinegar
  4 cloves garlic, halved

1. Combine eggplant, celery, onion, peppers and salt in a large bowl; place a layer of ice cubes on top; cover. Let stand for 3 hours; drain well.
2. Prepare jars and lids following General Directions, Steps 3 and 4, page 66.
3. Combine sugar, dill seeds and vinegar in a kettle or saucepan; bring to boiling, stirring constantly; stir in vegetables. Bring to boiling again, stirring occasionally; remove from heat.
4. Ladle into hot jars following General Directions, Steps 6-8; place 1 or 2 pieces of garlic in each jar. Process at simmering 15 minutes, following General Directions, Steps 9-13.

DILL PICKLE STICKS

Serve these pickles at your next barbecue.

Makes 12 pints.

 30 pickling cucumbers, about 4 inches long
     (about 7 pounds)
     Fresh dill
  8 cups white vinegar
  8 cups water
1½ cups sugar
  1 cup kosher salt
 ⅓ cup mixed pickling spices

1. Prepare jars and lids following General Directions, Steps 3 and 4, page 66.
2. Wash cucumbers well; drain on paper toweling; cut in half lengthwise. Following General Directions, Step 6, pack tightly into hot pint jars (wide-mouth jars are best); add 1 sprig of dill to each jar.
3. Combine vinegar, water, sugar and salt in a large kettle; tie mixed pickling spices in cheesecloth and add to kettle. Bring to boiling; lower heat; simmer 15 minutes.
4. Ladle into jars, leaving ¼-inch headroom. Seal and process 15 minutes in water-bath following General Directions, Steps 8-13 on page 66.

CANTALOUPE PICKLE

It's a spicy Southern treat to enjoy summer or winter.

Makes 6 to 8 servings.

 1 medium-size barely-ripe cantaloupe
 1 quart cold water
 4 tablespoons salt
 1 cup white vinegar
 1 cup light corn syrup
 1 cup sugar
 1 teaspoon whole cloves
 1 three-inch piece stick cinnamon
 1 teaspoon mustard seeds

1. Pare and remove seeds from cantaloupe and cut the flesh into strips about 2 inches by ½ inch. Dissolve the salt in the water and pour over the cantaloupe and let soak overnight.
2. Drain well and rinse cantaloupe in clear water.
3. In a saucepan combine the vinegar, corn syrup and sugar. Tie the cloves, cinnamon stick and seeds in a muslin bag and add to the syrup. Bring to a boil, and boil slowly 10 minutes. Add the cantaloupe and simmer very gently until it turns translucent, about 12 minutes. Pour into a hot, sterilized canning jar (see sterilizing directions under heading "When Making Jellies, page 67); cover, let cool. Store in the refrigerator and use within 3 months.

GARDEN MUSTARD PICKLES

When you have just a few of each vegetable, this is the recipe for you.

Makes 7 pints.

 1 small cauliflower, separated into flowerets
 1 pound small white onions, peeled
 6 green tomatoes, cored and cut into wedges
 6 pickling cucumbers, cut into 1-inch pieces
 2 large green peppers, halved, seeded and cut into 1-inch pieces
 2 large red peppers, halved, seeded and cut into 1-inch pieces
 ⅓ cup kosher salt
 ½ cup firmly packed brown sugar
 3 tablespoons dry mustard
 2 teaspoons turmeric
 2 teaspoons mustard seeds
 2 teaspoons celery seeds
 6 cups cider vinegar
 ½ cup all-purpose flour
 1 cup cold water

1. Combine cauliflower, onions, green tomato, cucumbers, green and red peppers in a large glass or ceramic bowl; sprinkle salt over vegetables; stir to blend well.

2. Cover bowl with plastic wrap; let stand 12 to 18 hours at room temperature. Next day, pour off all liquid from vegetables; spoon into kettle.
3. Add brown sugar, mustard, turmeric, mustard seeds and celery seeds; stir in cider vinegar.
4. Bring to boiling, stirring often; lower heat; simmer 15 minutes, or until vegetables are tender. While vegetables simmer, prepare jars and lids following General Directions, Steps 3 and 4, page 66.
5. When vegetables are almost cooked, combine flour and cold water in a small bowl to make a smooth paste. Stir slowly into bubbling liquid; cook, stirring constantly, until mixture thickens and bubbles 3 minutes.
6. Ladle into hot pint jars, leaving ½-inch headroom. Seal and process for 5 minutes in water-bath canner following General Directions, Steps 6 through 13 on page 66.

PICKLED PEACHES AND PEARS

Use this recipe when the crops from the orchards are at their peak. One preserving operation makes 2 products.

Makes 5 pints peaches and 6 pints pears.

 12 cups sugar
 4 cups cider vinegar
 4 three-inch pieces stick cinnamon, broken
 2 tablespoons whole cloves
 14 large peaches, peeled, halved and pitted (about 6 pounds)
 1 piece dry ginger root (optional)
 24 medium-size pears, peeled, halved and cored

1. Combine sugar, vinegar, cinnamon and cloves in a kettle. Bring to boiling, simmer 5 minutes.
2. Lower peach halves into kettle with a slotted spoon; bring to boiling; lower heat; simmer 15 minutes, or just until peaches are tender.
3. Remove kettle from heat; cover; let stand 12 to 18 hours at room temperature. Next day, bring mixture to boiling and prepare 5 jars and lids following General Directions, Steps 3 and 4, page 66. Ladle mixture into hot pint jars, leaving ½-inch headroom. Seal and process 20 minutes in water-bath, following General Directions, Steps 6-13.
4. Add dry ginger root to remaining syrup in kettle, if you wish. (You should have about 8 cups of syrup left.) Bring to boiling; lower pear halves into kettle with a slotted spoon; bring to boiling; lower heat; simmer 10 minutes, or just until pears are tender.
5. Remove kettle from heat; cover; let stand 12 to 18 hours at room temperature. Next day, bring mixture to boiling and prepare remaining 6 jars and lids following General Directions, Steps 3 and 4, page 66. Ladle into hot pint jars leaving ½-inch headroom. Seal and process 20 minutes in water-bath following General Directions, Steps 6-13.

PICKLED GREEN TOMATOES

Here's what to do with those green tomatoes still on the vine at season's end.

Makes 3 quarts.

12 green tomatoes, (about 2½ pounds)
3 cloves garlic
Fresh dill
6 cups water
3 cups white vinegar
¾ cup kosher salt

1. Prepare jars and lids following General Directions, Steps 3 and 4, page 66.
2. Wash tomatoes well; drain on paper toweling. Pack tightly in hot quart jars; add 1 clove garlic and a sprig of dill to each jar.
3. Combine water, vinegar and salt in a large kettle; bring to boiling; lower heat; simmer 5 minutes. Ladle into jars leaving ½-inch headroom. Seal and process 15 minutes in water-bath following General Directions, Steps 6-13. Store tomatoes at least 4 weeks before serving.

RUBY WATERMELON RELISH

The pink meat of the watermelon makes this a companion relish to the Spiced Watermelon rind recipe.

Makes 8 eight-ounce jars.

1 large watermelon (about 20 pounds)
4 cups sugar
2 cups cider vinegar
2 limes, thinly sliced
½ cup lime juice
1 teaspoon whole cloves
2 one-inch pieces stick cinnamon

1. Slice watermelon. Cut meat from rind, then into chunks. Save rind for Spiced Watermelon Rind, page 73.
2. Place about 1 cup chunks at a time in a square of double thickness cheesecloth. Squeeze to remove liquid. Remove seeds; measure pulp. (There should be 14 cups.) Place in large kettle.
3. Stir in sugar and vinegar. Heat to boiling; lower heat. Simmer, stirring often, 30 minutes.
4. While pulp is simmering, bring sliced limes to a boil in 2 changes of water (to remove bitterness). Drain.
5. Add sliced limes, lime juice, cloves and cinnamon. Cook, stirring often, 30 minutes longer, or until relish is thick. While mixture cooks, prepare jars and lids following General Directions, Steps 3 and 4, page 66.
6. Ladle mixture into hot jars; seal and process 15 minutes, following General Directions, Steps 6 through 13 on page 66.

PLUM CATSUP

A nice change-of-pace for the catsup bottle.

Makes 5 half pints.

4 pounds purple plums
1 large onion, chopped (1 cup)
¾ cup water
3½ cups sugar
1¼ cups cider vinegar
1 clove garlic, peeled
1 teaspoon salt
½ teaspoon ground cinnamon
⅛ teaspoon liquid red-pepper seasoning
⅓ cup mixed pickling spices

1. Wash plums; cut in half; remove and discard pits. Combine plums with onion and water in a large kettle. Bring to boiling; reduce heat; cover; simmer until plums are soft, about 30 minutes.
2. Press plum mixture through a fine sieve or food mill into a large bowl. Return plum puree to large kettle; stir in sugar, vinegar, garlic, salt, cinnamon and red-pepper seasoning.
3. Tie pickling spices in several layers of cheesecloth; add to kettle.
4. Bring mixture to boiling; reduce heat; simmer, stirring frequently, 30 minutes, or until catsup is very thick. Remove and discard garlic and spice bag. Note: While mixture cooks, prepare jars and lids (General Directions, Steps 3 and 4, page 66).
5. Ladle mixture into hot jars; seal and process 15 minutes, following General Directions. Steps 6-13.

PEACH AND PINEAPPLE RELISH

Serve this sweet-sour fruit relish with ham.

Makes 5 eight-ounce jars.

6 large peaches or nectarines, peeled, halved, pitted and chopped (6 cups)
1 large pineapple, sliced, pared, cored and chopped (5 cups)
1 jar (8 ounces) maraschino cherries
2 cups sugar
2 two-inch pieces stick cinnamon
1 teaspoon whole allspice

1. Combine peaches or nectarines and pineapple in a large kettle. Drain liquid from cherries into kettle; chop cherries; add. Stir in sugar. Tie cinnamon and allspice in cheesecloth; add to kettle.
2. Bring to boiling, stirring often. Reduce heat and simmer, stirring frequently near the end of cooking time to prevent scorching, 30 minutes, or until mixture thickens. Remove spice bag. While mixture cooks, prepare jars and lids following General Directions, Steps 3 and 4, page 66.
3. Ladle into hot jars; seal and process 15 minutes, following General Directions, Steps 6 through 13.

YANKEE CORN RELISH

To New Englanders, a traditional accompaniment for baked beans and brown bread.

Makes 8 half pints.

     12 ears corn
      2 large red or green peppers, halved, seeded
         and chopped
      1 large Bermuda onion, chopped
      1 cup sliced celery
      2 cups cider vinegar
      2 cups water
      2 tablespoons mustard seeds
      4 teaspoons salt
   1½ teaspoons turmeric
   1½ cups sugar
      ½ cup all-purpose flour

1. Prepare jars and lids following General Directions, Steps 3 and 4, page 66.
2. Peel husks and silk from corn. Place in a kettle of salted boiling water; return to boiling; simmer 5 minutes; drain and cool. Cut corn from cobs (you should have approximately 8 cups).
3. Combine corn, pepper, onion, celery, vinegar, water, mustard seeds, salt and turmeric in a large kettle. Bring to boiling; lower heat; simmer 20 minutes. Combine sugar and flour in a small bowl, stir into kettle slowly. Cook, stirring constantly, until mixture thickens and bubbles 3 minutes.
4. Ladle into hot half-pint jars, leaving ½-inch headroom; seal; process 15 minutes in waterbath canner, following General Directions, Steps 6-10.
5. Complete preparation of relish following General Directions, Steps 11-13.

RELISH-STUFFED PEPPERS

The peppers are stuffed and then packed tightly into sterilized jars.

Makes 5 or 6 one-and-one-half-pints.

      6 red peppers
      6 green peppers
      6 cups finely shredded green cabbage
      2 cups thinly sliced carrots
      1 cup salt
      4 quarts water
      2 tablespoons mustard seeds
      1 tablespoon celery seeds
      2 quarts white vinegar
      3 cups sugar

1. Cut stem ends from peppers and reserve. Remove seeds and white membranes from peppers.
2. Combine cabbage and carrots in a large bowl or kettle (not aluminum). Place the peppers and their stem ends on top. Dissolve salt in water; pour over vegetables to cover, let stand in cool

place 24 hours. Drain; rinse in cold water and drain thoroughly.
3. Prepare jars and lids following General Directions, Steps 3 and 4, page 66.
4. Combine cabbage and carrot mixture, mustard seeds and celery seeds in a large bowl; toss to mix well; fill peppers, dividing mixture evenly; replace stem ends.
5. Remove jars from water (General Directions, Step 6.) Pack stuffed peppers into the hot jars, mixing red and green.
6. In large saucepan, combine vinegar and sugar; bring to a full rolling boil, stirring occasionally. Pour boiling hot liquid over peppers in jars, leaving ½-inch space on top. Seal and process 15 minutes, following General Directions, Steps 8-13.

CALIFORNIA PEPPER RELISH

A new treat to serve with hamburgers. Have no red peppers? Green peppers will do just as well— or mix the two together.

Makes 8 eight-ounce jars.

     12 large red peppers
      3 tablespoons salt
      6 large tomatoes, peeled and chopped
      2 large onions, chopped (2 cups)
      3 cups sugar
      1 cup cider vinegar
      2 tablespoons mixed pickling spices

1. Halve, seed and chop peppers. (You should have 9 cups.) Layer with salt in a large glass bowl. Allow to stand at room temperature, stirring several times, 3 hours. Drain peppers well to remove all liquid.
2. Prepare jars and lids, following General Directions, Steps 3 and 4, page 66.
3. Combine drained peppers, tomatoes and onions in a large kettle; stir in sugar and vinegar. Tie mixed pickling spices in cheesecloth and crack with hammer. Add to kettle.
4. Bring to boiling, stirring often. Lower heat; simmer, stirring frequently near the end of the cooking time to prevent scorching, 30 minutes, or until mixture thickens. Remove spice bag.
5. Ladle into hot jars following General Directions, Steps 6-8. Process 10 minutes, following General Directions, Steps 9-13.

Top Center: Brandied Fruits. Second Row (from left to right): Spiced Watermelon Rind, Garden Mustard Pickles, Grape Lemon Jelly, Yankee Corn Relish and California Pepper Relish. Third Row: Dill Pickle Sticks, Tomato and Pear Marmalade and Garden Mustard Pickles (shown twice). Bottom: Relish-Stuffed Green and Red Peppers. Recipes for all are included in this chapter.

5

LAZY-DAY SALADS

*"Let first the onion
flourish there,
Rose among roots,
the maiden-fair
Wine-scented and poetic soul
Of the capacious salad bowl."*

UNDERWOODS, TO A GARDENER
ROBERT LOUIS STEVENSON (1887)

Sit back. Put your feet up. Relax. The lazy-day salad is here, and with it comes the answer to all kinds of menu demands. Make it a main dish, ahead of time; a side dish, at dinnertime; or, tote it along for a picnic, anytime. In this chapter we offer a good sampling of such salads, plus a section on salad dressings to make in five minutes or less. Mix the dressings ahead of time and store in the refrigerator until you're ready to drizzle one over a favorite salad, such as the Nicoise shown here. This salad's origin is French, but its popularity is universal, as you'll see when you try the recipe on page 85. Prepare the individual ingredients early in the day and then assemble at mealtime. In-between, enjoy a long, lazy day.

CAREFREE MOLDED CHICKEN AND CUCUMBER SALAD

This is a gelatin version of a summer favorite.

Makes 6 servings.

    3 whole chicken breasts, split (about 2¼
      pounds)
    1 large onion, quartered
    1 stalk celery with top, cut up
    3 teaspoons salt
    6 whole peppercorns
    3 cups water
    2 envelopes unflavored gelatin
    ¾ cup dry white wine
    2 medium-size cucumbers
    ¼ cup chopped green onion
    1 tablespoon chopped fresh dill or 1 teaspoon
      dried dillweed
    ¾ cup mayonnaise or salad dressing
    ½ cup dairy sour cream
      Lettuce
      Avocado slices
      Lemon wedges
      Dill

1. Combine chicken breasts, onion, celery, 2 teaspoons of the salt, peppercorns and water in large
saucepan. Bring to boiling; lower heat; simmer,
covered, 30 minutes, or until chicken is tender.
Remove from heat; cool in broth until cool
enough to handle.
2. Lift chicken from broth, remove and discard
skin and bones; dice meat; place in a large bowl.
3. Strain stock into a measuring cup; there
should be about 2 cups. Return broth to saucepan; bring to boiling.
4. Sprinkle gelatin over ½ cup of the wine; let
stand to soften, 5 minutes. Stir into hot broth
until dissolved. Measure out ¼ cup; combine with
remaining ¼ cup wine and pour into an 8-cup
mold. Place mold in a pan filled with ice and
water; chill until mixture is syrupy-thick. Cut 15
to 18 thin slices from one cucumber; arrange overlapping on gelatin, pressing down slightly.
5. Shred remaining cucumber coarsely. (You
should have about 2 cups.) Add to chicken along
with onion and dill or dillweed. Chill remaining
gelatin mixture until syrupy-thick; stir in mayonnaise or salad dressing, sour cream and the remaining 1 teaspoon salt until smooth. Pour over
chicken mixture; stir to mix. Carefully spoon into mold. Refrigerate several hours, or until firm.
6. Unmold onto serving plate. Garnish with crisp
lettuce, avocado slices, lemon wedges and sprigs
of dill as shown on page 89.

---

*Antipasto, long a favorite appetizer, is also a great
idea for supper. The ingredients are right out of
the supermarket and easily marinated in a peppy
Garlic Dressing. Recipe is included on page 84.*

MACARONI TOSS

*Pasta, one of the handiest meat stretchers, makes
its contribution to hearty warm-weather eating.*

Makes 4 servings.

    1 box (8 ounces) elbow macaroni
    1 cup mayonnaise or salad dressing
    3 tablespoons wine vinegar
    ¾ teaspoon salt
    ½ teaspoon leaf oregano, crumbled
    ⅛ teaspoon pepper
    1 can (12 ounces) pork luncheon meat, cubed
    1 cup chopped celery
    ½ cup chopped red pepper
    1 small onion, chopped (¼ cup)

1. Cook macaroni, following label directions;
drain; place in a large bowl; cool.
2. Blend mayonnaise or salad dressing, wine vinegar, salt, oregano and pepper in a small bowl.
3. Add luncheon meat, celery, red pepper and
onion to macaroni; spoon dressing over and toss
lightly to mix. Chill about 2 hours. Spoon into a
lettuce-lined salad bowl to serve, if you wish.

SUMMER SMORGASBORD

Here's a tangy salad for Viking appetites.

Makes 6 servings.

    1 jar (8 ounces) herring in wine sauce
    3 cups cooked diced potatoes
    1 can (1 pound) diced beets, drained
    1 large apple, pared, quartered, cored and
      diced
    1 small onion, diced (¼ cup)
    ¼ cup diced pared cucumber
    ½ cup cider vinegar
    1 hard-cooked egg yolk
    2 packages (6 ounces each) sliced tongue
    1 package (8 ounces) sliced caraway cheese,
      cut in triangles
      Watercress

1. Drain liquid from herring into a large bowl.
Dice herring.
2. Add potatoes, beets, apple, onion, cucumber
and herring to liquid in bowl. Drizzle with vinegar; toss lightly to mix. Spoon into a lightly oiled
6-cup bowl, packing mixture down firmly with
back of spoon. Chill at least 2 hours to season.
3. Just before serving, loosen salad around edge
with a knife; invert onto a large serving platter;
lift off bowl. Press egg yolk through a sieve on
top of salad.
4. Arrange tongue and cheese triangles around
each side of salad. Garnish serving platter with
some watercress or sprigs of parsley, if you wish.

TUNA SHELL SALAD

Here's tuna salad dressed up in a Mediterranean style.

Makes 4 servings.

    1 cup small macaroni shells
    1 can (about 7 ounces) tuna, drained and flaked
    ½ cup sliced celery
    1 medium-size green pepper, seeded and chopped
    ½ cup pitted ripe olives, halved
    1 small onion, chopped (¼ cup)
    ⅔ cup mayonnaise or salad dressing
    2 tablespoons wine vinegar
    ½ teaspoon salt
    ¼ teaspoon leaf oregano, crumbled
    ⅛ teaspoon pepper
    2 tablespoons chopped parsley
      Lettuce leaves
      Tomato slices

1. Cook macaroni shells in boiling salted water, following label directions; drain; cool.
2. Combine cooked macaroni with tuna, celery, green pepper, ripe olives and onion in a large bowl; toss to mix well.
3. Combine mayonnaise or salad dressing with vinegar, salt, oregano and pepper in a small bowl; blend well; fold into tuna mixture to coat well. Spoon into center of serving platter; sprinkle with parsley. Border with lettuce leaves topped with tomato slices sprinkled with salt and pepper and a few drops additional vinegar.

TUNA-MUSHROOM SALAD

A delightful tuna-vegetable salad; perfect for a luncheon menu.

Makes 4 servings.

    4 cups broken mixed salad greens
    ½ pound mushrooms, trimmed and sliced thin
    1 cup thinly sliced green onions
    1 can (about 7 ounces) tuna, drained
    4 slices bacon, crisply cooked
    ½ cup shredded Cheddar cheese
    ½ cup vegetable oil
    ¼ cup lemon juice
    1 small clove of garlic, minced
    1 teaspoon salt
    ½ teaspoon dry mustard
    ⅛ teaspoon pepper

1. Place salad greens in a large salad bowl; top with sliced mushrooms, then green onions, then tuna broken in large chunks.
2. Crumble bacon; toss with the shredded Cheddar cheese in a small bowl; sprinkle over salad.

3. Combine oil, lemon juice, garlic, salt, mustard and pepper in a small jar with tight-fitting lid; shake well. Pour dressing over salad in bowl; toss to coat well; serve immediately.

POLYNESIAN SALAD

Fish fillets combine with shrimp for this salad with an Oriental flavor.

Makes 6 servings.

    1 package (1 pound) frozen fillet of sole
    1½ cups water
    1 teaspoon salt
    2 slices lime or lemon
    1 package (8 ounces) frozen, shelled, deveined shrimp
    1 package (6 ounces) frozen Chinese snow peas and water chestnuts
    ⅔ cup vegetable oil
    ⅓ cup white wine vinegar
    2 tablespoons lime or lemon juice
    2 tablespoons soy sauce
    1 clove garlic, minced
    1 teaspoon ground ginger
    ½ teaspoon sugar
    4 cups thinly sliced Chinese cabbage
    2 cups thinly sliced romaine
    ½ cup sliced carrot
    ½ cup celery
    2 tablespoons toasted sesame seeds

1. Place fillet of sole in a medium-size skillet. Add 1 cup cold water to cover; sprinkle with 1 teaspoon salt; add lime or lemon slices; bring to boiling; lower heat; simmer, covered, 5 minutes, or until fish flakes easily when tested with fork. Remove fish from liquid; drain. Place in large shallow dish.
2. Bring fish liquid to boiling; drop in frozen shrimp; cook, following label directions, until shrimp are pink; drain. Place in separate mound in same dish.
3. Bring remaining ½ cup water to boiling in a small saucepan; drop in snow peas and water chestnuts; separate with fork; drain; place in small bowl. Refrigerate, covered, until well-chilled, at least 3 hours.
4. Combine oil, vinegar, lime or lemon juice, soy sauce, garlic, ground ginger and sugar in a jar with a tight-fitting lid; shake well to mix; drizzle ⅓ cup over fish and shrimp. Refrigerate, covered, until well-chilled, at least 3 hours. Refrigerate remaining dressing same length of time.
5. To serve: Line a large salad platter with Chinese cabbage and romaine. Arrange sole, shrimp, snow peas, water chestnuts, carrot and celery over greens; sprinkle with the 2 tablespoons of toasted sesame seeds. Pass oil-and-vinegar dressing; let everyone pour on the amount desired.

Plain unflavored yogurt is a good salad dressing stand-in for sour cream—only 125 calories a cupful instead of nearly 500! But be sure to use plain yogurt, not the sugared-up, fruit-flavored ones at more than double the number of calories!

CUCUMBER-YOGURT SALAD

A refreshing salad with a touch of mint.

Makes 8 servings.

    2 large cucumbers (about 1¼ pounds)
    1 container (8 ounces) plain yogurt
    ¼ cup sliced green onion
    2 large cloves garlic, minced
    1 tablespoon finely chopped fresh mint or
      1 teaspoon dried mint
    1 tablespoon white vinegar
    ½ teaspoon salt
    ¼ teaspoon white pepper

1. Pare cucumbers; cut into paper-thin slices. You should have enough for about 4 cups.
2. Combine yogurt, green onion, garlic, mint, vinegar, salt and pepper in a medium-size bowl. Add cucumbers; toss gently to coat; cover. Refrigerate at least 1 hour for flavors to develop. Garnish with additional fresh mint, if you wish.

SUMMER CHICKEN DIVAN

Here's a classic casserole we've transformed into a main-dish salad.

Makes 6 servings.

    3 large chicken breasts, about 12 ounces each
    1 small onion, peeled and sliced
    1 teaspoon salt
      Dash of pepper
      Water
    2 packages (10 ounces each) frozen asparagus spears
    1 envelope Parmesan salad dressing mix
      Vegetable oil
      Cider vinegar
    1 head Boston lettuce, separated into leaves
    2 cans (3 or 4 ounces each) whole mushrooms, drained
    ½ cup mayonnaise or salad dressing
    2 hard-cooked egg yolks

1. Combine chicken, onion, salt, pepper and 2 cups water in a large frying pan; cover. Simmer 30 minutes, or until chicken is tender. Remove from broth; cool until easy to handle, then pull off skin. Remove meat from each half of breast in one large piece; set aside. Strain broth and chill for soup another day.
2. While chicken cooks, cook asparagus, following label directions; drain; place in a shallow dish.
3. Prepare salad dressing mix with vegetable oil, vinegar and water, following label directions; drizzle ½ cup over asparagus; let stand 30 minutes to season.
4. Line a large shallow serving dish with lettuce; arrange asparagus spears over lettuce, then place chicken breasts, overlapping, in a row on top of asparagus. Pile mushrooms at each end.
5. Blend mayonnaise or salad dressing into remaining dressing in asparagus dish; drizzle over chicken. Press egg yolks through a sieve on top. Serve with additional Parmesan dressing.

CURRIED RICE AND CHICKEN SALAD

This make-ahead salad is simple to prepare, yet special enough for guests.

Makes 6 servings.

    1 broiler-fryer, about 2 pounds
    2 cups water
    1 teaspoon salt
    ¼ teaspoon pepper
    ¼ cup bottled oil and vinegar dressing
    2 whole pimientos, diced
    2 tablespoons vegetable oil
    2 teaspoons curry powder
    1 cup regular rice
    ½ cup mayonnaise or salad dressing
    ¼ cup lemon juice
      Leaf lettuce
    1 cup sliced green onions

1. Cut up chicken into serving-size pieces. Put chicken, water, ½ teaspoon of the salt and pepper in a large saucepan. Bring to boiling; lower heat; cover. Simmer 30 minutes, or until chicken is tender.
2. Remove chicken from broth; cool; cut into large pieces; combine with oil and vinegar dressing and pimiento in a small bowl; cover; chill several hours to blend flavors. Measure broth; add water, if necessary, to make 2½ cups; reserve.
3. Heat oil in a large saucepan; add curry powder; cook 2 minutes, stirring constantly. Stir in rice, remaining ½ teaspoon salt and broth mixture. Bring to boiling; lower heat; stir rice; cover. Simmer 25 minutes, or until rice is tender and liquid is absorbed.
4. Spoon rice into large bowl; fold in mayonnaise or salad dressing and lemon juice; cover; chill several hours to blend flavors.
5. Line serving platter with leaf lettuce; spoon rice salad onto platter; sprinkle green onion slices over; spoon the chicken and pimiento on the top.

MIDSUMMER COLESLAW

This crunchy coleslaw, complete with tangy dressing, can be made a day ahead.

Makes 6 to 8 servings.

   2 eggs, lightly beaten
   2 tablespoons sugar
   ½ teaspoon salt
   1 teaspoon dry mustard
   ¼ teaspoon freshly ground black pepper
   ½ cup vinegar
   2 tablespoons butter or margarine
   ½ cup heavy cream
   1 medium-size (3 pounds) head of cabbage, finely shredded
   2 ribs celery, finely chopped
   1 large green pepper, seeded and finely chopped

1. Several hours or a day ahead, beat the eggs and sugar together in a small saucepan. Beat in the salt, mustard, pepper, vinegar and butter.
2. Cook the mixture over medium heat or over hot water, while stirring vigorously, until mixture thickens. Do not allow to boil. Cool and chill.
3. Stir the cream into the chilled mixture. Combine the cabbage, celery and pepper, pour over the dressing, toss well and chill several hours.

ANTIPASTO SALAD

Here's how to make an hors d'oeuvre into a hearty main dish salad. Make it early in the day, so the flavors will mingle. (Shown on page 80.)

Makes 6 servings.

   1 can (1 pound, 4 ounces) chick peas, drained
   1 can (1 pound) red kidney beans, drained
   ½ cup chopped red onion
   ¼ cup chopped parsley
   1 cup Garlic Dressing (recipe is on page 88)
   1 medium-size zucchini, sliced
   ¼ pound thinly sliced prosciutto
     Small bread sticks (from a 3¼-ounce package)
   2 cans (4⅜ ounces each) sardines, drained
   1 jar (7¼ ounces) roasted red peppers
     Hot red cherry peppers (from a 16-ounce jar)
   1 package (6 ounces) Provolone cheese slices, quartered
   ¼ pound sliced salami, halved
     Oil-cured olives (from an 8-ounce jar)
   4 cups broken romaine

1. For Bean Salad: Combine chick peas, red kidney beans, chopped red onion, parsley and ⅓ cup Garlic Dressing in a medium-size bowl; toss to coat well; cover bowl with plastic wrap. Let

mixture marinate several hours in the refrigerator.
2. Cook zucchini slices in salted boiling water in a small saucepan 5 minutes, or just until tender. Drain and place in a small bowl; drizzle 3 tablespoons Garlic Dressing over; cover; let marinate in refrigerator.
3. To serve: Wrap prosciutto around bread sticks. Arrange all ingredients, except romaine, on a serving platter. Serve romaine in salad bowl. Let each person make his own salad selection to toss with romaine and remaining Garlic Dressing.

SALMON MOUSSE

Light and fluffy, this molded salmon salad is refreshing and satisfying for supper.

Makes 6 servings.

   2 envelopes unflavored gelatin
   2 cups water
   ¼ cup lemon juice
   1 envelope or teaspoon instant vegetable broth
   1 can (1 pound) salmon
   ¾ cup finely chopped celery
   ½ cup finely chopped seeded red pepper
   2 tablespoons chopped parsley
   2 tablespoons grated onion
   ½ teaspoon salt
   ¾ cup mayonnaise or salad dressing

1. Soften gelatin in 1 cup water in a medium-size saucepan. Heat, stirring constantly, until gelatin dissolves; remove from heat; cool; stir in 2 tablespoons lemon juice. Measure out ¾ cup of mixture and reserve.
2. Stir remaining 1 cup of water and instant vegetable broth into remaining mixture in saucepan. Heat, stirring constantly, just until hot.
3. Drain salmon and flake, removing bones and skin. Combine in medium-size bowl with celery, red pepper, parsley, grated onion, salt and mayonnaise or salad dressing. Stir in the ¾ cup gelatin mixture from Step 1. Reserve while preparing the fish-shape mold.
4. Pour half the remaining gelatin mixture into bottom of a 6-cup fish-shape mold; place in a large pan of ice and water; let stand, turning mold often from side to side, to form a thin coat of gelatin on bottom and sides of mold.
5. Spoon salmon mixture over gelatin-coated mold, spreading evenly to cover mold completely.
6. Chill in refrigerator at least 4 hours, or until gelatin mold is firm.
7. When ready to serve, run a sharp-tip thin-blade knife around top of salad; dip mold very quickly in and out of hot water. Cover with a chilled serving plate; turn upside down; shake gently; lift off mold. Garnish with cucumber slices and red pepper slices, and serve with some additional mayonnaise or salad dressing, if you wish.

SALAD NICOISE

A refreshingly simple salad that may be prepared earlier in the day, then assembled and served.

Makes 6 servings.

- 5 medium-size potatoes, cooked, drained and cooled
- ½ pound fresh green beans, cooked, drained and cooled
- ⅔ cup vegetable oil
- ⅓ cup wine vinegar
- 2 cloves garlic, crushed
- 1 tablespoon prepared mustard
- 1 tablespoon chopped parsley
- ½ teaspoon instant minced onion
- 1 teaspoon salt
- ¼ teaspoon ground pepper
- 2 large tomatoes, cut into wedges
- 1 red onion, cubed
- 1 small green pepper, seeded and cubed
- 6 ripe olives, halved
- 3 hard-cooked eggs, shelled and sliced
- 1 can (2 ounces) anchovy fillets, drained
- 2 medium-size heads of romaine
- 1 can (14 ounces) tuna fish, drained

1. Peel potatoes and cut into thick slices. Place in a shallow dish. Place beans in a second dish.
2. Combine oil, vinegar, garlic, mustard, parsley, onion, salt and pepper in a jar with a tight-fitting lid; shake well to mix. Drizzle ½ cup over potatoes and 2 tablespoons over beans; let each stand at least 30 minutes to season.
3. Layer vegetables, eggs, anchovies and romaine in a large salad bowl. Break tuna into chunks; arrange on top. Pour rest of dressing over; toss.

WHITECAP PEAR MOLD

Here's a side-dish salad that may very well steal the show!

Makes 8 servings.

- 1 package (6 ounces) lemon-flavor gelatin
- 2 cups boiling water
- 1½ cups cold water
- 1 tablespoon cider vinegar
- ¼ teaspoon salt
- ⅓ cup dairy sour cream
- ¼ cup mayonnaise or salad dressing
- ½ teaspoon dry mustard
- 1 can (1 pound, 13 ounces) pear halves, drained
- ½ pound seedless green grapes

1. Dissolve gelatin in boiling water in a medium-size bowl; stir in cold water, vinegar and salt.
2. Blend sour cream, mayonnaise or salad dressing, and mustard in a small bowl; beat in ½ cup of the gelatin mixture until smooth; pour into a 7-cup mold. Chill gelatin just until sticky-firm.
3. While dressing layer chills, place bowl of remaining gelatin mixture in a pan of ice and water to speed setting. Chill, stirring often, until as thick as unbeaten egg white.
4. Slice pear halves thin; fold into thickened gelatin with grapes. Carefully spoon over sticky-firm dressing layer in mold. Chill several hours, or until firm (overnight is best).
5. Just before serving, loosen salad around edge with a knife; dip mold very quickly in and out of hot water. Cover with a serving plate; turn upside down; gently lift off mold. Frame salad with small lettuce leaves, if you wish.

POTATO SALAD ROLL

This salad combines corned beef with popular potato salad in a pretty new shape.

Makes 4 servings.

- 6 medium-size potatoes, pared (about 1½ pounds)
- 1 can (12 ounces) corned beef
- 2 hard-cooked eggs, shelled and coarsely chopped
- 1 cup chopped celery
- 1 medium-size onion, chopped (½ cup)
- 2 teaspoons dry mustard
- 1 tablespoon lemon juice
- 1 teaspoon sugar
- 1 teaspoon salt
- ⅛ teaspoon pepper
- ¼ teaspoon caraway seeds, crushed
- 1 cup mayonnaise or salad dressing
  Parsley sprigs

1. Cook potatoes in boiling salted water in a large saucepan; drain; cool slightly. Cut into ½-inch cubes. (You should have about 4 cups.)
2. Remove corned beef from can; separate with a fork; combine with potatoes, eggs, celery and onion in a large bowl; reserve.
3. Blend dry mustard with lemon juice in a small bowl until smooth; stir in sugar, salt, pepper and caraway seeds. Stir in ¾ cup of the mayonnaise or salad dressing; blend well, gently fold into reserved potato mixture.
4. Spoon salad in a long strip on a double thickness of aluminum foil; roll up, enclosing in foil. Press to form an even cylinder, about 10 inches long. Fold in ends of foil to seal. Chill at least 4 hours, or overnight.
5. To serve, carefully unroll potato salad onto serving platter; it should be firm enough to hold its shape and slice easily. Spread with remaining ¼ cup mayonnaise or salad dressing; garnish with parsley sprigs. Border with cherry tomatoes and additional hard-cooked egg slices, if you wish. Cut the potato salad into even slices to serve.

SEAFOOD MACARONI SALAD

Here's a make-ahead main dish salad that's bound to become the kids' favorite.

Makes 6 servings.

      2 cups uncooked small shell macaroni
      5 tablespoons cider vinegar
      1 envelope Italian salad dressing mix
    ¼ cup mayonnaise or salad dressing
    ½ cup vegetable oil
      2 tablespoons chopped fresh parsley
    ½ teaspoon leaf basil, crumbled
      2 cans (about 7 ounces each) tuna, drained
  1½ cups fennel (anise) or 1 cup sliced celery
      1 small cucumber, thinly sliced (1½ cups)
          Lettuce
          Lemon wedges
          Grated Parmesan cheese

1. Cook macaroni shells following package directions; drain, then rinse in cold water and drain well again. Chill.
2. Combine vinegar, salad dressing mix and mayonnaise in a large bowl; beat with wire whisk until combined; gradually add oil, beating all the time. Stir in parsley and basil. Add tuna, fennel or celery, cucumber and macaroni; toss to coat well. Chill at least 2 hours for flavors to blend.
3. Just before serving, line salad bowl with lettuce; spoon salad on top. Garnish with lemon wedges and pass grated Parmesan cheese to sprinkle on, if you wish.

CALIFORNIA CHICKEN SALAD

Our version of one of California's best salads— handsome and hearty. The original, a specialty of the Brown Derby Restaurant in Hollywood, used finely chopped ingredients arranged in layers.

Makes 8 servings.

      4 cups broken romaine
      4 cups broken chicory
      2 ripe avocados, sliced
      3 ripe tomatoes, sliced
      1 small bunch watercress
      2 whole cooked chicken breasts, sliced
      8 slices crisp cooked bacon, crumbled
      2 hard-cooked eggs, sliced
      2 tablespoons chopped chives
          Roquefort French Dressing (recipe is on page 89)

1. Line a shallow salad bowl with the salad greens. Arrange avocados and tomatoes around edge. Mound watercress in center. Arrange chicken slices on top of watercress. Sprinkle with bacon. Garnish with egg slices; sprinkle with chives.
2. At the table, pour dressing over salad and toss.

CHEF'S SALAD CAESAR-STYLE

This combination of a Chef's and a Caesar salad is tossed with a special creamy dressing.

Makes 6 servings.

      1 package (3 ounces) cream cheese, softened to room temperature
    ⅓ cup mayonnaise or salad dressing
    ⅓ cup light cream or milk
      1 tablespoon lemon juice
    ¼ teaspoon garlic salt
      2 ounces Roquefort cheese (½ of a 4-ounce package), crumbled
      4 cups broken romaine leaves
      2 cups broken raw spinach leaves, loosely packed
      1 pint cherry tomatoes, cut in half
      2 medium-size zucchini, sliced ½-inch thick (about 3 cups)
      8 ounces cooked corned beef, cut into julienne strips (about 2 cups)*
      1 can (2 ounces) rolled anchovies with capers, drained
    ½ cup Italian-flavored croutons for salad

1. Beat cream cheese, mayonnaise, light cream, lemon juice and garlic salt in a small bowl with electric mixer until smooth. Stir in Roquefort. Refrigerate, covered, at least 1 hour.
2. Layer romaine, spinach, tomatoes and zucchini in a large salad bowl. Cover with plastic wrap; chill until serving time.
3. To serve: Arrange corned beef and anchovies over top of salad; sprinkle with croutons; pour dressing over all; toss to coat evenly.

* Turkey, chicken or ham may be used in place of corned beef.

CHICKEN SALAD DELUXE

Tender chicken is brightly flavored with a sour-cream-mayonnaise combination.

Makes 4 servings.

      1 broiler-fryer (about 3 pounds)
      4 cups water
      1 small onion, sliced
          Few celery tops
    ¼ teaspoon salt
    ⅓ cup mayonnaise or salad dressing
    ⅓ cup dairy sour cream
      1 tablespoon lemon juice
    ¼ teaspoon pepper
    ¾ cup chopped celery
      1 medium-size onion, chopped (½ cup)
    ¼ cup chopped dill pickle
          Lettuce
          Paprika

1. Combine chicken with water, sliced onion, celery tops and salt in a kettle or Dutch oven. Heat to boiling; reduce heat; cover; simmer about 1 hour, or until chicken is tender. Remove from broth and cool until easy to handle. (Save broth to start a soup another day.)
2. Skin the chicken and take meat from bones. Cut meat into bite-size pieces; put in medium-size bowl.
3. Blend mayonnaise or salad dressing, sour cream, lemon juice and pepper in a small bowl. Combine celery, onion and dill pickle with chicken; add the dressing; toss until evenly coated. Cover; chill at least an hour in the refrigerator to season and blend flavors.
4. Line salad bowl with lettuce leaves. Spoon salad into bowl. Sprinkle with paprika.

SEA-FARE SALAD

Here's an inexpensive main dish salad for the fishermen in the family!

Makes 6 servings.

 1 cup macaroni shells
1½ cups water
 2 slices lemon
 3 peppercorns
 1 bay leaf
 1 package (1 pound) frozen fillets of flounder or sole
 1 package (10 ounces) frozen mixed vegetables, cooked and drained
 1 cup chopped celery
 1 medium-size onion, chopped (½ cup)
½ cup bottled Italian-style dressing
 2 tablespoons lemon juice
⅛ teaspoon pepper
¼ cup mayonnaise or salad dressing
   Salad greens
 1 medium-size cucumber, sliced
   Radish roses

1. Cook macaroni shells following label directions; drain well.
2. Combine water, lemon slices, peppercorns and bay leaf in a skillet; bring to boiling. Place frozen block of fillets in skillet; cover. Simmer about 10 minutes, or until fish just flakes; drain. Flake lightly with a fork; cool.
3. Combine macaroni, fish, mixed vegetables, celery and onion in a large bowl. Mix Italian-style dressing with lemon juice and pepper; add to macaroni mixture. Toss salad lightly. Cover; refrigerate 3 hours, or until well-chilled.
4. At serving time, add mayonnaise or salad dressing to marinated mixture; toss lightly. Line a serving platter with salad greens; mound salad in center. Garnish with sliced cucumber and radish roses, if you wish; serve salad immediately.

CAROLINA COLESLAW

"This isn't a fancy recipe," says its creator, Mrs. Oscar McCollum of Rockingham County, North Carolina. "But we like it. And it just gets better and better the longer it sits in the refrigerator."

Makes 6 to 8 servings.

 1 large cabbage (about 3 pounds), trimmed, quartered and cored
 1 medium-size sweet green pepper, cored, seeded and minced (for color, use ½ green pepper and ½ sweet red pepper)
 1 medium-size sweet onion (Bermuda or Spanish), peeled and chopped fine
 2 carrots, grated

DRESSING:
 1 cup sugar
 1 teaspoon salt
 1 teaspoon dry mustard
 1 teaspoon celery seeds
 1 cup cider vinegar
⅔ cup vegetable oil

1. With a sharp knife, slice each cabbage quarter very fine; combine with green pepper, onion and carrots in a large bowl and toss to mix.
2. Mix sugar, salt, mustard and celery seeds in a small saucepan; add vinegar and oil and let come to a boil over moderate heat, stirring until sugar dissolves. Pour over cabbage and toss well. Cool, then cover and refrigerate until ready to serve.

BAVARIAN BAKED POTATO SALAD

This warm robust salad is chock-full of chunky frankfurters.

Makes 6 servings.

 5 medium-size potatoes (about 2 pounds)
 1 pound frankfurters, cut into 1-inch pieces
 2 tablespoons vegetable oil
 1 medium-size onion, chopped (½ cup)
 2 tablespoons flour
 3 tablespoons brown sugar
 1 teaspoon salt
 1 teaspoon dry mustard
⅛ teaspoon pepper
 1 cup water
⅓ cup vinegar
 1 cup thinly sliced celery
½ cup chopped green pepper
¼ cup chopped pimiento
 1 package (8 ounces) process sliced American cheese

1. Cook potatoes in boiling salted water in a large pan 30 minutes, or until tender; drain. Cool, then peel and dice. Place in a medium-size bowl.

2. Brown frankfurters in oil in a medium-size skillet; remove with a slotted spoon to the bowl with potatoes.

3. Sauté onion in same skillet until soft. Combine flour, sugar, salt and dry mustard; stir into drippings; cook, stirring constantly, until bubbly. Stir in water and vinegar; continue cooking and stirring until dressing thickens and bubbles 1 minute.

4. Add celery, green pepper and pimiento; cook 1 minute longer. Pour over potatoes and frankfurters. Spoon one half of the potato mixture into an 8-cup baking dish; layer with 4 slices of cheese; spoon remaining potato mixture into dish. Top with remaining cheese slices cut into triangles.

5. Bake in moderate oven (350°) 15 minutes, or until cheese is slightly melted. Serve warm.

FIVE-MINUTE SALAD DRESSINGS

CLASSIC FRENCH DRESSING

It's great for green salads.

Makes 1 cup.

  ⅔ cup vegetable or olive oil
  ½ cup cider or wine vinegar
  ½ teaspoon sugar
  1 teaspoon salt
  ¼ teaspoon pepper

Combine all ingredients in a screw-top jar with a tight-fitting lid. Shake well to blend; chill.

GARLIC DRESSING

A great choice for hors d'oeuvres- or main-dish-antipasto (see page 84).

Makes about 1 cup.

  ⅔ cup olive or vegetable oil
  ⅓ cup red wine vinegar
  3 cloves garlic, crushed
  1 teaspoon mixed Italian herbs, crumbled
  1 teaspoon salt
  ¼ teaspoon freshly ground pepper

Combine oil, vinegar, garlic, mixed Italian herbs, salt and pepper in a 2-cup jar with a screw top. Cover jar securely; shake to blend well.

WEIGHT-WATCHING TIP

Add olive flavor to salad dressings (without the oil calories) simply by adding the olive instead of the oil! Mince up an olive in any of our low-calorie salad dressing recipes and it'll taste as if it's based on lots of calorie-rich olive oil!

"MAYONNAISE" SALAD DRESSING

For a change of pace, try this interesting mayonnaise-type dressing. It's made with oil and vinegar and a touch of egg yolk to give it stability and body.

Makes about ⅔ cup.

  4 teaspoons Dijon mustard
  4 teaspoons red wine vinegar
  1 egg yolk
  ½ teaspoon Worcestershire sauce
    Dash of liquid red-pepper seasoning
  ½ cup peanut or olive oil
    Salt and freshly ground pepper to taste
  4 teaspoons heavy cream

1. Place the mustard, vinegar, egg yolk, Worcestershire sauce and liquid red-pepper seasoning in a salad bowl.

2. Use a wire whisk and start beating the mixture rapidly. Gradually add the oil, beating constantly. The mixture should be like a thin mayonnaise. Add salt and pepper to taste and the cream. If you wish a thinner dressing, beat in a little water. And, if desired, add a little fresh lemon juice.

Variations: Add about a teaspoon or more of finely chopped parsley, basil or chives or a combination of all three.

HERBED FRENCH DRESSING

This is a refreshing dressing for crispy vegetable salads.

Makes 1 cup.

  1 cup Classic French Dressing (at left)
  ½ teaspoon leaf basil, crumbled
  ½ teaspoon leaf tarragon, crumbled
  2 tablespoons grated Parmesan cheese

Combine all ingredients in a screw-top jar with a tight-fitting lid. Shake well to blend; chill.

TANGY FRENCH DRESSING

This dressing is one cabbage lovers will enjoy. Serve in on a cabbage slaw or plain cabbage.

Makes 1 cup.

  1 cup Classic French Dressing (above left)
  1 teaspoon Worcestershire sauce
  1 teaspoon prepared mustard
  1 clove garlic, peeled and halved

Combine all ingredients in a screw-top jar with a tight-fitting lid. Shake well to blend; chill well.

ROQUEFORT FRENCH DRESSING

Here's a zesty dressing that's perfect on ripe tomatoes or with our California Chicken Salad (see recipe on page 86).

Makes about 1½ cups.

- ⅓ cup tarragon vinegar
- 1½ teaspoons salt
- ¼ teaspoon pepper
- 1 tablespoon chopped parsley
- 1 tablespoon chopped chives
- ⅔ cup vegetable oil
- 1 package (4 ounces) Roquefort or blue cheese, crumbled

Combine vinegar, salt, pepper, parsley, chives and oil in a jar with tight-fitting lid; shake jar well until blended. Add cheese. Refrigerate at least 2 hours for dressing flavors to blend thoroughly.

TOMATO FRENCH DRESSING

Here's a delightful dressing for crisp chilled lettuce wedges.

Makes about 2⅓ cups.

- 1 cup Classic French Dressing (see page 88)
- 1 can condensed tomato soup
- 1 clove garlic, peeled and halved
- 1 tablespoon prepared mustard
- 1 tablespoon minced onion

Combine all ingredients in a large screw-top jar with a tight-fitting lid. Shake well to blend; chill.

Carefree Molded Chicken and Cucumber Salad is a perfect main-dish choice for hot nights because it can be made early in the day and refrigerated. Recipe can be found on page 81.

6

COMPANY MEALS ON A SHOESTRING

*"He was a wealthy man,
and kindly to his fellow men;
for dwelling in a house by
the side of the road,
he used to entertain
all comers."*
THE ILIAD, BK VI, L. 14.
HOMER (C. 700 B.C.)

This chapter takes you on a vacation from routine cooking. In its place, candlelight, soft music and all our best recipes for feeding a crowd—without breaking the bank. This is enjoyable cooking, too, as the dinner we show here illustrates. It starts with Ham Bolognese, a main course large enough for a long guest list, and the only time-consuming recipe on the menu. It's served with easy-to-make Rice Pilaf, a tossed green salad (with bottled dressing), wine and, for dessert, Pineapple and Peach in Cassis. Turn the page for these and other recipes guaranteed to take you on a very pleasant dinnertime journey—on a shoestring.

MEXICAN FONDUE

This south-of-the-border version of cheese fondue is livened with chili powder and hot peppers. Serve with crusty bread, sliced vegetables and corn chips for varied taste—and festive color.

Makes 8 servings.

   1 pound Cheddar cheese, shredded (4 cups)
   1 pound Monterey Jack cheese,
      shredded (4 cups)
   ¼ cup all-purpose flour
   2 teaspoons chili powder (or more)
   1 large green pepper
   1 large red pepper
   1 pint (2 cups) cherry tomatoes
   2 large avocados
   1 loaf sourdough or French bread
   1 clove garlic, halved
   1 can (12 ounces) beer
   1 can (4 ounces) hot green chili peppers,
      seeded and chopped
   1 bag (6 ounces) corn chips

1. Combine Cheddar and Monterey Jack cheeses

with flour and chili powder in a large bowl until the ingredients are well-blended.

2. Halve, seed and cut green and red peppers into thin strips; wash and stem cherry tomatoes; halve, pit and peel avocados; cut into 1-inch cubes. Cut bread into 1-inch cubes, leaving some crust on each piece. (This much can be done ahead, if you wish. Wrap each food separately in plastic wrap and refrigerate until serving time.)

3. When ready to serve, rub the garlic along the inside of a ceramic fondue or flameproof ceramic baking dish; add beer and heat slowly, just until beer stops foaming and begins to bubble.

4. Gradually add cheese mixture, a handful at a time, stirring constantly, until cheese is melted and smooth; add hot green peppers. Place pan over a candle warmer and serve on a tray with groups of pepper strips, avocado pieces, bread chunks, cherry tomatoes and corn chips.

Mexican Fondue, a south-of-the-border version of the classic fondue, is a great way to entertain because guests help you cook! The recipe for this easy meal-in-a-pot begins in the column at left.

SHRIMP SZECHUAN STYLE

Shrimp and green onions are stir-fried, then simmered in a peppery tomato sauce—in less than 30 minutes.

Makes 4 servings.

- ¼ **cup catsup**
- 2 **tablespoons soy sauce**
- 1 **tablespoon dry sherry**
- ½ **teaspoon sugar**
- ½ **teaspoon ground ginger**
- ¼ **teaspoon crushed red pepper**
- 2 **tablespoons vegetable oil**
- 1 **pound shelled and deveined shrimp (frozen or fresh)**
- 4 **cloves garlic, finely chopped**
- ½ **cup green onions, cut in ¼-inch pieces**

1. Combine catsup, soy sauce, sherry, sugar, ginger and red pepper in a 1-cup measure.
2. Heat vegetable oil in a wok or large skillet over high heat. Toss in shrimp. Cook, stirring constantly, until shrimp turns pink and firms up, about 2 minutes. Remove to a heated plate with a slotted spoon.
3. Add garlic to oil remaining in wok. Stir-fry 15 seconds. Stir in green onions, adding more oil, if necessary. Stir-fry 1 to 2 minutes, or until onions become soft. Add catsup mixture. Cook, stirring constantly, over medium heat until bubbly.
4. Return shrimp to wok; heat 1 minute more. Serve with hot boiled rice, if you wish.

MEAT LOAF SAUERBRATEN WITH NOODLES AND RED CABBAGE

Delightfully quick and true to the long-cooking original in flavor, this loaf is a skillet special.

Makes 8 servings.

- 2 **pounds ground beef**
- ½ **cup packaged bread crumbs**
- 3 **tablespoons instant diced onion**
- 2 **teaspoons salt**
- ¼ **teaspoon ground cloves**
- ¼ **cup milk**
- 2 **eggs**
- 2 **tablespoons butter or margarine**
- ½ **cup cider vinegar**
- ½ **cup dry red wine**
- ½ **cup water**
- 8 **gingersnaps**
- 1 **package (8 ounces) wide noodles, cooked Red Cabbage (recipe on page 95)**

1. Combine beef, bread crumbs, onion, salt, cloves, milk and eggs in a large bowl. Mix lightly until well-blended. Turn out onto wet surface; mold the mixture into an oval-shaped meat loaf.
2. Heat butter or margarine in a large deep skillet. Brown meat loaf on one side over medium heat, 5 minutes; carefully turn with 2 wide spatulas and brown other side 5 minutes.
3. Add vinegar, wine and water. Heat to boiling; lower heat; cover; simmer 45 minutes.
4. Remove loaf to heated platter, keep hot. Stir gingersnaps into liquid in skillet. Heat, stirring constantly, until gravy thickens and is bubbly hot.
5. To serve: Arrange cooked noodles and red cabbage on platter with meat loaf; spoon some of gravy over meat.

CLAM PIE

Ask a New Englander for a clam pie recipe, and you'll find no two are alike—but here's one we particularly like.

Bake at 450° for 25 minutes.
Makes 6 servings.

- ½ **package piecrust mix**
- 2 **medium potatoes (¾ pound) cooked in skin, peeled and cut into ¼-inch slices**
- 4 **slices bacon**
- 1 **large onion, sliced (1 cup)**
- 2 **cans (8 ounces each) minced clams**
- ½ **cup milk**
- ¼ **cup (½ stick) butter or margarine**
- 2 **tablespoons flour**
- ¾ **teaspoon leaf savory, crumbled**
- ½ **teaspoon salt**
- ¼ **teaspoon pepper**

1. Prepare piecrust mix, following label directions. Place in refrigerator until ready to use.
2. Cook bacon in a large skillet until crispy; remove and reserve. Add sliced onion to bacon fat (about 3 tablespoons); cook until tender.
3. Drain liquid from clams, measuring liquid into a 2-cup measure; add milk to equal 1¾ cups liquid; reserve.
4. Add the minced clams to sliced onions, crumble in bacon and reserve.
5. Melt butter in a small saucepan; add flour, savory, salt and pepper; cook until bubbly, 1 minute. Stir in clam-milk liquid; cook over medium heat until thickened; stir into clam mixture.
6. Arrange potato slices on bottom of a 9-inch pie plate; spoon clam mixture over potatoes.
7. Roll out pastry to an 11-inch round; cut out several slits near center to let steam escape; cover pie. Trim overhang to ½ inch; fold under flush with rim; flute to make a stand-up edge. Roll pastry trimmings, cut out into fancy shapes; decorate top of pastry, if you wish. Brush top of pie with remaining clam juice or milk.
8. Bake in a very hot oven (450°) for 25 minutes, or until the crust is golden. Let the pie stand for about 15 minutes before slicing and serving.

MUSTARD SAUCE

Makes about ½ cup.

- ¼ **cup dry mustard**
- ¼ **cup cold water**
- ¼ **cup honey**

Combine dry mustard and cold water in a cup to make a smooth paste; stir in honey until well-blended. Keep in refrigerator.

COQUILLES SAINT JACQUES, MORNAY

A creamy main dish named after the French word for scallop.

Bake at 450° for 10 minutes.
Makes 6 servings.

- 1½ **pounds fresh or frozen unbreaded scallops or 2 packages (12 ounces each) frozen Greenland turbot, cod or pollock fillets**
- 1 **can (3 or 4 ounces) chopped mushrooms**
  Dry white wine
- 1 **tablespoon mixed pickling spices, tied in cheesecloth**
  Instant mashed potatoes (to make 4 servings)
- 1 **cup frozen peas (from a 1½- to 2-pound bag)**
- 1 **egg**
  Butter or margarine
- 3 **tablespoons grated Parmesan cheese**

1. Wash scallops or cut frozen fish fillets into 1-inch pieces with a sharp knife.
2. Drain liquid from mushrooms into a 1-cup measure; add enough wine to make 1 cup. Pour liquid into a large skillet; add pickling spices.
3. Heat liquid to bubbling; add fish; lower heat; cover skillet. Simmer 5 minutes.
4. While fish poaches, measure the water and salt called for on instant-mashed-potato label into a medium-size saucepan; add frozen peas; heat to boiling, simmer 3 minutes. Remove peas with a slotted spoon; reserve.
5. Remove saucepan from heat; beat in potato flakes, egg and the butter or margarine called for on label until mixture is thick and smooth.
6. Remove fish from skillet with slotted spoon; reserve. Discard spice bag.
7. Stir mushroom soup into liquid in skillet until smooth; add cooked fish and peas. Divide mixture among 6 scallop shells or 1-cup baking dishes.
8. Fit a pastry bag with a fancy tip; fill with prepared potatoes; edge shells or baking dishes with fluted potato; sprinkle cheese over potato.
9. Bake in very hot oven (450°) 10 minutes, or until golden.
Note: This dish can be prepared ahead of time and refrigerated. Increase baking time to 20 minutes, or until the scallop mixture is bubbly-hot.

COQ AU VIN BLANC

It doesn't take a lot of ingredients to cook à la Francaise; the essentials are here.

Bake at 350° for 40 minutes.
Makes 8 servings.

- 4 **whole chicken breasts (10 ounces each), split**
- 2 **cups (½ of a 1½-pound bag) frozen small whole onions**
- 2 **cups (½ of a 1½-pound bag) frozen small whole or cut-up carrots**
- 1 **cup dry white wine**
- 1 **can (15 ounces) beef gravy**

1. Arrange chicken breasts, skin side down, in a cold Dutch oven; heat slowly to brown. Turn; brown other side. Drain off accumulated fat.
2. Add onions and carrots; sauté briefly. Pour in wine and beef gravy. Bring to boiling; cover.
3. Bake in moderate oven (350°) 40 minutes, or until chicken and vegetables are tender. Garnish with mushrooms and croutons, if you wish.

MONGOLIAN HOT POT

Your guests cook skewered vegetables, turkey and shrimp in a bubbly broth. Three accompanying sauces offer hot, sweet and pungent dips to please all tastes.

Makes 6 servings.

- 1½ **pounds frozen turkey breast fillets, thawed**
- ½ **pound green beans**
- 1 **bunch green onions**
- ½ **pound fresh spinach**
- ½ **pound fresh mushrooms**
- 1 **medium-size zucchini**
- 1 **medium-size yellow squash**
- 2 **cans condensed chicken broth**
- 2½ **cups water**
- 1 **package (8 ounces) frozen, shelled, deveined, raw shrimp, thawed**
  Mustard Sauce (recipe in column at left)
  Duck sauce or ham glaze (from a 10-ounce jar)
  Hawaiian teriyaki sauce (from a 5-ounce bottle) or soy sauce
  Hot rice

1. Cut turkey fillets into 1-inch squares; tip green beans and cut into 2-inch pieces; trim green onions and cut into 3-inch pieces; wash and trim spinach; cut mushrooms, crosswise, into thin slices; tip and slice zucchini and yellow squash. (This can be done ahead of time, if you wish. Wrap each food separately and refrigerate until serving time.)
2. At serving time: Pour chicken broth and water into a Mongolian hot pot or electric wok; heat to simmering, following manufacturer's directions.

Arrange prepared foods with shrimp in rows on a large flat tray. Spoon Mustard Sauce and duck sauce into small bowls; pour teriyaki sauce into a third small bowl.

3. Each guest spears assorted foods onto a fondue fork or bamboo skewer and cooks in broth 3 minutes, or until vegetables are crisply tender. Serve with Mustard Sauce, duck sauce and teriyaki sauce over rice.

4. When all the food has been cooked, ladle remaining broth into tiny cups and pass to guests.

ORANGE-GLAZED LAMB CHOPS WITH MINT AND RAISIN PILAF

A spiral of glistening lamb chops crowns a buttery pilaf flecked with peas, carrots and golden raisins. It all goes together fast, and if you brown the chops in the broiler instead of a skillet, you'll save both cooking and clean-up time.

Makes 4 servings.

    8 rib lamb chops
    ½ teaspoon salt
    ¼ teaspoon leaf rosemary, crumbled
    ⅛ teaspoon pepper
    2 tablespoons butter or margarine, melted
Glaze:
    ¼ cup tart orange marmalade
    1 tablespoon vinegar
    1 tablespoon bottled grenadine syrup
Pilaf:
    1 cup frozen chopped onion
    4 tablespoons butter or margarine
    ½ cup golden raisins
    ⅔ cup toasted slivered almonds
 2¼ cups water
    2 envelopes instant chicken broth
    3 tablespoons frozen concentrate for orange juice
    1 tablespoon brown sugar
    1 tablespoon dried mint flakes, crushed
    ⅛ teaspoon leaf rosemary, crumbled
    ¼ teaspoon bottled lemon-flavored salt
    1 cup uncooked converted rice
    1 package (10 ounces) frozen peas and carrots

1. Sprinkle lamb chops lightly with salt, rosemary and pepper, then brush with melted butter; arrange in a single layer on a broiler pan so that curved ribs all face the same way. Broil 5 inches from the heat 3 to 4 minutes until nicely browned.
2. Meanwhile, heat marmalade, vinegar and grenadine in a small saucepan until marmalade melts. Brush tops of broiled chops with glaze and let stand at room temperature while preparing pilaf. Keep glaze warm.
3. Sauté onion in butter in a large skillet 3 minutes until soft. Add raisins, almonds, water, broth, orange juice, sugar, mint, rosemary and lemon-flavored salt. Simmer for about 2 to 3 minutes.

4. Stir in rice, bring to boiling; pour into a 12-cup paella pan or *au gratin* dish. Cover with foil. Bake in a moderate oven (375°) 20 minutes until rice is almost tender and most of the liquid absorbed. Add peas and carrots, tossing lightly to mix; arrange chops, browned sides up, in a spiral around edge of pan with rib ends pointing toward the center; brush with glaze.
5. Re-cover and bake 20 minutes; uncover, brush chops with glaze and bake 10 minutes longer.

RED CABBAGE

Makes 8 servings.

    1 small red cabbage (about 1½ pounds) finely shredded
    1 red apple, washed, quartered, cored and sliced
    ¼ cup red currant jelly
    ¼ cup water
    1 teaspoon salt

1. Combine cabbage, apple, jelly, water and salt in large saucepan; cover.
2. Cook over medium heat, stirring occasionally, 30 minutes, or until cabbage is tender but still a little crisp. (See Meat Loaf Sauerbraten with Noodles and Red Cabbage, on page 93.)

OLD-FASHIONED CORN & HAM PUDDING

Old-fashioned and thrifty, too, this end-of-the week supper dish is one most men enjoy.

Makes 4 servings.

    2 tablespoons butter or margarine
    ¼ cup minced green pepper
    1 small onion, minced (¼ cup)
    1 tablespoon flour
    1 can (1 pound) cream-style corn
    ¾ to 1 cup minced lean leftover cooked ham
    3 eggs, separated
    2 to 3 dashes liquid red-pepper seasoning
      Dash Worcestershire sauce
    ⅛ teaspoon pepper
    ½ teaspoon salt

1. Preheat oven to 350°. Butter a 6-cup shallow baking dish.
2. Melt the butter in a large heavy skillet. Add the green pepper and onion. Cook, stirring constantly, until vegetables are soft. Stir in flour; add corn and ham; blend; remove from heat to a large bowl. Cool to lukewarm.
3. Add egg yolks, pepper seasoning, Worcestershire, salt and pepper; blend well.
4. Beat egg whites until stiff. Fold into corn mixture. Pour into prepared baking dish.
5. Bake in a preheated 350° oven until firm, about 25 minutes. Serve immediately.

STUFFED CHICKEN ROMA

This recipe puts a continental flavor into back-yard cooking.

Makes 6 servings.

6 chicken breasts, about 12 ounces each
2 tablespoons finely chopped green onion
½ cup (1 stick) butter or margarine
1½ cups fresh bread crumbs
¼ pound soft salami, finely chopped

1. Bone chicken breasts, leaving skin in place. Place flat, skin side down, on a cutting board.
2. Sauté onion in 3 tablespoons of the butter or margarine until soft in a small frying pan; stir in bread crumbs and salami until evenly moist.
3. Divide stuffing into 6 parts; spoon along hollows in chicken breasts. Fold edges of chicken over stuffing to cover completely; fasten with wooden picks.
4. Melt remaining butter or margarine in a small saucepan on grill; brush part over chicken. Place breasts on grill, buttered side down, about 6 inches above hot coals. Grill 20 minutes. Brush again with melted butter or margarine; turn. Grill 20 minutes longer, or until chicken is tender and golden. Place on a large serving platter; remove picks. Garnish with carrot curls and sprigs of chicory, if you wish.
Note: If traveling a distance to your eating spot, make stuffing and chill well, then stuff into chicken breasts and keep chilled until cooking time.

HUNGARIAN BEEF GULYÁS

The generous use of paprika identifies this stew as a native dish in the land of the Magyars.

Makes 8 servings.

4 slices bacon, diced
1 large onion, chopped (1 cup)
2 cloves garlic, crushed
1½ tablespoons paprika
3 pounds beef round, cut into 1½-inch cubes
1 can condensed beef broth
1½ teaspoons salt
½ teaspoon caraway seeds
1 pound small white onions, peeled
4 tablespoons flour
6 tablespoons water
Hot cooked egg noodles
Dairy sour cream

1. Sauté bacon until crisp in Dutch oven; remove with slotted spoon; reserve.
2. Brown beef cubes, half at a time, in the bacon fat; remove to a bowl as they brown.
3. Sauté onion in fat in pan until soft and golden; stir in garlic and paprika; cook, stirring the onion

and the garlic constantly, for about two minutes.
4. Return browned beef to pan; stir in beef broth, salt and caraway seeds. Heat to boiling; lower heat; cover. Simmer 1½ hours.
5. Add onions and bacon. Simmer 45 to 60 minutes longer, or until beef and onions are tender. Mix flour and water to a smooth paste; stir into boiling Gulyás; cook, stirring constantly, until sauce thickens and bubbles 1 minute. Gulyás may now be refrigerated and then reheated just before serving.
6. Spoon Gulyás onto a heated deep platter; arrange egg noodles around edge. Garnish with sautéed green peppers and chopped parsley, if you wish. Pass sour cream at the table.

STEWED LENTILS WITH LAMB RIBS

This economical casserole is good with rice and a cucumber salad.

Makes 4 servings.

1¼ pounds meaty lamb ribs
2 cups (12 ounces) lentils
1 medium-size onion, chopped
1 large carrot, diced
2 chopped canned tomatoes with liquid
1 large clove garlic, minced
3 to 4 cups water
1 bay leaf
1 teaspoon thyme
1 teaspoon salt
½ teaspoon black pepper

1. Cut lamb ribs apart and trim off heavy excess fat. With a meat axe or a sharp knife, cut each rib across into thirds, so that each piece is about 1½ to 2 inches long. Wash lentils and pick over, but do not soak.
2. Place lamb ribs in cold skillet and gradually heat until they are frying and their fat melts. Turn frequently so all sides brown. When lamb is golden brown on all sides, remove to a 2-quart casserole or stew pot.
3. Add onion and carrot to skillet with hot lamb fat and sauté over moderate heat until golden brown. Stir in tomatoes and liquid, bring to a boil, and scrape in coagulated pan juices with a wooden spatula or spoon. Pour the sauce over lamb ribs in casserole.
4. Add garlic, bay leaf, thyme, salt and pepper and 2 cups water. Bring to a boil, then gently stir in lentils. Add enough additional boiling water to come just to the level of the lentils. Bring to a boil, cover, reduce to a simmer and cook steadily but gently for about 2 hours, or until lentils and lamb are tender. Add boiling water as needed during cooking and stir gently every half hour or so. Adjust seasonings, adding a few drops of vinegar if you like.

BAKED HAM BOLOGNESE

The Northern Italians always had a way with cheeses and herbs, especially in pastas, and on pizzas. We borrowed that idea and stuffed a ham with cheeses and herbs.

Bake at 325° for about 2 hours.
Makes 6 servings with some leftovers.

    1 cup shredded mozzarella cheese
    ¼ cup finely chopped green onion
    2 tablespoons chopped parsley
    1 teaspoon leaf oregano, crumbled
    ½ teaspoon leaf basil, crumbled
    ½ fully cooked ham (butt half) weighing about
       8 pounds
    2 tablespoons grated Parmesan cheese
    3 tomatoes, cut into wedges
    2 green peppers, seeded and cut into strips

1. Mix mozzarella, onion, parsley, oregano and basil in a small bowl.
2. Trim any skin and excess fat from ham. Make deep cuts, about 1 inch apart, in fat side of ham. Press cheese mixture into cuts; pack in well. Place ham fat side up in small shallow roasting pan.
3. Bake in slow oven (325°) 15 minutes per pound. About 30 minutes before ham is done, skim fat from drippings in pan. Add peppers and tomatoes to pan; stir to cover with drippings. Sprinkle ham with Parmesan cheese.
4. Bake 30 minutes longer, or until ham and vegetables are done. Place ham on serving platter; spoon peppers and tomatoes around base. Sprinkle with more cheese and parsley, if you wish.

RICE PILAF

After a minimal amount of preparation, this side dish goes in the oven until serving time. It's shown on page 90.

Bake at 325° for 45 minutes.
Makes 8 to 10 servings.

    4 tablespoons vegetable oil
    1 large onion, thinly sliced
    1½ cups uncooked regular rice
    3½ cups canned chicken broth (2 cans, about
       13¾ ounces each) or bouillon
       Chopped parsley

1. Sauté onion in oil until golden in large skillet; remove with slotted spoon.
2. Add rice to skillet and sauté, stirring constantly, until slightly browned. Stir in chicken broth; heat to boiling. Spoon into an 8-cup baking dish; add onion; cover.
3. Bake in moderate oven (325°) 45 minutes, or until liquid is absorbed and rice is tender. Fluff up rice with a fork and sprinkle with the parsley.

PINEAPPLE AND PEACH IN CASSIS

This make-ahead dessert is a beautiful choice for a summer buffet. It's pictured on page 91.

Makes 8 to 10 servings.

    3 cans (1 pound each) peach halves, drained
    1 small ripe pineapple
    ½ cup creme de cassis
       Lime or lemon, cut into wedges

1. Cut top from pineapple; cut lengthwise into quarters. Remove core and rind, including the eyes, from each quarter, then slice fruit crosswise into ½-inch thick slices.
2. Arrange pineapple and peach halves in large serving bowl. Pour creme de cassis over. Chill until serving time, at least 1 hour.
3. To serve: Spoon fruits and liquid into individual dessert dishes. Garnish each with a wedge of lime or lemon to squeeze over fruits if desired.

SHRIMP CHEESE SQUARES

A deep-sea version of popular Quiche Lorraine. Delicious warm or cold.

Bake at 450° for 15 minutes, then at 350° for 15 minutes.
Makes 35 squares.

    1 package piecrust mix
    1 cup chopped green onions
    1 tablespoon butter or margarine
    1 package (8 ounces) Swiss cheese, shredded
       (2 cups)
    1 package (1 pound) frozen shrimp, shelled,
       deveined and cooked
    8 eggs
    4 cups light cream
    2 teaspoons salt
    ⅛ teaspoon pepper
    ⅛ teaspoon cayenne

1. Prepare piecrust mix, following label directions, or make double-crust pastry recipe. Roll out, half at a time, to 9x6-inch rectangle; fit both halves into 15½x10½x1-inch jelly-roll pan. Seal together edges of halves. Prick with fork.
2. Bake in hot oven (425°) 5 minutes; remove to wire rack; cool slightly. Increase oven temperature to 450°.
3. Sauté green onions in butter or margarine till soft, in skillet, 5 minutes. Sprinkle cheese evenly in a layer in pastry shell; add onions and shrimp.
4. Beat eggs slightly in a large bowl; slowly beat in cream, salt, pepper and cayenne, then pour into pastry shell.
5. Bake in hot oven (450°) for 15 minutes; lower heat to moderate (350°). Bake 15 minutes more, or until the center of quiche is almost set.

CRABMEAT FLOUNDER ROLLS

Delicate rolls of flounder filled with a savory onion-mushroom-crabmeat filling, sauced with wine and Swiss cheese! Elegant party fare that seems extravagantly rich for its scant calorie count.

Bake at 400° for 30 minutes.
Makes 8 servings.

  2 pounds frozen flounder fillets, thawed
  1 can (4 ounces) mushroom stems and pieces, drained
  3 tablespoons minced onion
  1 can (7½ ounces) crabmeat, drained and picked over
  ¼ cup fine dry bread crumbs
  1 tablespoon parsley flakes
  1 teaspoon salt
  ⅛ teaspoon pepper
  3 tablespoons flour
  1½ cups skim milk
  ¼ cup dry white wine
  2 ounces process Swiss cheese, shredded (½ cup)
    Paprika

1. Separate flounder fillets; trim into 8 pieces.
2. Chop mushrooms finely; combine with onion, crabmeat, bread crumbs, parsley, ½ teaspoon of the salt and pepper. Spread over fillets; roll up. Place rolls, seam-side down, in a shallow 8-cup baking dish. Tuck any remaining filling around the flounder rolls.
3. Combine flour, milk, wine and remaining ½ teaspoon salt in saucepan. Cook over moderate heat, stirring constantly, until sauce thickens and bubbles. Add cheese; stir until melted. Pour over fish rolls. Sprinkle lightly with paprika.
4. Bake in hot oven (400°) 30 minutes, or until fish flakes easily with a fork.

HERBED FRIED CHICKEN

A crispy, crackly fried chicken to please all the perfectionists in the family.

Makes 4 servings.

  1 broiler-fryer (about 2½ pounds)
  2 eggs
  ¾ cup flour
  1½ teaspoons salt
  1 teaspoon leaf basil, crumbled
  ½ teaspoon leaf thyme, crumbled
  ½ teaspoon pepper
  ¼ teaspoon ground nutmeg
    Shortening or vegetable oil

1. Cut chicken into serving-size pieces.
2. Beat eggs in a shallow dish. Mix flour, salt, basil, thyme, pepper and nutmeg in a plastic bag.

3. Dip chicken pieces in eggs, allowing excess to drip off; shake in flour mixture to coat well. Dip again in egg and shake in flour mixture to form a thick coating. Place chicken pieces on wire rack for 15 minutes to allow coating to set.
4. Melt enough shortening, or pour enough oil into a large heavy skillet with a cover to a 1-inch depth. Place over medium heat. When a few drops of water sizzle when flicked into the hot fat, add the chicken pieces, skin-side down. Cook slowly, turning once, 20 minutes, or until golden.
5. Reduce heat; cover skillet. Cook 30 minutes longer, or until chicken is tender. Remove cover for last 5 minutes for a crunchy crust.

SWISS-STYLE CHICKEN CUTLETS

This is one of the many variations that can be done with breaded chicken cutlets. Vary the nuts in the breading and the cheese in the filling to your heart's content.

Makes 6 servings.

  6 chicken cutlets
  ¼ teaspoon salt
  ⅛ teaspoon pepper
  2 tablespoons Swiss cheese cut in ⅛-inch cubes
  2 tablespoons chopped walnuts
  2 tablespoons chopped parsley
  2 tablespoons flour
  1 egg
  1 teaspoon each vegetable oil and water
    Salt and pepper
  ⅓ cup packaged bread crumbs mixed with 2 tablespoons finely chopped walnuts
  ¼ cup butter or margarine, melted

1. Cut a pocket in each cutlet. Sprinkle with salt and pepper. Mix the Swiss cheese, walnuts and parsley well, and fill each cutlet with 1 tablespoon of the mixture. Seal the edges of each cutlet well by pressing together.
2. Flour each cutlet. Beat the egg with the oil and water and a pinch each of salt and pepper until very liquid. Mix the bread crumbs and walnuts on a piece of wax paper.
3. Brush a fine film of beaten egg on the first side of each cutlet, then invert it into the crumb and nut mixture. Brush the second side with egg also and coat with the crumb nut mixture. Pat smartly between hands to discard excess crumbs.
4. Heat the fat or oil in a large skillet. Panfry the cutlets until golden, about 8 to 10 minutes.

COOK-SAVER TIP
Break rather than cut off the woodish ends of asparagus. The stalks will snap easily where the tender top ends and tough base begins.

BRATWURST BAKE

Meaty bratwurst and a rich tomato sauce combine to satisfy the biggest of outdoor appetites.

Bake at 350° for 45 minutes.
Makes 6 servings.

- **6 fully-cooked bratwurst**
- **1 tablespoon vegetable oil**
- **1 large onion, peeled and sliced**
- **1 clove garlic, minced**
- **1 can (1 pound) Italian tomatoes**
- **1 can (6 ounces) tomato paste**
- **1 tablespoon leaf oregano, crumbled**
- **1½ teaspoons salt**
- **¼ teaspoon pepper**
- **1 tablespoon bottled steak sauce**
- **2 cans (1 pound, 4 ounces each) chick-peas, drained**

1. Brown bratwurst in vegetable oil in a Dutch oven; remove from pan with a slotted spoon.
2. Add onion and garlic to drippings in Dutch oven; sauté until soft.
3. Stir in tomatoes and paste, oregano, salt, pepper, steak sauce and chick-peas. Heat 3 minutes, or until bubbly. Arrange bratwurst on top. Do not cover. Bake in moderate oven (350°) 45 minutes, or until bubbly.
Note: Chill if made ahead, then reheat on grill at your picnic spot.

DOUBLE SAUSAGE WINDERS

Frankfurters, long a barbecue standby, take center stage when stuffed with smoky sausage links and dressed with a colorful tomato relish.

Makes 8 servings.

- **2 medium-size tomatoes, finely chopped**
- **1 medium-size onion, finely chopped (½ cup)**
- **3 tablespoons finely chopped celery**
- **2 tablespoons finely chopped sweet red pepper**
- **1 tablespoon vinegar**
- **¾ teaspoon salt**
- **⅛ teaspoon pepper**
- **8 frankfurters**
- **4 heat-and-serve sausage links**
- **8 slices bacon, partly cooked**
- **8 frankfurter rolls**
- **4 tablespoons (½ stick) butter or margarine**
- **1 teaspoon leaf thyme, crumbled**

1. Mix tomatoes, onion, celery, red pepper, vinegar, salt and pepper in a small bowl. Chill several hours, or overnight to season.
2. Slit each frankfurter lengthwise almost to bottom; quarter sausages lengthwise. Stuff 2 quarters into each frankfurter; wrap slice of partly cooked bacon around each; fasten with wet wooden picks.

3. Place on grill about 6 inches above hot coals. Grill, turning several times, 8 minutes, or until bacon is crisp and frankfurters are heated through.
4. While meat cooks, toast rolls on side of grill. Melt butter or margarine in a small saucepan on grill; stir in thyme; brush over cut side of rolls.
5. Serve frankfurters in rolls; top with relish.
Note: Stuff frankfurters and wrap with bacon ahead, then carry, ready to grill, to your eating spot. Take along relish in a covered jar.

SPAGHETTI WITH RED CLAM SAUCE

Pasta, as Italians have long known, is a great penny stretcher. Seafood, too—if you catch it yourself or if you take advantage of relatively low-cost canned minced clams. Here's an updated, Americanized version of an Italian favorite that substitutes canned clams for fresh.

Makes 6 servings.

- **2 tablespoons olive oil**
- **2 medium-size onions, peeled and chopped**
- **1 clove garlic, peeled and minced**
- **1 bay leaf, crumbled**
- **¼ teaspoon leaf basil, crumbled**
- **1 teaspoon salt**
- **⅛ teaspoon freshly ground black pepper**
- **2 teaspoons honey or light brown sugar**
- **1 can (1 pound, 13 ounces) tomatoes**
- **1 can (6 ounces) tomato paste**
- **¼ cup dry white wine**
- **¼ cup minced parsley**
- **1 can (10½ ounces) minced clams**
- **1 pound thin spaghetti, cooked, following package directions**
- **Grated Parmesan cheese (topping)**

1. Heat olive oil in a large heavy skillet over moderate heat; add onion and garlic and sauté, stirring occasionally, 8 to 10 minutes, until golden. Add bay leaf, basil, salt, pepper, honey or brown sugar, tomatoes, tomato paste, wine, parsley and the liquid drained from the canned clams; reserve clams. Simmer, uncovered, stirring now and then, 1 hour, until flavors mingle and sauce is about the consistency of gravy. Mix in clams and heat 5 minutes longer.
2. Drain spaghetti well; mound on a large heated platter and top with the Red Clam Sauce. Sprinkle with grated Parmesan and serve (pass grated Parmesan so that everyone can help himself).

MONEY-SAVING TIP

Don't throw away leftover rice. Save and reheat next day. Store it overnight in a covered container in the refrigerator, then when you're ready to reheat it, empty the rice into a strainer set over simmering water; cover and steam until fluffy.

MONTEREY SUPPER SPECIAL

Tuna, a family dinner standby, is skillfully blended with packaged and frozen mixes for a fast-mix casserole.

Bake at 400° for 20 minutes.
Makes 4 servings.

- 1 package (about 6 ounces) Spanish-rice mix
- 1 package (10 ounces) frozen Mexican-style kidney beans, corn and peas in sauce.
- 1 can (7 ounces) tuna, drained and flaked
- 2 medium tomatoes, sliced
- 3 slices Monterey Jack cheese (from an 8-ounce package)

1. Combine Spanish-rice mix, water called for on label and Mexican-style vegetables in a flameproof 6-cup casserole or a large skillet.
2. Heat to boiling; simmer 2 minutes, breaking up sauce cubes from vegetables with the back of a spoon. If a skillet was used in Step 1, pour mixture into a 6-cup baking dish.
3. Stir tuna into rice mixture; cover dish.
4. Bake in hot oven (400°) 20 minutes, or until liquid is absorbed.
5. Arrange tomato slices on casserole; top with cheese. Bake 3 minutes, or until cheese melts.

OVEN IRISH STEW

This stew has all the flavor of the longer-cooking variety, yet it is ready in less than an hour.

Bake at 400° for 45 minutes.
Makes 6 servings.

- 6 shoulder lamb chops (about 2 pounds)
- 1 package (1 pound, 8 ounces) frozen stew vegetables
- 1 can condensed chicken broth
- 1 teaspoon onion salt
- 1 tablespoon chopped fresh mint or
  1 teaspoon leaf marjoram, crumbled

1. Trim excess fat from chops. Melt several pieces in a large skillet until there are 2 tablespoons of fat. Remove and discard remaining fat.
2. Brown chops, 3 at a time, in fat in skillet; remove and reserve. Brown stew vegetables in fat remaining in pan. Stir in chicken broth, onion salt and mint or marjoram. Heat to boiling.
3. Arrange browned chops down the center of a shallow 8-cup baking dish; spoon vegetables and liquid around chops; cover dish.
4. Bake in hot oven (400°) 45 minutes, or until chops are fork tender. Garnish with a bunch of fresh mint, if you wish.
Note: Two tablespoons flour may be sprinkled over browned vegetables and stirred lightly before adding broth, if you want a gravy.

ASAPAO DE PESCADO

This Caribbean fish stew takes a grand total of 30 minutes to make.

Bake at 400° for 20 minutes.
Makes 6 servings.

- 1 clove garlic, minced
- 2 tablespoons vegetable oil
- 1 can (1 pound) stewed tomatoes
- 1 can (13¾ ounces) chicken broth
- 1 package (6 ounces) Spanish-rice mix
- 1 package (10 ounces) frozen Italian-style vegetables in sauce
- ½ teaspoon leaf savory, crumbled
- 1 package (1 pound) frozen fillet of sole
- 1 can (1 pint, 8 ounces) bucket of steamed clams with shells

1. Sauté garlic in vegetable oil in a skillet until soft. Add tomatoes, chicken broth, rice mix, vegetables and savory. Cover; bring to boiling.
2. Transfer to 8-cup casserole. Cut fillet of sole into cubes and add to casserole with clams and ½ cup of the clam liquid; cover.
3. Bake in hot oven (400°) for 20 minutes, or until it is bubbly-hot.

BAKED PORK CHOPS

Crumb-coated pork chops are served with an easy mushroom gravy.

Bake at 425° for 30 minutes.
Makes 4 servings.

- 8 loin pork chops, cut ½ inch thick (about 1½ pounds)
  Milk
- 1 package seasoned coating mix for pork
- 1 can condensed golden mushroom soup
- ½ cup water
- 2 tablespoons vinegar

1. Dip pork chops in milk and shake in seasoning bag, following label directions. Arrange chops in single layer in a shallow baking pan.
2. Bake chops 30 minutes, or until golden-brown. Place chops on a hot platter and keep warm.
3. Stir mushroom soup, water and vinegar into drippings in baking pan. Cook, stirring constantly, until mixture is bubbly-hot. Serve gravy separately.

The three casseroles pictured at right are all easy to prepare, will wait almost indefinitely for latecomers and allow you to escape from the kitchen once preparations are done. Shown are Monterey Supper Special (near right); Oven Irish Stew (far right) and Asapao de Pescado (bottom). The recipes for all three casseroles are above.

7

THIRST QUENCHERS

BEVERAGES & COLD SOUPS

*"If all be true that I do think,
There are five reasons we
should drink:
Good wine—a friend—
or being dry—
Or lest we should be by and by—
Or any other reason why."*
FIVE REASONS FOR DRINKING
HENRY ALDRICH (1647-1710)

There's nothing under a summer sun more refreshing than a drink—be it a tall, cool beverage you sip slowly and contentedly while watching sea gulls glide across the sea; or, a hearty chilled soup to quaff between hoisting anchor and sail. This chapter has them all, beginning with the thirst quenchers shown here. From left to right in the photo: Apricot-Banana Royale, Spiced Tea, Red & Silver Fizz, California Sipper and Sangria. Also shown: A luscious assortment of fruits to serve as edible stirrers and garnishes. The recipes begin on the next page.

COLD DRINKS

PEACH FROSTY

It's an easy blender beverage milk-shake fans will enjoy.

Makes 4 servings.

  1 can (8 ounces) cling-peach slices with syrup
  2 cups milk
  ¾ pint (1½ cups) vanilla ice cream
  ¼ teaspoon almond extract

Place cling-peach slices and syrup in an electric blender container. Add milk, ice cream and extract; cover. Beat until creamy-smooth. (Or beat peaches until smooth in a bowl with an electric beater; slowly beat in remaining ingredients.) *Note:* If your blender container holds less than 4½ cups, prepare half of each mixture at a time.

CHOCOLATE EGG CREAM

One of New York's most popular drinks!

Makes 2 servings.

  2 cups chocolate-flavor milk
  ½ pint vanilla ice cream
  Carbonated water (from a 6-ounce bottle)

Combine milk and ice cream in container of electric blender. Cover; whirl at high speed for 30 seconds. Pour into 2 tall glasses. Add carbonated water to fill glasses; serve immediately.

CARIOCA COOLER

Coffee and chocolate served ice-cold make a winning team.

Makes 4 tall drinks.

  ⅓ cup instant cocoa mix
  2 tablespoons instant coffee
  ¼ cup sugar
  ¼ teaspoon ground cinnamon
  ¼ cup hot water
  4 cups cold milk

Dissolve cocoa mix, coffee, sugar and cinnamon in hot water in a tall pitcher. Stir in milk until blended. Pour into 4 tall glasses.

Three summer punches, left, can add a refreshing note to any hot day. From left to right in photo: Cranberry Wine Cooler, Jamaican Citrus Punch and Pina Colada. Recipes are in this chapter.

RED AND SILVER FIZZ

This thirst quencher not only tastes delicious—it looks it, too, as you can see in the photograph on page 102.

Makes 8 to 10 servings.

  2 cans (6 ounces each) frozen fruit juicy-red Hawaiian Punch, undiluted
  1 can (6 ounces) frozen pineapple juice, undiluted
  1 juice can cold water
  3 bottles (12 ounces each) club soda, chilled
  Ice cubes
  Fresh or canned pineapple chunks for garnish

1. Combine Hawaiian Punch, pineapple juice and cold water in large mixing bowl; beat with wire whisk until melted and well combined. Slowly stir in club soda.
2. Ladle into ice-filled glasses and serve immediately with red and white straws; garnish with pineapple chunks, if you wish.

CRANBERRY WINE COOLER

A light and refreshing addition for any warm-weather get-together.

Makes 6 to 8 servings.

  1 bottle sweet white wine, chilled
  3 cups cranberry juice cocktail, chilled
  ¼ cup orange-flavored liqueur
  ¼ cup light corn syrup
  Ice cubes
  Orange and lime slices

1. Combine wine, cranberry juice cocktail, liqueur and corn syrup in large pitcher. Stir to mix. Chill until ready to serve.
2. Just before serving, add ice cubes and orange and lime slices as a garnish.

STRAWBERRY BLUSH

Canned fruit cocktail goes into this invitingly cool refresher.

Makes 4 servings.

  1 can (about 8 ounces) fruit cocktail
  ½ cup bottled grenadine syrup
  1 pint (2 cups) strawberry ice cream
  2 cups milk

Combine all ingredients in an electric blender container; cover; beat until creamy-smooth. (Or combine all ingredients in a bowl and beat with an electric beater.) Pour into tall glasses; serve.

PIÑA COLADA

Direct from St. Croix, U.S. Virgin Islands, this drink is made with pineapple juice, coconut milk and just a little rum to give it zing!

Makes 6 servings.

   2 cups pineapple juice
   1 cup coconut milk or cream (from 1-pound can)
   1 cup golden or light rum
   2 tablespoons lime juice
   1 cup ice cubes
   Grated nutmeg (optional)

1. Combine pineapple juice, coconut milk, rum, lime juice and ice cubes in large container of electric blender; cover; whirl at high speed for 1 minute, or until ice cubes are crushed.
2. Pour over ice in glasses; sprinkle with nutmeg and garnish with a kabob of lime wedges and cubed pineapple, if you wish. Serve immediately.

SANGRÌA

Fast becoming a favorite party punch, this fruity wine drink is so refreshing.

Makes 25 half-cup servings.

   ½ gallon red wine (2 quarts)
   1 cup orange juice
   4 tablespoons lime juice
   ⅔ cup sugar
   ½ cup Cointreau or Curacao
   2 bottles (12 ounces each) club soda, chilled
   Ice cubes
   Orange slices
   Lime slices

1. Combine wine, orange and lime juices and sugar in a large pitcher; stir until sugar is dissolved; add liqueur; chill.
2. Just before serving, add club soda, ice cubes and orange and lime slices for garnish.

MAPLE-PECAN MILK SHAKE

Flavor booster: Bottled maple-blended syrup.

Makes 4 servings.

   ¼ cup maple-blended syrup
   2 cups skim milk
   ½ pint (1 cup) butter-pecan ice cream

Combine all ingredients in an electric blender container; cover; beat until creamy-smooth. (Or combine all ingredients in a bowl and beat with an electric beater.) Pour into four tall glasses.

APRICOT-BANANA ROYALE

Fresh bananas and ice milk make this summertime smoothie.

Makes 4 servings.

   1 medium-size ripe banana, peeled and sliced
   2 tablespoons sugar
   2 cups milk
   ½ cup bottled apricot-sour cocktail mix
   ½ pint (1 cup) vanilla ice milk

Place banana in container of an electric blender. Add sugar, milk, apricot-sour cocktail mix and ice milk; cover. Beat until creamy-smooth. (Or mash banana in bowl, then beat in remaining ingredients with an electric beater.)
NOTE: If your blender container holds less than 4½ cups, prepare half of mixture at a time.

CALIFORNIA SIPPER

Orange juice and apricot nectar give this fruity drink its golden color.

Makes 6 tall drinks.

   1 can (6 ounces) frozen concentrate for orange juice, thawed
   1 can (12 ounces) apricot nectar
   1 bottle (28 ounces) ginger ale

Combine orange juice and apricot nectar in a tall pitcher. Stir in ginger ale. Pour into 6 tall glasses filled with ice cubes. Add a twist of orange, if you wish, and serve immediately.

SPICED TEA

Cloves and cinnamon lend a spicy pick-up to this summer standard.

Makes 4 one-cup servings.

   Cinnamon sticks
   ½ teaspoon whole cloves
   4 cups water
   6 tea bags
   Lemon slices

1. In a medium-size saucepan, combine 2 three-inch cinnamon sticks, broken in pieces, cloves and water. Heat to boiling; simmer 5 minutes.
2. Strain into a 4-cup measure; add boiling water to make 4 cups. Pour over tea bags in a large pitcher; steep 3 minutes; remove tea bags. Cover; let stand at room temperature until ready to serve.
3. Pour over ice in tall glasses. Garnish each with a long cinnamon stick topped with 2 half slices of lemon, and serve with sugar, if you wish.

KEY LARGO PUNCH

Cool lime and lemon sherbet quench big thirsts.

Makes 10 servings.

- 1 envelope unsweetened lemon-lime instant soft drink mix
- ½ cup water
- 2 bottles (28 ounces each) ginger ale
- 1 pint lemon sherbet
  Lemon and lime slices

Combine soft drink mix and water in a small punch bowl. Stir in ginger ale. Drop small scoop of sherbet into punch. Garnish with lemon and lime slices. Let everyone ladle own servings.

PLANTERS PUNCH

A St. Thomas specialty made with simple ingredients, this tantalizing drink is sure to make your next party unforgettable.

Makes 6 servings.

- ¾ cup orange juice
- ⅓ cup lemon juice
- ¼ cup lime juice
- ⅓ cup superfine sugar
- 1½ cups golden rum
- ¼ cup grenadine
  Chilled carbonated soda water
  Orange slices and maraschino cherries

1. Combine orange juice, lemon juice, lime juice and sugar in small pitcher; stir until sugar dissolves; add rum and grenadine and stir well.
2. To serve: Fill 6 tall glasses with ice cubes; pour punch over, dividing evenly; fill glasses up with soda water. Garnish with orange slices and cherries, if you wish. Serve with a straw.

ORANGE MINT TEA

Cooling mint jelly and orange rind steep along with the tea bags.

Makes 4 one-cup servings.

- ¼ cup mint jelly
- 4 cups water
- 2 teaspoons grated orange rind
- 6 tea bags

In a medium-size saucepan, heat mint jelly and water to boiling. Pour over grated orange rind and tea bags in a large pitcher; steep 3 minutes; remove tea bags. Cover; let stand at room temperature until ready to serve. Pour over ice in tall glasses. Serve with sugar and some lemon wedges.

TROPICAL FRUIT PUNCH

The ice cubes are part of the flavor!

Makes 10 servings.

- 1 can (6 ounces) frozen concentrate for lemonade
- 1 can (48 ounces) cherry-flavor tropical fruit punch
- 1 bottle (28 ounces) lemon-lime flavored carbonated beverage
- ¼ cup light corn syrup

Prepare concentrate for lemonade; freeze in 2 large ice cube trays. Place in punch bowl. Stir in remaining ingredients. Garnish with fresh mint.

CRANBERRY FIZZ

This cooler is one you'll want to take on picnics.

Makes 6 tall drinks.

- 1 bottle (32 ounces) cranberry juice cocktail, chilled
  Fresh mint leaves
- 1 bottle (28 ounces) grapefruit-flavor carbonated beverage
  Lemon peel

Combine cranberry juice cocktail and mint leaves in a tall pitcher filled with ice cubes, and crush leaves slightly. Stir in grapefruit-flavor beverage. Garnish with lemon peel, if you wish.

PINK TEA PUNCH

Instant tea makes this punch a cinch to prepare.

Makes 6 one-cup servings.

- 2 tablespoons instant tea
- 4 cups water
- 1 can (6 ounces) thawed frozen concentrate for raspberry-lemonade
- ½ cup bottled grenadine
- 1 bottle (7 ounces) lemon-lime flavor carbonated beverage

In a large pitcher, blend tea and water; stir in raspberry-lemonade concentrate and grenadine syrup. Just before serving, stir in carbonated beverage. Pour over ice in tall glasses.

ICE CUBE TIP

For a refreshing addition to cold beverages, make fruit-flavored ice cubes. Pour orange juice (or any other favorite) into a sectioned ice cube tray. Freeze and use ice cubes in lemonade or iced tea.

CHOCOLATE-CHERRY COOLER

Need a 4 o'clock pickup? Mix this good-for-you treat in an instant.

Makes 4 servings.

2 cups chocolate milk
1 pint (2 cups) cherry ice cream
1 teaspoon rum flavoring or extract

Combine all ingredients in an electric blender container; cover; beat until creamy-smooth. (Or combine all ingredients in a bowl and beat with an electric beater.) Pour into tall glasses.

ORANGE-PINEAPPLE WHIRL

It's a creamy-smooth blender treat.

Makes 4 servings.

1 can (6 ounces) frozen concentrate for orange-pineapple juice, thawed
2 cups milk
½ pint (1 cup) pineapple ice cream
¼ cup light corn syrup

Place all ingredients in container of electric blender; cover. Beat until creamy-smooth. (Or combine all ingredients in a bowl and beat with an electric beater.) Pour into tall glasses.
NOTE: If your blender container holds less than 4½ cups, prepare half of each mixture at a time.

GRAPEFRUIT FIZZ

Flavor is spicy yet tangy. And it's so refreshing on a hot day.

Makes 6 servings.

1 cup sugar
2 cups water
3 whole allspice
3 whole cloves
1 can (6 ounces) frozen concentrate for grapefruit juice
1 bottle (28 ounces) ginger ale
Green food coloring
Ice cubes
1 lemon, cut in 6 slices
6 maraschino cherries

1. Combine sugar, water, allspice and cloves in a medium-size saucepan; heat to boiling, then simmer 5 minutes. Strain into a pitcher; cool.
2. Stir in frozen grapefruit juice until thawed, then ginger ale and a few drops food coloring.
3. Pour over ice cubes in 6 tall glasses; garnish each with lemon and a maraschino cherry.

CRANBERRY BANANA FLOAT

It's delicious!

Makes 3 servings.

1 cup cranberry juice cocktail
1 ripe banana, peeled and cut up
½ cup milk
¼ cup orange juice
½ pint lemon sherbet

1. Combine cranberry juice, banana, milk and orange juice in container of electric blender; cover; whirl at high speed until smooth, about 1 minute.
2. To serve: Pour into tall glasses; garnish with small scoops of lemon sherbet; serve with straws.

SUMMER SOUPS

TOMATO-CLAM APPETIZER

This soup is not only quick to make—it's also quick to disappear.

Makes 4 servings.

1 can condensed tomato soup
1 cup buttermilk
1 teaspoon Worcestershire sauce
¼ teaspoon salt
1 can (about 8 ounces) minced clams

1. Beat tomato soup with buttermilk, Worcestershire sauce and salt until smooth in a large bowl. Stir in clams and liquid; cover. Chill several hours, or overnight.
2. Ladle into cups or small bowls; garnish each serving with a sprig of parsley, if you wish.

TOMATO FRAPPE

Serve this well-seasoned tomato broth before dinner.

Makes 6 servings.

6 large ripe tomatoes, chopped
1½ teaspoons salt
⅛ teaspoon pepper
⅛ teaspoon ground thyme
3 whole cloves
1 large bay leaf
½ teaspoon onion juice
1 tablespoon lemon juice
Cucumber slices

1. Combine tomatoes, salt, pepper, thyme, cloves, bay leaf and onion juice in a medium-size saucepan. Heat to boiling; cover. Cook for 20 minutes.

2. Press mixture through a fine sieve into a medium-size bowl; stir in lemon juice. Pour into a shallow pan, 9x9x2; freeze several hours, or until firm.
3. Just before serving, break up frozen soup; crush fine in an ice crusher or an electric blender. (Or place pieces in a double-thick transparent bag; crush with a mallet.)
4. Spoon into cups or small bowls; garnish each serving with several cucumber slices.

SUMMER SALMON CHOWDER

Serve this soup with rolls and butter for a delightful luncheon break.

Makes 4 servings.

    1 can condensed cream of celery soup
 1⅓ cups milk
 ⅛ teaspoon pepper
    1 can (about 4 ounces) salmon
 ¼ cup chopped pared cucumber

1. Blend soup, milk and pepper in a medium-size bowl.
2. Remove skin and bones from salmon. Flake salmon; add to soup mixture. Beat vigorously with a rotary or electric beater; stir in cucumber; cover. Chill several hours, or overnight.
3. Ladle into cups or small bowls; garnish each serving with a cucumber slice.

JELLIED LEMON STRATA

Chopped eggs go between the delicious gelatin layers.

Makes 4 servings.

    1 envelope unflavored gelatin
    1 can (about 14 ounces) chicken broth
    1 teaspoon grated lemon rind
    2 tablespoons lemon juice
 ¼ teaspoon salt
    2 hard-cooked eggs, shelled
    2 tablespoons chopped parsley

1. Soften gelatin in 1 cup of the chicken broth in a small saucepan; heat, stirring constantly, until gelatin dissolves; remove from heat.
2. Stir in remaining chicken broth, lemon rind, lemon juice and salt; pour into a baking dish, 9x9x2. Chill several hours.
3. Chop eggs coarsely; toss with the chopped parsley in a small bowl.
4. Cut gelatin mixture lengthwise and crosswise into ¼-inch cubes; spoon half into tall cups or parfait glasses. Top with egg mixture, then remaining gelatin mixture. Garnish each serving with a sprig of fresh parsley, if you wish.

CHILLED BEET SOUP

This blender soup is truly the essence of chopped beets, simmered in a beef broth.

Makes 6 servings.

 ¼ cup (½ stick) butter or margarine
    1 large leek, chopped (¾ cup)
    1 carrot, pared and chopped (½ cup)
    1 parsnip, pared and chopped (½ cup)
 ½ cup chopped celery
    2 tablespoons chopped parsley
    1 medium-size onion, chopped (½ cup)
    2 cups chopped cooked beets
    2 cans (10¼ ounces each) condensed beef broth
 ½ teaspoon salt
 ⅛ teaspoon pepper
 ¼ cup lemon juice
    1 cup (½ pint) dairy sour cream

1. Melt butter or margarine in a large saucepan; sauté leek, carrot, parsnip, celery, parsley and onion until almost tender. Add the cooked beets and beef broth; cover.
2. Bring to boiling; lower heat; cover; simmer 10 minutes. Remove from heat; cool slightly.
3. Pour part of the soup at a time into container of electric blender; cover. Whirl until smooth. (Or purée through sieve or food mill.) Pour into a large bowl. Stir in salt, pepper and lemon juice. Chill at least 4 hours.
4. Pour into chilled serving bowl. Garnish with sour cream. Sprinkle with chopped chives, if you wish. Serve icy cold.

HOT-WEATHER CHEDDAR SOUP

Here's an easy-to-make cooler that uses process-cheese spread and canned soup as main ingredients. It's shown on page 113.

Makes 6 to 8 servings.

    2 cans condensed cream of celery soup
    1 cup water
    1 cup milk
    1 jar (8 ounces) process Cheddar cheese spread
    1 cup light cream or table cream
 ¼ teaspoon pepper

1. Blend celery soup, water and milk in a medium-size saucepan. Heat slowly, stirring several times, to boiling; remove from heat.
2. Stir in cheese until blended, then cream and pepper. Pour into a medium-size bowl; cover. Chill several hours, or overnight.
3. Ladle into cups or small bowls. Garnish each serving with a spoonful of unsweetened whipped cream, shredded Cheddar cheese and a dash of paprika, if you wish. Serve immediately.

PLUM CHILLER

Serve soup for a breakfast change-of-pace.

Makes 8 servings.

  2 pounds ripe red plums
  ¾ cup sugar
  ¼ teaspoon grated orange rind
  1 two-inch piece stick cinnamon
  4 cups water
  3 tablespoons quick-cooking tapioca

1. Wash plums; halve and pit. Combine with sugar, orange peel, cinnamon stick and water in a large saucepan. Heat to boiling, then simmer 20 minutes, or until plums are very soft; remove cinnamon stick.
2. Press mixture through a coarse sieve into a bowl; return to saucepan; stir in tapioca.
3. Heat, stirring constantly, to a full rolling boil, then simmer, stirring several times, 10 minutes, or until mixture thickens slightly. Pour into a medium-size bowl; cover. Chill several hours, or overnight in the refrigerator.
4. Ladle into cups or small bowls; float a thin slice of orange on each serving, if you wish.

CHILLED WATERCRESS SOUP

Prepare this early in the day and let the refrigerator take over until it's icy cold.

Makes 6 servings.

  1 large bunch watercress
  6 tablespoons (¾ stick) butter or margarine
  4 large leeks, chopped (2 cups)
  3 tablespoons flour
  3 envelopes or teaspoons instant chicken broth
  1 teaspoon salt
  1 teaspoon leaf basil, crumbled
  3 cups water
  2 cups plain yogurt

1. Wash and pick over watercress. Remove stems and measure leaves. (You should have 2 cups.)
2. Melt butter or margarine in a large heavy saucepan; sauté leeks and watercress just until wilted, but do not allow to brown.
3. Stir in flour, instant chicken broth, salt and basil. Cook, stirring constantly, until mixture bubbles, about 1 minute; stir in water. Heat slowly to boiling, lower heat; cover; simmer 15 minutes. Remove saucepan from heat; cool.
4. Pour part of the soup at a time into container of electric blender; cover. Whirl until smooth.
5. Pour into a large bowl. Stir in yogurt. Cover; chill at least 4 hours.
6. Pour into chilled serving bowl. Garnish with sprigs of watercress and slices of radish, if you wish. Serve while soup is still icy cold.

CUCUMBER CUP

Dill-seasoned and delicious.

Makes 4 servings.

  1 envelope unflavored gelatin
  1½ cups water
  1 envelope instant chicken broth or 1 teaspoon granulated chicken bouillon
  1 small onion, peeled and grated
  2 tablespoons lemon juice
  2 tablespoons fresh chopped dill
  ¼ teaspoon salt
  ⅛ teaspoon pepper
  1 medium-size cucumber
  2 teaspoons dairy sour cream

1. Soften gelatin in water in a small saucepan. Heat, stirring constantly, until gelatin dissolves; remove from heat.
2. Stir in chicken broth until dissolved, then onion, lemon juice, dill, salt and pepper; pour into a medium-size bowl. Chill 30 minutes, or until as thick as unbeaten egg white.
3. While gelatin mixture chills, pare cucumber; quarter lengthwise and scoop out seeds; dice cucumber fine. Fold into thickened gelatin mixture. Chill again until firm.
4. Spoon into cups or small bowls; top each with ½ teaspoon sour cream and a sprig of dill.

CHILLED ASPARAGUS SOUP

Top this cooler with a dollop of sour cream, and a sprig of parsley.

Makes 8 servings.

  2 large leeks, chopped (1 cup)
  ¼ cup (½ stick) butter or margarine
  3 envelopes or teaspoons instant chicken broth
  3 cups water
  2 packages (10 ounces each) frozen asparagus pieces
  ¼ cup flour
  1 teaspoon salt
  ⅛ teaspoon pepper
  2 cups light cream

1. Sauté leeks in butter or margarine until soft in a large skillet.
2. Combine chicken broth and water in a large saucepan; bring to boiling; add asparagus and cook 5 minutes. Remove and add to leeks.
3. Stir flour into the asparagus and leeks until absorbed; add chicken broth, salt and pepper. Simmer 3 minutes.
4. Pour part of the soup at a time into container of electric blender; cover. Whirl until smooth. (Or purée through sieve or food mill.)
5. Pour into a large bowl; stir in light cream;

cover bowl. Chill at least 4 hours, or overnight.
6. Pour into chilled serving bowl. Garnish with lightly salted whipped cream and parsley, if you wish. Serve icy cold.

CREAMY CHILLED ONION SOUP

Here's a hot weather switch on a popular French classic.

Makes 8 servings.

    4 large onions, chopped (4 cups)
 ¼ teaspoon leaf rosemary, crumbled
    6 tablespoons (¾ stick) butter or margarine
    2 cans (13¾ ounces each) chicken broth
    2 egg yolks
    1 cup light cream
    2 teaspoons lemon juice
    1 teaspoon salt
 ¼ teaspoon white pepper

1. Sauté onion and rosemary in butter or margarine until very soft in a large heavy saucepan, but do not allow onions to brown. Remove from heat and cool.
2. Pour part of the onion mixture into container of electric blender; cover. Whirl until smooth. (Or purée through a sieve or food mill.)
3. Combine purée with chicken broth in same saucepan. Heat to boiling; lower heat; simmer for about 5 minutes.
4. Beat egg yolks slightly in small bowl; beat in cream until smooth. Beat egg-cream mixture slowly into remaining mixture in saucepan. Cook, stirring constantly, 1 minute.
5. Remove from heat; add lemon juice, salt and pepper. Pour into a large bowl. Cover; chill at least 4 hours.
6. Pour into chilled serving bowl. Garnish with sprigs of parsley, if you wish. Serve icy cold.

CHILLED CURRIED CARROT SOUP

It has a smooth, exotic taste!

Makes 6 to 8 servings.

 ¼ cup (½ stick) butter or margarine
    1 large onion, chopped (1 cup)
    1 package (1 pound) carrots, pared and sliced (3 cups)
 ¾ teaspoon curry powder
    1 thin strip lemon peel
    1 can condensed chicken broth
 1½ teaspoons salt
 ¼ teaspoon pepper
    1 cup light cream

1. Melt butter or margarine in a large saucepan; sauté onion and carrots until onion is tender, about 5 minutes. Add curry powder and lemon peel; cook 3 minutes longer.
2. Pour chicken broth into a quart measure; add water to make a quart of liquid; add to onion-carrot mixture. Bring to boiling; lower heat; cover; simmer about 20 minutes, or until carrots are tender. Remove from heat; cool slightly.
3. Pour part of the soup at a time into container of electric blender; cover. Whirl until smooth. (Or purée through sieve or food mill.)
4. Pour into a large bowl. Stir in salt, pepper and cream. Cover; chill at least 4 hours.
5. Pour into chilled serving bowl. Garnish with thin slices of carrot and green onion, if you wish. Serve icy cold.

CHILLED LOBSTER BISQUE

This smooth soup takes on a heavenly flavor with clam broth, dry white wine and light cream.

Makes 8 servings.

    1 package (8 ounces) frozen lobster tails
    3 tablespoons butter or margarine
    2 tablespoons vegetable oil
    2 large leeks, chopped (1 cup)
    1 large onion, chopped (1 cup)
    4 large carrots, chopped (2 cups)
    1 clove of garlic, minced
 ¼ cup Cognac
    2 cups dry white wine
    2 bottles (8 ounces each) clam broth
 1½ teaspoons salt
 ½ teaspoon paprika
    2 cups light cream
      Watercress

1. Sauté lobster tails in butter or margarine and vegetable oil in a large heavy saucepan until lobsters turn a bright red. Remove from saucepan; reserve for next step.
2. Sauté leeks, onion, carrots and garlic in same pan until very soft and golden, about 10 minutes. Return lobster tails to saucepan. Heat Cognac in a small metal cup; pour over lobsters and ignite carefully with a long match. Stir until flames die.
3. Add wine, clam broth, salt and paprika. Heat slowly to boiling; lower heat; cover; simmer 15 minutes. Remove saucepan from heat; cool.
4. Remove lobster tails from soup; cool. Remove meat from tails in one piece and slice. Reserve some for garnish.
5. Pour part of the soup at a time into container of electric blender; add part of the lobster; cover. Whirl until smooth. (Or purée through sieve or food mill.)
6. Pour into a large bowl. Stir in cream. Cover; chill at least 4 hours.
7. Pour into chilled serving bowl. Garnish with reserved lobster slices and sprigs of watercress, if you wish. Serve while soup is still icy cold.

CHILLED SENEGALESE SOUP

This is a delicious blend of chicken, tart apple, curry and light cream.

Makes 8 servings.

    4 **tablespoons (½ stick) butter or margarine**
    1 **large onion, chopped (1 cup)**
    1 **medium-size tart apple, pared, quartered, cored and chopped**
    2 **teaspoons curry powder**
    1 **whole chicken breast, split (12 ounces)**
    ¼ **cup flour**
    1 **teaspoon salt**
    1 **bay leaf**
    4 **cups water**
    1 **cup light cream**

1. Melt 2 tablespoons of the butter or margarine in a large heavy saucepan; sauté onion and chopped apple until soft; stir in curry powder; cook for 1 minute; remove mixture; reserve. Add remaining butter or margarine to saucepan; sauté chicken 5 minutes on each side; stir in flour; cook until bubbly; add salt, bay leaf and water.
2. Heat slowly to boiling; lower heat; cover; simmer 30 minutes. Remove saucepan from heat and allow to cool.
3. Remove chicken and bay leaf from soup. Skin and bone chicken; chop.
4. Pour part of the soup at a time into container of electric blender; add part of the chicken; cover. Whirl until smooth. (Or purée through sieve or food mill.)
5. Pour into a large bowl. Stir in cream. Cover; chill at least 4 hours.
6. Pour into chilled serving bowl. Garnish with slivers of red apple and mint leaves, if you wish. Serve icy cold.

FROSTY FISH BISQUE

Make this one in your blender.

Makes 8 servings.

    1 **package (1 pound) frozen perch fillets**
    1 **teaspoon seasoned salt**
    1 **bay leaf**
    2 **slices lemon**
    1 **cup water**
    2 **cans frozen condensed cream of potato soup, thawed slightly**
    2 **cups milk**
    1 **cup light cream or table cream**

1. Combine frozen fish, seasoned salt, bay leaf, lemon slices and water in a medium-size frying pan. Heat to boiling; cover. Simmer 10 minutes, or until fish flakes easily; remove bay leaf and lemon slices from cooking liquid in frying pan.
2. Break fish into pieces; place fish and cooking liquid in an electric-blender container; cover. Beat until smooth; pour into a large bowl. (If you do not have a blender, flake fish very fine with a fork, then mix with cooking liquid. Soup won't be as smooth but will taste just as good.)
3. While fish cooks, combine potato soup with 1 cup of milk in a medium-size saucepan; heat, stirring several times; just to boiling. Cool slightly; pour into an electric blender container; cover. Beat until smooth. Stir into fish mixture with remaining 1 cup milk and cream; cover. Chill several hours, or overnight.
4. Ladle into cups or small bowls; float a thin green-pepper ring and several fish-shape crackers on each serving, if you wish.

CREAMY SPINACH COOLER

Evaporated milk is the "cream" in this hot-weather soup.

Makes 6 servings.

    1 **package (10 ounces) frozen chopped spinach**
    2 **tablespoons butter or margarine**
    3 **tablespoons flour**
    1 **envelope instant chicken broth or 1 teaspoon granulated chicken bouillon**
    ½ **teaspoon salt**
    ⅛ **teaspoon pepper**
    2 **cups milk**
    1 **large can evaporated milk**
    1 **small onion, choppen fine (¼ cup)**
    1 **tablespoon lemon juice**

1. Unwrap spinach; let stand at room temperature while making sauce.
2. Melt butter or margarine in a medium-size saucepan; stir in flour, chicken broth, salt and pepper; cook, stirring constantly, until bubbly. Stir in milk and evaporated milk; continue cooking and stirring until sauce thickens and boils 1 minute. Remove from heat.
3. Cut partly thawed spinach into ½-inch pieces; stir into hot sauce until completely thawed. Stir in onion and lemon juice. (If you prefer a smoother mixture, pour soup into an electric blender container; cover. Beat until smooth.) Pour soup into a large bowl; cover. Chill in the refrigerator several hours, or overnight.
4. Ladle into cups or small bowls. Garnish each serving with a sprig of watercress, if you wish.

Cold soups rescue wilted palates any time of day. Clockwise from top: Tomato Frappé, Plum Chiller, Creamy Spinach Cooler, Jellied Lemon Strata, Frosty Fish Bisque, Hot-Weather Cheddar Soup and Cucumber Cup. The recipes for these delightful chilled soups are included in this chapter.

8

JUST DESSERTS

"Curlylocks, Curlylocks,
Wilt thou be mine?
Thou shalt not wash dishes
Nor yet feed the swine,
But sit on a cushion
And sew a fine seam
And feed upon strawberries,
sugar and cream."
CURLYLOCKS/ANONYMOUS

In the nursery rhyme above, Curlylocks might have been won over by the strawberries her suitor offered. But we can guarantee you'll succumb to the selection of desserts in this chapter. They include fruit desserts, cakes, pies, strudels, mousses and crepes. In addition, you'll find a special section on ice cream and sherbet desserts, complete with step-by-step directions for making homemade flavors. Before you turn the page, however, feast your eyes on our Peach Melba Finale at left. It's made with peach ice cream, peach halves, whipped cream and raspberry sauce—and all the work can be done ahead of time. What, we ask, could be more just?

SANGRÍA ORANGE CUPS

A popular summer beverage becomes a tangy cool dessert.

Makes 6 servings.

3 large oranges
1¾ cups sangría or 1¾ cups red wine
1 package (3 ounces) orange-flavor gelatin

1. Mark a guideline, lengthwise, around middle of each orange with the tip of paring knife. Then make even scallop cuts into orange above and below line, all the way around. Pull halves apart.
2. Remove orange sections from orange halves with a grapefruit knife and reserve; scoop shells clean with a large spoon.
3. Heat sangría or red wine, just to boiling, in a small saucepan; stir in orange gelatin until dissolved; pour into a bowl.
4. Chill 30 minutes, or until mixture is beginning to thicken. Fold in orange sections and any orange juice into gelatin. Chill 2 hours.
5. Put orange shells into sherbet glasses. Spoon gelatin mixture into shells. Chill.

STRAWBERRY CREAM PIE

Here's one of summer's favorite make-ahead pies.

Bake shell at 450° for 12 minutes.
Makes 1 nine-inch pie.

1 frozen ready-to-bake 9-inch piecrust
⅔ cup sugar
4 tablespoons cornstarch
3 tablespoons flour
½ teaspoon salt
2½ cups milk
2 eggs
2 tablespoons butter or margarine
1 teaspoon vanilla
½ teaspoon orange extract
2 cups (1 pint) strawberries
½ cup cream for whipping

1. Thaw piecrust, following label directions; place in a 9-inch pie plate; reflute edge to make slightly higher. Prick shell well all over with a fork.
2. Bake in very hot oven (450°) 12 minutes, or until the crust is golden; cool completely in pie plate on a wire rack.
3. Mix sugar, cornstarch, flour and salt in the top of a double boiler; stir in milk. Cook, stirring often, over simmering water until mixture thickens; cover. Cook 15 minutes longer, or until mixture mounds softly on spoon; remove from heat.
4. Beat eggs slightly in a small bowl; slowly blend in about ½ cup of the hot cornstarch mixture; slowly stir back into remaining mixture in double boiler. Cook, stirring constantly, over simmering water 3 minutes; remove from heat. Stir in butter or margarine until melted, then vanilla and orange extract. Pour into a medium-size bowl; cover. Cool completely.
5. Wash strawberries; reserve half for topping. Hull remainder and halve.
6. Beat cream until stiff in a small bowl; fold into cooled cornstarch mixture. Pour half into prepared pastry shell; place halved strawberries in a single layer on top; spoon in remaining filling. Chill at least 3 hours, or until firm enough to cut.
7. Just before serving, halve reserved berries; arrange, cut side down, on pie.

SWEDISH PANCAKES

These light little cakes are irresistible served piping hot with fruity toppings. (Shown on page 116.)

Makes 12 servings.

1¼ cups sifted all-purpose flour
2 tablespoons sugar
½ teaspoon salt
3 eggs
3 cups milk
4 tablespoons (½ stick) butter or margarine, melted
Cream-style cottage cheese (optional)
Preserved lingonberries, cranberry relish, apricot preserves or orange sections

1. Sift flour, sugar and salt onto wax paper. Beat eggs until light in a medium-size bowl; add dry ingredients; blend until smooth. Stir in milk to make a thin batter.
2. Cover; let stand at room temperature 1 hour.
3. Heat a large heavy skillet or a Swedish pancake pan over low heat. Test temperature by sprinkling on a few drops of water; when drops bounce about, temperature is right. Lightly grease pan with butter or margarine.
4. Use 1 to 2 tablespoons of batter for each pancake; bake until top appears dry and underside is golden; turn, lightly brown other side. Repeat, lightly greasing skillet before each baking. You will have about 48 pancakes.
5. Place on heated serving platter and keep warm while making the rest of the pancakes. Fill with a small amount of cottage cheese and top with lingonberries, cranberry relish, apricot preserves, fresh orange sections or the following topping:
Orange Butter Topping: Beat 1 stick (½ cup) butter or margarine with ½ teaspoon grated orange rind, 1 tablespoon orange juice and 1 teaspoon sugar until mixture is light and fluffy.

Swedish Pancakes, left, are served with a cottage cheese filling, orange sections and three kinds of jam. The recipe for this dessert is at right.

MELON BASKET MEDLEY

This is a beautiful and practical dessert or salad for a big buffet. (Shown on page 62.)

Makes 12 servings.

1 **elongated watermelon, weighing about 15 pounds and measuring about 15 inches in length**
1 **large honeydew melon**
1 **large cantaloupe melon**
Fresh mint
Lemon and lime slices

1. Trim a thin slice from watermelon, if needed, so it will stand flat (as shown in photograph on page 62). Using wood picks, mark off a 1½-inch wide strip across center of melon for basket handle; make deep cuts on both sides of handle and also 1 inch in from both ends, halfway through melon. Cut in from sides, being careful not to cut through handle and end pieces. Remove the 2 pieces from top.
2. Cut watermelon meat from under handle. Scoop out meat from watermelon with large melon-ball cutter. Cut balls from honeydew and cantaloupe and place in separate bowls.
3. Arrange watermelon balls in basket, top with honeydew and cantaloupe as pictured. Garnish with sprigs of mint and lemon and lime slices.

ORANGE CHARLOTTE

A citrus-cool dessert, and so little bother to make. It's really a smooth Bavarian cream in a shell.

Makes 8 servings.

1 **package (3 ounces) ladyfingers**
3 **tablespoons Curacao (optional)**
2 **envelopes unflavored gelatin**
½ **cup sugar**
4 **eggs, separated**
1 **can (6 ounces) frozen concentrate for orange juice, thawed**
1¼ **cups water**
1 **cup heavy cream**

1. Separate ladyfingers; place on a cooky sheet; drizzle part of the Curacao over; let stand.
2. Combine gelatin and ¼ cup of the sugar in a heavy saucepan; beat in egg yolks, orange juice concentrate and water until smooth.
3. Cook over medium heat, stirring constantly, until mixture thickens and just coats spoon. Pour mixture into a large bowl; stir in remaining Curacao. Chill 30 minutes, or until slightly thickened.
4. While gelatin chills, stand ladyfingers around edge of an 8-inch springform pan, and in the bottom of the pan, arrange remaining ladyfingers.
5. Beat egg whites until foamy-white and double

in volume in a medium-size bowl; beat in remaining ¼ cup sugar, 1 tablespoon at a time, until meringue forms soft peaks. Beat heavy cream until stiff in a small bowl.
6. Fold whipped cream, then meringue into thickened gelatin mixture until no streaks of white remain. Spoon into prepared pan, swirling top with spoon. Chill 4 hours, or until firm.
7. To serve: Release spring and carefully lift off side of pan; slide dessert on its metal base, onto a serving plate. Garnish with whipped cream and thin orange slices, if you wish.

ZABAGLIONE

Fresh fruit is the perfect accompaniment for this fluffy meringue.

Makes 8 servings.

3 **egg yolks**
¼ **cup sugar**
⅓ **cup cream sherry or ⅓ cup Marsala wine**
Strawberries, peaches or apricots

1. Beat egg yolks in the top of a double boiler (glass is best) until thick and lemon-colored.
2. Beat in sugar, gradually, until mixture is very thick and light in color. Beat in wine slowly.
3. Place top of double boiler over simmering water. (If using a metal double boiler, do not allow the water to touch the bottom of the pan.)
4. Beat at high speed for 5 minutes, or until mixture has thickened and become very fluffy.
5. Spoon over fruit of your choice and serve while mixture is still warm.

FROSTY FRUIT CUP

Frozen peaches combined with quick-setting gelatin give you a speedy molded fruit dessert.

Makes 6 servings.

2 **cups seedless green grapes, halved**
1 **package (10 ounces) frozen peaches in quick-thaw pouch**
¾ **cup apple juice**
1 **package (3 ounces) orange-flavor gelatin**
6 **to 8 ice cubes**
2 **tablespoons dairy sour cream**

1. Combine grapes and peach slices in a large bowl; break up peaches; mix.
2. Heat apple juice to boiling in a small saucepan; combine with orange gelatin in container of electric blender; whirl at low speed until dissolved. Add ice cubes and whirl at medium to high speed until creamy-thick and foamy; blend in sour cream.
3. Spoon fruit into individual dessert dishes and pour the orange-gelatin mixture over fruit. Chill.

PINEAPPLE CROWN

Shown on page 62, this delightful fruit boat can be served as a salad or as a light dessert.

Makes 6 servings.

- 1 large pineapple
- 2 cups (1 pint) strawberries
- 2 medium-size seedless oranges
- 1 cup seedless green grapes
- 1 banana, sliced
- ½ cup dairy sour cream
- ½ cup mayonnaise or salad dressing
- ¼ cup 10X (confectioners' powdered) sugar

1. Lay pineapple on its side on cutting board; cut in half lengthwise with a sharp knife, cutting through leafy crown. Remove core; cut fruit away from rind in as large pieces as possible, leaving two ¼- to ½-inch shells. Slice pineapple pieces into bite-size chunks; place in a large bowl.
2. Wash, hull and halve strawberries. Pare and section 1 of the oranges. Add strawberries, orange sections, grapes and banana to pineapple; toss.
3. Grate 1 teaspoon rind from remaining orange, then squeeze 2 tablespoons juice; blend both with sour cream, mayonnaise or salad dressing, and 10X sugar in a small bowl.
4. To serve: Arrange pineapple shells on a large serving plate; spoon fruit mixture into shells. Serve dressing separately.

CHOCO-RASPBERRY ICEBOX CAKE

An old favorite with a new twist. Chill it awhile to let the flavors mellow and make slicing neat.

Makes 8 servings.

- ½ cup raspberry preserves
- 2 tablespoons orange-flavored liqueur
- 2 packages (2 ounces each) whipped topping mix
- 1 cup cold milk
- 2 teaspoons vanilla
- 1 package (8½ ounces) chocolate wafers

1. Combine preserves and orange-flavored liqueur in a cup. Prepare whipped topping mix with milk and vanilla, following label directions.
2. Spread raspberry mixture on one side of a chocolate wafer and whipped topping on second side. Make 10 stacks of cookies until all are coated.
3. Turn the first cooky stack on its side on serving tray; spread last cooky with whipped topping and press on the next stack. Repeat until all cookies are joined in a long roll.
4. Frost cake generously with whipped topping. Fit a pastry bag with a fancy tip. Fill bag with remaining whipped topping. Pipe a double row of swirls down the center of cake. Pipe remaining whipped topping around sides and bottom of cake. Carefully spoon remaining raspberry preserves down the top of frosted cake.
5. Chill at least 3 hours. To serve: Cut cake into thin diagonal slices.

CHOCOLATE MOUSSE

Let your electric blender make this fabulous dessert in minutes!

Makes 6 servings.

- ⅓ cup very hot coffee
- 1 package (6 ounces) semisweet chocolate pieces
- 4 egg yolks
- 2 tablespoons creme de cacao liqueur
- 4 egg whites
  Whipped cream
  Chopped pistachio nuts

1. Combine hot coffee and chocolate pieces in the container of an electric blender. Cover blender; whirl at high speed until the mixture is very smooth, about 30 seconds.
2. Add egg yolks and liqueur. Cover blender; whirl at high speed 30 seconds, or until the mixture is thick and smooth.
3. Beat egg whites until stiff in a small bowl. Pour chocolate mixture over egg whites and fold in until no streaks of white remain. Pour into a serving bowl. Chill at least 1 hour.
4. To serve: Garnish top of mousse with whipped cream and chopped nuts.

QUICK APPLE STRUDEL

Makes 1 large strudel.

- 1 can (1 pound, 5 ounces) prepared apple pie filling
- ¼ cup golden seedless raisins
- 1 teaspoon grated lemon rind
- ⅛ teaspoon ground cinnamon
- ⅛ teaspoon ground nutmeg
- 1 package (10 ounces) frozen ready-to-bake puff pastry shells
- ¼ cup packaged bread crumbs
- 1 tablespoon sugar
  Confectioner's sugar

1. Place apple pie filling in a small bowl. With a knife, using a chopping motion against the sides of the bowl, cut apple slices into very small pieces.
2. Add raisins, lemon rind, cinnamon and nutmeg.
3. Prepare pastry shells according to directions for Quick Cherry Strudel, page 120, eliminating almonds, and sprinkling pastry with 1 tablespoon sugar instead of 2, as called for in Cherry Strudel. To serve, dust with confectioner's sugar.

GREAT GRANDMA'S SOFT GINGER CAKE

An old English recipe that moved west across America with the wagon trains. It was economical a hundred years ago and it's economical today.

Bake at 350° for 30 minutes.
Makes 12 servings.

2½ cups sifted all-purpose flour
1¾ teaspoon baking soda
 1 teaspoon ground ginger
 1 teaspoon ground cinnamon
 ¼ teaspoon ground cloves
 ¼ teaspoon salt
 1 cup sugar
 ½ cup vegetable shortening
 1 cup molasses
 1 cup boiling water
 2 eggs, well-beaten

1. Sift together flour, soda, spices and salt and set aside for Step 3.
2. Cream sugar with shortening and molasses until well-blended.
3. Add sifted dry ingredients to creamed mixture alternately with boiling water, beginning and ending with dry ingredients. Stir in eggs.
4. Pour into a well-greased 13x9x2-inch baking pan and bake in a moderate oven (350°) for 30 minutes, or until center springs back when lightly pressed with fingertip. Cool upright in pan to room temperature. Cut in large squares and serve.

QUICK CHERRY STRUDEL

Time of preparation is cut to a minimum for this elegant strudel, when convenient, frozen puff pastry and prepared pie filling are used.

Makes 1 large strudel.

 1 package (10 ounces) frozen ready-to-bake puff pastry shells
 1 can (1 pound, 5 ounces) prepared cherry pie filling
 2 teaspoons grated lemon rind
 ¼ cup packaged bread crumbs
 1 tablespoon milk
 ¼ cup sliced unblanched almonds
 2 tablespoons sugar

1. Preheat oven to 450°.
2. Let pastry shells soften at room temperature for about 20 to 30 minutes.
3. Combine cherry pie filling and lemon rind in a small bowl; reserve.
4. On a *cloth-lined, well-floured board,* overlap pastry shells in a straight line. Using a *floured stockinette covered* rolling pin, press down onto the pastry shells. (*Note:* You may use a floured rolling pin without the stockinette, but flour the

rolling pin frequently to prevent the pastry shells from sticking.) Roll out from center of shells to a 16x22-inch rectangle; do not tear pastry.
5. Sprinkle pastry with bread crumbs.
6. Spoon cherry pie filling down length of pastry closest to you into a 2-inch strip and within 2 inches of edges. Fold in sides, keep filling in.
7. Using the pastry cloth, grasp at both ends and gently lift the cloth up and let the strudel roll itself up. Carefully slide onto a cooky sheet, keeping seam down; form into a horseshoe shape.
8. Brush top generously with milk; sprinkle on almond slices, pressing well in order to keep in place. Then sprinkle with sugar.
9. Lower oven heat from 450° to 400° and bake strudel 25 minutes, or until golden brown; let cool on baking sheet 10 minutes. Serve warm.

RHUBARB COMPOTE

Whipped cream and spices add a touch of elegance to fresh rhubarb.

Makes 8 servings.

 2 pounds fresh rhubarb
 2 cups sugar (for rhubarb)
 ½ teaspoon ground cardamom
 2 cups water (for rhubarb)
 6 tablespoons cornstarch
 ¾ cup cold water
 2 teaspoons vanilla
 1 cup cream for whipping
 2 tablespoons sugar (for topping)
   Fresh mint

1. Trim rhubarb and cut into ½-inch pieces. Combine with 2 cups sugar, cardamom and 2 cups water in a large saucepan.
2. Heat slowly to boiling; cover; reduce heat. Simmer 10 minutes, or until rhubarb is tender.
3. Blend cornstarch and ¾ cup cold water to make a smooth paste in a small bowl. Stir into simmering rhubarb. Cook, stirring constantly, until mixture thickens and bubbles 1 minute. Remove from heat; stir in 1 teaspoon of the vanilla. Chill completely.
4. Beat cream with 2 tablespoons sugar and remaining vanilla until stiff in a small bowl.
5. Pour chilled rhubarb into a glass bowl. Pipe whipped cream through pastry bag with fancy tip, or drop by spoonfuls onto rhubarb and garnish with mint leaves, if you wish.

LEFTOVER TIP

A good way to use up stale pound or angel cake: Break into bite-size pieces and place in a medium-size bowl. Drizzle lightly with sweet sherry, port or Madeira. Stir in vanilla pudding (made from a mix), then serve, topping each portion with a dollop of raspberry or strawberry jam.

The Carefree Summer Ice Cream Guide

HOW TO MAKE ICE CREAM IN AN ELECTRIC OR NON-ELECTRIC ICE CREAM FREEZER

Follow the directions below when using an ice cream freezer for the homemade ice cream and sherbet recipes in this section. If your ice cream freezer is smaller than the 4-, 5- or 6-quart sizes called for in the recipes, freeze half the mixture at a time.

1. Wash the ice cream can, dasher and cover in hot sudsy water, rinse thoroughly in hot water and then in cold water. Dry well.
2. Crush ice cubes by pounding in a canvas bag with the flat of a hammer or a wooden mallet or use an ice crusher if you have one. (You will need between 6 and 10 trays of ice to make 16 to 20 cups of crushed ice. Empty ice trays a day or so ahead and store in plastic bags for a good supply.) Or buy the ice cubes from your supermarket or neighborhood ice dealer.
3. Measure out 2½ cups rock salt or 1½ cups table salt. (The rock salt will give a smoother ice cream because the ice-and-water will be colder.)
4. Pour chilled mixture into freezer can. Insert dasher; place can in freezer bucket. Put crank unit in place, following manufacturer's directions.
5. Start machine cranking, either electrically or by hand. Spread a 2-inch depth of crushed ice in bottom of bucket. Add about ¼ cup rock salt; continue layering in the same proportions of crushed ice and rock salt until bucket is filled. (You will need about 16 cups crushed ice and 2½ cups rock salt to fill the bucket of the 4-quart ice cream maker. If using table salt, layer with 3 tablespoons salt to each 2-inch depth crushed ice.) Add 1 cup of water to start melting of ice.
6. Check the drain hold in the bucket occasionally to be sure that it has not been obstructed, so that excess water will drain out of bucket. Add 4 cups crushed ice and ¼ cup rock salt as needed to keep bucket well packed with this mixture.
7. Allow ice cream to churn until motor slows or stops, or when hand model becomes difficult to turn. Disconnect electric model as soon as it stops, to prevent motor damage. (Ice cream mixture will be the consistency of whipped cream and sherbet will be a mushy consistency.)
8. Spoon ice cream or sherbet into plastic freezer containers, allowing a ½-inch space at the top of the container for expansion; cover. Freeze ice cream or sherbet until firm, at least 2 hours.

HOW TO UNMOLD SHERBET

Run a thin-bladed knife around edge of mold or bowl. Invert mold onto a chilled serving plate. Moisten a clean cloth under hot running water; wring out as well as possible; press cloth against side of mold. Continue with hot cloths until sherbet melts just enough for mold to loosen; lift off mold. Return sherbet to freezer until serving time.

ALL-AMERICAN VANILLA ICE CREAM

The all-time favorite among ice cream lovers, delicious by itself and extra special when served with an ice cream topping.

Makes about 2 quarts.

　1½　cups sugar
　¼　cup flour
　　　Dash of salt
　2　cups milk
　4　eggs, slightly beaten
　1　quart (4 cups) heavy cream
　2　tablespoons vanilla

1. Combine sugar, flour and salt in a large saucepan; stir in milk. Cook, stirring constantly, over medium heat, until mixture bubbles 1 minute.
2. Stir half the hot mixture slowly into beaten eggs in a medium-size bowl; stir back into remaining mixture in pan. Cook, stirring, 1 minute.
3. Pour into a large bowl; stir in cream and vanilla. Chill at least 2 hours.
4. Pour mixture into a 4-to-6-quart freezer can; freeze, following directions above.
5. Pack in plastic containers; freeze until firm.

APRICOT ICE CREAM

Sweet-tart tang of apricots, blended with rich custard, freezes velvet soft.

Makes about 2 quarts.

　1　package (8 ounces) dried apricots
　1½　cups water
　1¾　cups sugar
　¼　cup flour
　　　Dash of salt
　1½　cups milk
　4　eggs, slightly beaten
　1　quart (4 cups) heavy cream
　1　tablespoon vanilla

1. Cover apricots with water in a small saucepan. Heat to boiling. Cover saucepan and remove from heat. Allow to stand 1 hour, or until almost all of the water has been absorbed. Pour apricots and liquid into container of electric blender; whirl until puréed, or press through sieve or food mill.
2. Combine sugar, flour and salt in a large saucepan; stir in milk. Cook, stirring constantly, over medium heat, until mixture thickens and bubbles 1 minute. Remove from heat.
3. Stir half of the mixture slowly into beaten eggs in a bowl; stir back into remaining mixture in pan. Cook, stirring constantly, 1 minute.
4. Pour into a large bowl; cool; stir in apricot purée, cream and vanilla. Chill.
5. Pour mixture into a 4-to-6-quart freezer can; freeze, following directions at left.
6. Pack in plastic containers; freeze until firm.

FRESH STRAWBERRY ICE CREAM

Juicy red strawberries are deep-frozen in this creamy custard mixture.

Makes about 2 quarts.

1¼ cups sugar
    Dash of salt
3 tablespoons flour
1½ cups milk
3 eggs, slightly beaten
3 cups heavy cream
1 pint (2 cups) strawberries, washed and hulled
    Few drops red food coloring

1. Combine 1 cup of the sugar, salt and flour in a medium-size saucepan; add milk gradually. Cook over medium heat, stirring, until mixture thickens and bubbles. Remove from heat.
2. Stir half the mixture slowly into beaten eggs in a medium-size bowl; stir back into remaining mixture in saucepan. Cook, stirring constantly, 1 minute. Remove from heat; pour into a large bowl; cool; stir in cream. Chill.
3. Mash strawberries with a potato masher or a fork in a large bowl; stir in remaining ¼ cup sugar. Blend strawberries into chilled mixture; add food coloring for a deeper pink, if you wish.
4. Pour mixture into a 4-to-6-quart freezer can; freeze, following directions on page 122. Pack in plastic containers; freeze until firm.

MINT CHOCOLATE CHIP ICE CREAM

Mint-cool and speckled with nuggets of chocolate.

Makes 2 quarts.

1½ cups sugar
¼ cup flour
    Dash of salt
2 cups milk
4 eggs, slightly beaten
1 quart (4 cups) heavy cream
¾ teaspoon green food coloring
2 teaspoons peppermint extract
1 square semisweet chocolate, finely chopped

1. Combine sugar, flour and salt in a medium-size saucepan; add milk gradually. Cook over medium heat, stirring constantly, until mixture thickens and bubbles. Remove from heat.
2. Stir one half the mixture slowly into beaten eggs in a medium-size bowl; stir back into remaining mixture in saucepan. Cook, stirring constantly, 1 minute. Remove from heat; pour into a large bowl; cool. Stir in cream, food coloring and peppermint extract; chill.
3. Pour into a 4-to-6-quart freezer can; freeze, following directions on page 122.
4. Fold chocolate into soft ice cream.
5. Pack in plastic containers; freeze until firm.

PHILADELPHIA ICE CREAM

A most deluxe ice cream, so rich you will only want to serve a little at a time.

Makes 1 quart.

1 quart (4 cups) heavy cream
¾ cup sugar
¼ teaspoon salt
1 two-inch piece vanilla bean or 2 tablespoons vanilla

1. Combine 2 cups of the cream, sugar and salt in a medium-size saucepan.
2. If using vanilla bean, cut in half, lengthwise, and scrape out the tiny seeds. Add seeds and pod to cream mixture in saucepan.
3. Heat, stirring often, just until sugar dissolves. Pour into a bowl and add remaining 2 cups cream and vanilla. Chill for at least 1 hour.
4. If vanilla bean is used, remove pod from mixture before pouring into a 4-to-6-quart freezer can; freeze, following directions on page 122.
5. Pack in plastic containers; freeze until firm.

LEMON SHERBET

Tangy, but not too tart, this is the perfect dessert for summer suppers.

Makes 1½ quarts.

1¼ cups sugar
1 envelope unflavored gelatin
2¼ cups water
1 tablespoon grated lemon rind
½ cup lemon juice
1½ cups milk
2 egg whites
¼ cup sugar

1. Combine 1¼ cups sugar and unflavored gelatin in a medium-size saucepan; stir in water and lemon rind.
2. Heat, stirring often, until mixture comes to boiling; *lower heat and simmer 5 minutes;* remove saucepan from heat; stir in lemon juice. Strain mixture into a 13x9x2-inch metal pan.
3. Cool at room temperature 30 minutes. Stir in milk until well-blended. Freeze mixture, stirring several times so that sherbet freezes evenly, until almost frozen, about 4 hours.
4. Beat egg whites until foamy and double in volume in a small bowl. Beat in the ¼ cup sugar gradually, until meringue forms soft peaks.
5. Spoon frozen mixture into a chilled large bowl; beat with an electric mixer until very smooth.
6. Fold in meringue quickly. Spoon into a 6-cup mold or bowl; cover with foil or plastic wrap.
7. Freeze in food freezer for at least 6 hours, or overnight. Unmold, or scoop right from the bowl.

KONA CHOCOLATE ICE CREAM

This ice cream blends two favorite flavors—deep chocolate with a whisper of fragrant coffee.

Makes 2 quarts.

1½ cups sugar
 ¼ cup flour
 2 teaspoons instant coffee powder
   Dash of salt
 2 cups milk
 4 squares unsweetened chocolate
 4 eggs, slightly beaten
 1 quart (4 cups) heavy cream
 2 tablespoons vanilla

1. Combine sugar, flour, coffee and salt in a large saucepan; stir in milk and chocolate.
2. Cook, stirring constantly, over medium heat. until chocolate melts and mixture thickens.
3. Stir half the mixture slowly into beaten eggs in a medium-size bowl; stir back into remaining mixture in saucepan. Cook, stirring, 1 minute.
4. Pour chocolate-egg mixture into a large bowl; stir in cream and vanilla. Chill.
5. Pour mixture into a 4-to-6-quart freezer can; freeze, following directions on page 122.
6. Pack in plastic containers; freeze until firm.

ORANGE SHERBET

Golden and smooth, try a scoop on fresh fruit.

Makes 1½ quarts.

1¼ cups sugar
 1 envelope unflavored gelatin
2¼ cups water
 1 tablespoon grated orange rind
 1 can (6 ounces) frozen concentrate for orange juice
 1 cup milk
 2 egg whites
 ¼ cup sugar

1. Combine the 1¼ cups sugar and gelatin in a medium-size saucepan; stir in water and rind.
2. Heat, stirring often, until mixture comes to boiling; *lower heat and simmer 5 minutes.* Remove saucepan from heat; stir in frozen orange-juice concentrate until thawed. Strain mixture into a 13x9x2-inch metal pan.
3. Cool at room temperature 30 minutes. Stir in milk until well-blended. Freeze mixture, stirring several times so that sherbet freezes evenly, until almost frozen, about 4 hours.
4. Beat eggs whites until foamy and double in volume in a small bowl. Beat in the ¼ cup sugar gradually, until merinuge forms soft peaks.
5. Spoon frozen mixture into a chilled large bowl. Beat immediately with an electric mixer until

the frozen mixture is very smooth in consistency.
6. Fold in meringue quickly. Spoon into a 6-cup mold or bowl; cover with foil or plastic wrap.
7. Freeze about 6 hours, or overnight. Unmold, or scoop directly from bowl.

LEMON VELVET ICE CREAM

The refreshing flavor of lemon combines with an egg-rich cream for a unique flavor treat.

Makes 3 quarts.

 2 cups sugar
 ¼ teaspoon salt
 3 tablespoons flour
3½ cups milk
 6 egg yolks, slightly beaten
 2 tablespoons grated lemon rind
 ⅔ cup lemon juice
 3 cups heavy cream

1. Combine sugar, salt and flour in a large saucepan; add milk gradually. Cook over medium heat, stirring constantly, until mixture thickens and bubbles. Remove from heat.
2. Stir half the mixture slowly into beaten egg yolks; stir back into remaining mixture in saucepan. Cook, stirring constantly, 1 minute. Remove from heat; pour into a large bowl; cool. Add lemon rind and lemon juice. Stir in cream; chill.
3. Pour mixture into a 4-to-6-quart freezer can; freeze, following directions on page 122.
4. Pack in plastic containers; freeze until firm.

WALNUT CRUNCH ICE CREAM

Buttery, crunchy nut candy is stirred through the delicious vanilla ice cream.

Makes 1 quart.

 ¼ cup (½ stick) butter or margarine
 6 tablespoons sugar
 ½ teaspoon light corn syrup
 1 tablespoon water
   Dash of salt
 ¼ cup chopped walnuts
   All-American Vanilla Ice Cream (see recipe on page 122)

1. Combine butter or margarine, sugar, corn syrup, water and salt in a small, heavy saucepan. Cook over medium heat, stirring constantly, until a candy thermometer reaches 305°. Add nuts; mix well.
2. Pour quickly onto buttered cooky sheet. Cool.
3. Chop hardened candy into small pieces.
4. Stir candy pieces into freshly made All-American Vanilla Ice Cream.
5. Pack in plastic containers; freeze until firm.

ROMAN HOLIDAY SHERBET

The combination of a tangy citrus trio enhanced with wine puts this sherbet in the "special occasion" class.

Makes 1½ quarts.

    2 oranges
    2 lemons
    2 limes
1¼ cups sugar
    1 envelope unflavored gelatin
    1 cup water
    2 cups dry white wine
    2 egg whites
    ¼ cup sugar

1. Grate rind from oranges, lemons and limes. Squeeze fruits and strain juices into a 2-cup measure, adding water, if necessary, to make 1½ cups.
2. Combine the 1¼ cups sugar and gelatin in a medium-size saucepan; stir in water and rinds.
3. Heat, stirring often, until mixture comes to boiling; *lower heat and simmer 5 minutes.* Remove saucepan from heat; stir in fruit juices. Strain mixture into a 13x9x2-inch metal pan.
4. Cool at room temperature 30 minutes. Stir in wine until well-blended. Freeze mixture, stirring several times so that sherbet freezes evenly, until almost frozen, about 4 hours.
5. Beat egg whites until foamy and double in volume in a small bowl. Beat in the ¼ cup sugar, about a tablespoon at a time, until the meringue forms soft, glossy peaks.
6. Spoon frozen mixture into a chilled large bowl; beat with an electric mixer until very smooth.
7. Fold in meringue quickly. Spoon into a 6-cup mold or bowl; cover with foil or plastic wrap.
8. Freeze about 6 hours, or overnight. Unmold, or scoop directly from bowl.

PEACH MELBA FINALE

An elegant ending to company dinners, this easy ice cream dessert is as luscious to look at as it is to eat. (See picture on page 114.)

Makes 8 to 10 servings.

    2 tablespoons cornstarch
    ¼ cup sugar
    1 cup water
    1 package (10 ounces) frozen raspberries, thawed
    1 pint heavy cream, whipped
    ½ gallon peach ice cream, scooped into balls
    1 can (1 pound, 14 ounces) peach halves, drained

1. Combine cornstarch and sugar in a small saucepan; blend well. Stir in water. Cook over medium heat, stirring constantly, until sauce thickens and becomes clear. Chill thoroughly.
2. Spoon about ⅓ of the cream onto the bottom of a large-size serving dish. Arrange ice cream balls and peach halves alternately around outer edge of dish on top of heavy cream. Gently spoon chilled raspberry sauce around outer edge of bowl, between peaches and ice cream.
3. Continue to arrange peaches, ice cream, sauce and heavy cream until bowl is filled. Place in freezer until serving time.

PEACH MELBA RIPPLE ICE CREAM

Swirls of raspberry sauce ripple through this fresh peach ice cream.

Makes 2 quarts.

    1 cup sugar
    3 tablespoons flour
      Dash of salt
1½ cups milk
    3 eggs, slightly beaten
    3 cups heavy cream
    ½ teaspoon almond extract
    2 packages (10 ounces each) frozen peaches, thawed and drained
    1 package (10 ounces) frozen raspberries, thawed
    2 tablespoons sugar (for raspberries)
    1 teaspoon cornstarch

1. Combine 1 cup sugar, flour and salt in a medium-size saucepan; add milk gradually. Cook over medium heat, stirring constantly, until mixture thickens and bubbles. Remove from heat.
2. Stir half the mixture slowly into beaten eggs in a medium-size bowl; stir back into remaining mixture in saucepan. Cook, stirring constantly, 1 minute. Remove from heat; pour into a large bowl; cool. Stir in cream and almond extract; chill.
3. Crush peaches with potato masher or fork in a medium-size bowl; reserve.
4. Press raspberries through a fine sieve into a small saucepan; add 2 tablespoons sugar. Mix cornstarch and 1 tablespoon water in a cup; add to raspberries. Cook over medium heat, just until thickened and bubbly, about 1 minute. Cool the raspberry sauce completely; reserve.
5. Pour ice cream mixture into a 4-to-6-quart freezer can; add peaches; freeze, following directions on page 122.
6. When ice cream is frozen, working very fast, spoon about one-fifth of the ice cream into a large plastic container or bowl; drizzle raspberry sauce over. Continue to layer the ice cream and sauce this way. Freeze until firm.
Note: If you wish to use fresh peaches in your ice cream, peel and crush 3 large peaches with ½ cup sugar (you should have about 2 cups crushed peaches). Continue as above (see Step 3).

PHOTOGRAPHS

All photographs by George Nordhausen except the following: Douglas Kirkland, pages 36-37. Rudy Muller, page 54. Gordon Smith, pages 1, 2-3, 14-15, 21, 24-25, 29, 44-45, 65, 78-79, 90-91, 102-103, 121. Stan Young, page 113.

ACKNOWLEDGMENTS

The editor gratefully acknowledges the help of the Film Promotion Office, Department of Commerce, St. Thomas, U.S. Virgin Islands, as well as the following companies, organizations and individuals in St. Thomas: P. Boatwright; Bolongo Bay Beach & Tennis Club (pages 24-25); Casa Venegas; Continental, Inc.; Cowpet Bay Villas (page 1); Indies House Hotel (pages 14-15); Mr. and Mrs. T. Moran (pages 78-79, 90-91); Stinky Moran; M. Perry Associates, Cowpet Bay; and A.H. Riise Gift Shop. Plus: The Annala Orchards, Hood River, Oregon (pages 52-53); and the Frozen Potato Products Institute.

BUYER'S GUIDE

Pages 24-25: CopCo barbecue grill from Continental, Inc., St. Thomas, V.I., 00801; Dansk Koben Style Saucepan #706 from Continental, Inc., and other major department stores.
Pages 78-79: Glass salad bowl and pitcher from Rosenthal Studio Haus, New York, N. Y., 10036.
Pages 90-91: Tablecloth and white Dansk Koben Style casserole from Continental, Inc., St. Thomas, V.I., 00801; wine glasses from Casa Venegas, St. Thomas, V.I., 00801; wood salad bowl from Rosenthal Studio Haus, N. Y. 10036; Orrefors Sweden Ljuslykta Candleholder with Shade from B. Altman, New York, N. Y. 10016; flowers by Katherine; candles from Hallmark.
Page 101: Glass by Corning.
Pages 102-103: From left to right —glass and bowl for fruit by Boda from A. H. Riise Gift Shop; pitcher and individual stemmed glass, Casa Venegas; pitcher, A. H. Riise, all in St. Thomas, V.I., 00801. Sangria pitcher (far right) from Rosenthal Studio Haus, New York, N. Y. 10036.